VERSIONS OF SURVIVAL

SUNY Series in Modern Jewish
Literature and Culture
Sarah Blacher Cohen, Editor

VERSIONS OF SURVIVAL

THE HOLOCAUST AND THE HUMAN SPIRIT

Lawrence L. Langer

Professor of English
Simmons College

State University of New York Press
Albany

Published by
State University of New York
Press, Albany

© 1982 State University of
New York

For information, address State
University of New York Press,
State University Plaza, Albany,
N.Y., 12246

Library of Congress Cataloging in Publication Data

Langer, Lawrence L.
Versions of survival.

  (SUNY series in modern Jewish literature and
culture)
    Includes index.
    1. Holocaust, Jewish (1939-1945), in literature.
2. Holocaust, Jewish (1939-1945)—Personal narra-
tives—Addresses, essays, lectures. I. Title.
II. Series.
PN56.H55L3   809'.93358   81-14560
ISBN 0-87395-583-8   AACR2
ISBN 0-87395-584-6 (pbk.)

For Sandy
again and always

They stole away the meaning words used to have. It's like learning a whole new language in a strange new world. As if you can teach people to get used to anything—that you are and at the same time, you aren't, that you exist, and at the same time, you don't, that you're lying and telling the truth all together. I feel like I've come back from some other planet.

Arnost Lustig,
Darkness Casts No Shadow

CONTENTS

PREFACE

A friend, whose odyssey of survival during the Holocaust is too long and too painful to rehearse here, furnished me with an image, visual and intellectual, that illuminates the central tension explored in this book. For months during the War, she and her family hid from the Nazis, spending one night in a field, another in a loft, never knowing if they would greet the following dawn alive. One day, apparently near the end of her emotional tether, her mother exclaimed wearily: "This is no life; it's a chess game, in which you play the white pieces and the black pieces at the same time!" The lucidity of this formulation, which captures so precisely the essential moral agony of the Holocaust victim, has haunted me ever since: each move one made in the "game" of survival *included* a gesture that insured, for another if not for oneself, a form of human defeat. Even if he survived—another hour, another day, another lifetime—the "victor" carried with him the memory of checkmated millions, and of his own exhausted moral vitality, that did nothing and could have done nothing to rescue them from their hopeless situation.

The pietistic mode may be one legitimate response to atrocity, but I have chosen not to follow it here. The habit of finding old spiritual categories and vocabulary to sanctify the meaningless new deaths (to say nothing of the lucky survivals) of the Holocaust has never seemed to me a fruitful way of entering the darkest recesses of that horror. Viewing the destruction of European Jewry in the context of eternal verities like martyrdom, human dignity, or whatever rhetorical label we choose can be seen as a consoling and, for some, a psychologically necessary form of avoidance. Attempts to cope with the Holocaust subsequent to that event have confirmed one of the deepest instincts in the civilized mind: the need to establish a principle of causality in human experience, retrospectively (and sometimes retroactively). The danger, of course, is that we conjure up a principle where none existed and reduce the complex survival ordeal to a matter of mere inner strength, of clinging to values that somehow insured continuing existence. This view compels us to ignore the doom of those less fortunate, for to ascribe to the victims an inner weakness or an abandonment of values is to introduce an implicit reproach too infamous to consider. But to accept pure chance as the key to survival is to admit into the universe of atrocity a randomness that damages our precious image of the civilized mind.

The material I explore and the views I develop in this book are not intended as a refutation of that image, but a confirmation of the urgency to enlarge it to include the universe of atrocity. Perhaps we need to pay greater homage to the legacy of Melville's Ishmael in *Moby Dick*: "Not ignoring what is good," he announces, "I am quick to perceive a horror." He loved to sail forbidden seas and to land on barbarous coasts. Those coasts are now much closer to home than during Ishmael's whaling days, nor must we go in search of horrors, which attend us uninvited. For many, the existence of Auschwitz suspended the link between the human and the divine. But it went further, by shattering the bond between the human and the moral—and not only for the culprits. The Nazis left no room for the *exemplary* value of human behavior: the authentic martyrs in the deathcamps, who voluntarily chose death when through some compromise they might meaningfully have chosen life, may be counted on the fingers of two hands. This is not to denigrate the victims, but to describe accurately their moral situation, which was not of their own making.

Auschwitz and the other deathcamps taught the abasement, not the infinitude of the private man, a doctrine departing so radically

from our lingering heritage of romantic possibility that we resist
its gloomy message as if our spiritual salvation depended on it.
This book begins with a chapter assessing the limitations of
viewpoint of some commentators on the Holocaust who still
cherish that potential infinitude, even though their emphases
differ; it continues with a chapter on works, both autobiographical
and literary, but all by survivors, exploring soberly how
Auschwitz has modified the affirmative image of man; turns next
to an evaluation of how a single survivor, Elie Wiesel, in a
substantial body of writing over an extended period of time, has
met in his imaginative vision the challenge of man's divided
nature during and after the deathcamp era; and concludes with a
study of two poets, Gertrud Kolmar and Nelly Sachs, the first of
whom (a victim of Auschwitz) never surrendered her faith in the
infinitude of the poet's voice, and the second of whom wrestled
with the problem of how the Holocaust had reduced the
resonance of her verse to a lyric whisper.

By calling this book *Versions of Survival*, I do not mean to
question the accuracy, so far as that accuracy is within the
author's control, of accounts of the deathcamp experience. But in
the collision between memory and truth, intention sometimes
meets stubborn resistance from a very complex and often
unconscious method of reclaiming the facts. Tillers in the field of
atrocity sometimes suffer from a disconcerting uncertainty about
the process of recollection itself. The dilemma has been stated
concisely by a critic who happens to be writing about Lillian
Hellman's autobiographical volumes, though the relevance to
writing about the Holocaust is immediately evident:

> Even as we recall the past our memories reshape it until it is
> hard to tell if we remember original experiences or only
> earlier memories of them. At the same time, the process of
> remembering is interpretive, and creates new
> self-understanding, so that we change ourselves through our
> recollections. Any quest after objective truth which employs
> memory as the tool of vision must of necessity then be
> frustrated by both the initial selectivity of perceptions which
> later furnished memories; then by the gradual alteration of
> memory through repetition and interpretation; and finally by
> the particular configuration of the self at the moment of
> actual recall.[1]

In this sense, every survivor memoir must be read, at least partially, as a work of the imagination, which selects some details and blocks out others for the purpose of shaping the reader's response—indeed, for the purpose of organizing the author's own response too. But we must guard against establishing too rigid a rhetoric of deathcamp commentary, lest future generations mistake the rhetoric for the ultimately ungraspable reality itself. An axiom of the narrative mode, from which survivor memoirs are not exempt, is that all telling modifies what is being told. This book is no exception.

I am grateful to the National Endowment for the Humanities for a Fellowship for Independent Study and Research that released me from academic duties and made possible the writing of this book. I am also indebted to the President, Corporation, and Alumnae Association of Simmons College, without whose continued support through the Alumnae Endowed Chair this work would not have been possible. Finally, and most important, to my immediate family and the small community of friends who return my love with their own, I owe the chance to balance my desperate public vision of our unhappy century with the precious private opportunity for human devotion and fulfillment.

ONE

LANGUAGE AS REFUGE

As the attempted extermination of European Jewry recedes in
time, students of that unparalleled effort at total genocide find
themselves wrestling with a question that grows more complex
with the appearance of each new volume on the subject: how to
reclaim for the Holocaust, in the words of a recent commentator,
"the veracity of its own specific pain." [1] We write about the
Holocaust from what we think we know; and what we think we
know is inspired by what we have seen, heard, and experienced,
or what we interpret from the narratives of others. Memory and
insight collaborate with fact to create visions of a dolorous past.
But visions are made up of many versions, and the impact of our
journey through the universe of annihilation often depends on the
witnesses we choose as our guides.

For example: one signpost at the entrance to this realm might be
the portrait painted in 1943 by Lea Lilienblum, a survivor of the
Warsaw ghetto, of the Jewish poet and dramatist Itzhak
Katzenelson, who died in Auschwitz. A shaven skull with
shrunken cheeks and lips awry, the visage is already inhabited by
impending atrocity. The eyes stare away from sight and into an
inner darkness, as if they had been scooped from their sockets or

1

turned around, to shut out the normal light of day. In the caverns that were once his eyes dwells the mystery of his "specific pain"; what he "sees" spreads desolation across his face—and his faith. It appears to be so terrible that it has atrophied his vital signs with a paralyzing despair. Haunting the hollows of those eyes is an internal vision of the eclipse of man—and possibly the eclipse of God.[2]

The analogy with Sophocles' hero is inevitable—but inexact. Polluted Oedipus, self-blinded, partial agent of his tragic fate, stumbles from the scene to accept his suffering until, forgiven, he regains the favor of the gods. Not so Katzenelson, who in that moment of perception captured by the painter seems to be struggling with the difference between the dignity of a tragic destiny and the total abasement of extermination. The implications are too awful to absorb. Words hover on the verge of expression, but the spectacle that silences his soul has also stilled his tongue. To the viewer, this face transformed into a death mask by such blinding anguish vividly illustrates what we mean when we speak of the Holocaust as an event unimaginable and indescribable. What he "sees" is a sealed doom, like the boxcars that brought him to Auschwitz.

A shift from ravaged eyes to shining flesh may seem abrupt and disconcerting, but no more so than many other bizarre fluctuations in the concentration camp universe. The unsuspecting reader will be surprised by another painting, a watercolor called "Internee Bathing" by Malvina Schalkova, who spent the war years in Theresienstadt. Whereas the substance of Katzenelson's physical presence has been eroded by his inner vision of annihilation, Schalkova's potential victim, a naked woman, is shown in the life-affirming act of keeping the body clean. Surrounded by elementary accoutrements of ablution—pitchers and basins and buckets, a primitive stove, and, most astonishing of all, complete privacy—the woman in the watercolor enacts a principle of survival stressed by numerous commentators on the camp ordeal: keeping one's appearance as normal and healthy as possible. This too was a form of resistance, postponing and perhaps helping to avert the certainty of extermination that clouded the clarity of Katzenelson's eyes.

For the student of the Holocaust, which included Auschwitz *and* Theresienstadt, extermination *and* the desperate effort to avoid contamination, such contradictory visions may cause confusion.

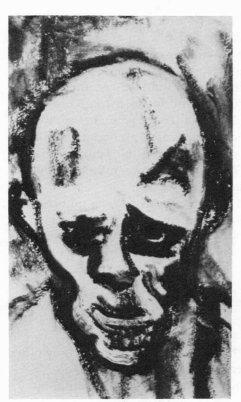

Left: **Lea Lilienblum,** Portrait of
Yitzhak Katzenelson, 1943
Gouache on paper, 14½" x 8½"
Used by permission
Ghetto Fighters' House,
Kibbutz Lohamei Haghettaot,
Israel

Below: **Malvina Schalkova,**
Internee Bathing, undated
Watercolor on paper, 12½" x 18¼"
Used by permission
Ghetto Fighters' House,
Kibbutz Lohamei Haghettaot,
Israel

One barrack in Auschwitz contained a single water faucet for two thousand women; Charlotte Delbo reports that she was encrusted with filth when she finally was able to bathe (in a stream) after more than two months without water for washing. The image of an internee bathing, like Katzenelson's horrorstruck eyes, projects a partial truth, and warns anyone who would recover the specific pains—and they must be pluralized—of the deathcamp ordeal to be wary of formulas and single truths. Those who attempt to generate such truths, as we shall see, sacrifice ambiguity for the sake of coherence, seeking to construct a possible future from the debris of an impossible past. The tension between the two will be a primary source of concern in this study.

Responses to the Holocaust must be governed by a number of other cautions, the first of which is cogently stated by Benzion Dinur, coeditor of the initial volume in the *Yad Washem Studies on the European Jewish Catastrophe and Resistance.* Commenting on the crucial importance of "memoirs and reminiscences of persons who witnessed and experienced the horrors of the European catastrophe" (and this includes victims and persecutors), Dinur admonishes:

> These memoirs must be treated in the same way as any other testimony and must, of course, be properly examined. The plain and unvarnished character of the narration and the presence of the narrator on the spot at the time constitute in themselves no guarantee of the authenticity of such memoirs. The reason need not be any desire to "amend" or "improve" upon actual events for any ulterior purpose. It is difficult for the individual to liberate himself from his own personality. He has a propensity to see the past and his own past experiences, from the vantage point of the present. In such evidence every effort must be made to establish all the facts relating to the narrator, his location and status during the period of the catastrophe, and his subsequent career. We must keep in mind that one of the requisite qualities for writing reminiscences is that of recreating the "climate" existing at the time and thereby to reconstruct the past.[3]

Every narrative about the deathcamps includes an encounter between fact and memory, persuasive horror and the will to disbelieve. "Today," writes Charlotte Delbo as an epigraph to the account of her ordeal in Auschwitz, "I am not sure that what I have written is true *(vrai)*. But I am sure that it happened that way *(véridique)*." [4] In part, she tries to distinguish between verbalized observation and the event itself, which we gain access to, which even *she* regains access to through the inadequate mediating efforts of the word. It is the difference between the "true" (can I portray the unspeakable, which you did not experience, so that it will seem authentic to you?) and the "veracious" (which memory confirms, even as language hesitates). The internal vision invariably sacrifices some of its truth as it struggles to find an idiom that will make the events of atrocity seem veracious to the outsider.

Not all writers on the subject approach it with such honest diffidence. Delbo is wary of the temptation to see her own past in Auschwitz from the vantage point of the present, and builds that tension into her narrative. Contemporary explanations, she implies, try to clarify *now* what was shadowy *then*:

> I stand in the midst of my comrades and I think that if I return one day and want to explain this inexplicable thing, I will say: "I used to say to myself: you must stand, you must stand for the entire roll call. You must stand again today. It is because you will have stood again today that you will return, if you do return one day." And this will be false. I did not say anything to myself. I did not think anything. The will to resist no doubt lay in a much deeper and more secret mechanism which has since broken; I shall never know. [5]

Since the victim as witness is not a recording machine but a fallible human being—the same, to be sure, can be said of anyone who sifts through the rubble of the Holocaust in search of fragments of meaning—it is useful to distinguish between visions of deathcamp reality, limited only by the imagination of the narrator, and versions of that reality, determined by the personality of the author—from which, as Benzion Dinur proposed, it is difficult to liberate oneself. Memory alone, as Delbo insists, is an uncertain monitor of atrocity.

Our entry into the world of the Holocaust thus depends on who tells the tale—and how. Not everyone need tell the same story; not everyone does. Hermann Langbein, author of *Menschen in Auschwitz*, an exhaustive documentation of the camp he himself survived, offers this succinct warning, a classic statement for anyone undertaking an investigation of survival:

> Each of us carries within him his own personally colored memory, each has experienced "his" Auschwitz. The perspective of someone who was always hungry is different from the perspective of a prisoner functionary; Auschwitz of the year 1942 was essentially unlike the Auschwitz of the year 1944. Every single sub-camp in the larger complex was a world of its own. For this reason many survivors of Auschwitz object to particular descriptions: "that's not the way I saw it—that's totally new to me."[6]

Benedict Kautsky, another survivor, confirms this view: "When you talk about a concentration camp, it's not enough to give merely its name. . . . Even when you're talking about the same period of time, prisoners in the same camp lived as if on different planets, depending on the work they had to do." [7] Thus we are faced not only with the problem of verifying the truth, but of knowing which truths we are trying to verify.

An even more complex question arises when we consider the image of himself or herself that the survivor must maintain in order to exist. Gitta Sereny, in her study of Franz Stangl, commandant of Sobibor and Treblinka, adds some crucial insight into this dilemma:

> One of the most extraordinary things about delving into this period now is the different interpretation given to individual events by different people. This is less the result of failing memories or deliberate manipulation, than because most people now represent these events and their part in them with a view to seeming—to themselves even more than to others—what they would have *liked* to have been, rather than what they were.[8]

Although Sereny is speaking principally of Stangl, whom she interviewed extensively in prison, her words apply equally to other kinds of "survivors," ranging from victims like Bruno Bettelheim and Viktor Frankl to convicted war criminals like Albert Speer and Rudolph Hoess—all of whom divide their verbal energy between recapturing the truth and rescuing their image for themselves and for posterity.

For survivor and nonsurvivor, normal ideas of time, space, and identity oppose a remote experience that stubbornly eludes attempts to bring it into a familiar focus. Primo Levi in *Survival in Auschwitz* tells how the Allied landings in the west and the Russian offensive in the east bred only short-lived hopes that help would soon arrive. Words like "east" and "west" evoked for inmates a vague sense of distance; the notion of "soon" belonged to a time scheme that was irrelevant to the unpredictable life of the deathcamp. "Day by day," says Levi,

> everyone felt his strength vanish, his desire to live melt away, his mind grow dim; and Normandy and Russia were so far away, and the winter so near; hunger and desolation so concrete, and all the rest so unreal, that it did not seem possible that there could really exist any other world or time other than our world of mud and our sterile and stagnant time, whose end we were by now incapable of imagining.[9]

At Auschwitz, the flow of chronological and historical time that governs our lives today stopped, while space was hermetically sealed by barbed-wire fences that defined the frontiers of one's hopes—and one's despair.

In trying to recreate the climates of that experience we are faced with the same polarities—hope and despair—though the locale has reversed, since what was unreal for Levi in Auschwitz is the substance of *our* reality. After more than thirty years, the human need persists to see those worlds in terms of each other, so that motive and behavior in Auschwitz do not cancel out the belief in moral action that forms the basis of our civilization. Survivor accounts, as we shall see, often vacillate between Levi's "sterile and stagnant time, whose end we were . . . incapable of imagining," and a more fluid image of the ordeal, which permits certain modes of conduct to link the individual with normality and to reduce the sense of alienation between the world of the deathcamps and our own. As the distressed reader drifts between elegy and eulogy, presentation and justification, the agony of extermination and the triumph of survival, he seems to find evidence for one commentator's compelling formulation that an "art of the holocaust must also be an art of the phoenix." [10]

This may be true for the artist of the Holocaust (as well as for the historian and for those others whose very voices include the future as they write), but whether it accurately describes the situation of the victim before his literal survival remains an exasperating question. Although some witnesses argue that a passionate inner commitment to hope made endurance easier and survival and rebirth more possible, others suggest that the experience lacks temporal analogy. But the impulse to find one continues, and cannot be discounted as mere self-deception. Part of the meaning of the Holocaust, its "truth" if not its "veracity," is the one imposed on it by those who refuse to interpret its message as a revelation of moral chaos. All survivor accounts, and all narratives about survivors and their experience, are limited by a number of inescapable restrictions. They speak of a world where the values cherished by western civilization were moribund; but they speak *to* (and from) a world where those values presumably remain intact. They must depend on a vocabulary that finds little resonance in the universe of the deathcamps: "suffocation in the gas chamber" grates harshly against more consoling descriptions like "salvation through suffering" or "tragic insight." But some writers on the Holocaust find it so difficult to absorb this abrasive contradiction that instead of altering our perception of moral reality, they try to adapt the fact of extermination to ideas of suffering and heroism that have governed man's secular or religious fate throughout the Judeo-Christian era. Authors like Viktor Frankl and Bruno Bettelheim, whose works on the subject are among the most widely read and often quoted, seem unwilling to abandon the possibility of individual choice and heroic gesture even in the extreme situation of atrocity, although evidence, including some of their own, repeatedly undermines many of their conclusions. Is it an image of man they are loath to sacrifice, or an image of themselves?

This is far from a frivolous question. A few long-standing reputations are much less important to post-Holocaust generations than a valid vision of the options open to survivors, within the camps and after the liberation. To accept any single voice as authoritative is to betray the complexity of the event and to risk diminishing the full horror of the doom of its victims—and the world that destroyed them. Some voices seem to choose their memories, others to be chosen by them; and although all are writing about the same historical episode, the images of man emerging often resemble creatures from alien universes. It is as if the living collide at every verbal turn with murmuring masses of the dead, who echo the high priests in *Aida*: "Justify thyself!"

More than thirty years later we still need to assess the impact which that huge quantity of uncompleted living permanently denied the possibility of expression has made on the imaginations of those who survived the ordeal.

There are moments when one feels that a gesture other than verbal might be more effective in helping us to penetrate that stronghold of meaningless death. Consider the story of Stella, told by Dorothy Rabinowitz in her *New Lives*, an account of Holocaust survivors in America.[11] An apparently inexplicable impulse drives Stella in 1974 from her comfortable New York home, despite her husband's protests, back to Poland and the site of the Majdanek concentration camp outside Lublin, which she had survived in part because her older sister had taken her place among a group of women selected for the gas chamber. Stella's pilgrimage is silent and solitary; her Lublin friends, who reluctantly accompany her to the camp, think her perverse. And though words recount the event, our imagination crosses the distance between idea and action through Stella's pantomime as she climbs the rail separating her from the oven and crawls into the narrow crematorium opening in search of—of what? A token of her sister's fate? (She does gather some ashes in a vinyl pouch, ashes, we are told, left there by the Russians when they liberated the camp.) Communion with the dead? Homer, Virgil, and Dante provide us with no patterns for this unique encounter, while language falters as it gropes for terms to animate an incomprehensible act. Purgation of guilt? Tragic remorse? Rebirth through suffering? Journey into the past? Quest for meaning? Vocabulary mocks the event, while the event mocks our vocabulary. The very title of the book, *New Lives*, unwittingly burlesques Stella's efforts to establish contact with an old death. The tomb is empty, and ashes are a poor substitute for the ceremony of remembering. Whatever phoenix she may find there remains mute and incommunicable.

Indeed, if we need a myth to verify the results of our encounter with extermination, a griffin or gorgon might be more suitable than the youthful freshness of the risen phoenix. Unless the mythifying impulse acknowledges a monstrosity etched permanently on that page of history we call the Holocaust, it falsifies the event and allows us too easy an escape from the voracious maw of those years. Expressions like "tragic suffering" and "heroic resistance," ostensibly intended to define the response of the victim, unobtrusively divert our attention from the event to our attitude toward it. Confronted with the idea of tragedy, the imagination instinctively retreats to that long roll call of literary figures who achieved status and stature even in defeat. But the victims at Auschwitz faced a different kind of roll call; unlike the regal heroes of tragedy, they possessed neither power nor freedom of choice. In this world of shrunken options, their "defeat" can only charitably be designated "inhuman." In literature, the courage and intelligence of an Oedipus may have pacified that offstage threat we call the Sphinx; but at Auschwitz the devouring beast held center stage, and no human resource seemed able to solve the riddle of its insatiable hunger.

The language of heroism is incommensurate with the experience of annihilation, but in the absence of a more adequate idiom, commentators continue to rely on its code words. Such efforts take an existence without form and void and through a kind of verbal transmutation create a suggestion of order where none prevailed. They define the victim's ordeal with a familiar vocabulary, but beneath the verbal level lurks the psychological urge to support a tottering self-esteem, crushed by the memory of extermination. Many students of the Holocaust seem dismayed by how easily that event undermined men's sense of their physical and spiritual worth. The Nazi purpose was to obliterate the victim, not merely punish or defeat him: to nullify his spirit, grind up his bones, disperse his ashes, until he literally vanished from the face of the earth. Although the full purpose miscarried, the attempt is still very much alive to the human imagination, which must now rebuild a sense of worth in a universe that was willing to see so many perish for nothing. But let us be honest about the implications of this process. Words can be used to strip the facade from atrocity, or to masquerade a dignified image of the humiliated self.

Yet somehow we must wrestle with the paradox of the unspeakable; we cannot offer a blank tablet to history and require future generations to inscribe it with the unreliable details of fading recollections. Because we suffer from an absence of unusual analogies, we draw on familiar ones, in a desperate attempt to lead the imagination from normal living through abnormal dying and back to life. We describe the camp experience as Hell on earth, ignoring the simple fact that Hell was a place for the punishment of sins, whereas the Jews of Europe

were innocent. A critic as distinguished as George Steiner
develops this comparison with melodramatic fervor:

> We know from the plans of those who built them and from
> the testimony of inmates, that the death camps constituted a
> complete, coherent world. They had their own measure of
> time, which is pain. The unbearable was parceled out with
> pedantic nicety. The obscenities and abjections practiced in
> them were accompanied by prescribed rituals of derision and
> false promise. There were regulated gradations of horror
> within the total, concentric sphere. *L'univers concentrationnaire*
> has no true counterpart in the secular mode. Its analogue is
> Hell. The camp embodies, often down to minutiae, the
> images and chronicles of Hell in European art and thought
> from the twelfth to the eighteenth centuries. It is these
> representations which gave to the deranged horrors of Belsen
> a kind of "expected logic." [12]

Even if this analogy were accurate—which it is not—one wonders
what consolation the imagination is supposed to derive from the
idea that meaningless death in a place like Auschwitz resembles a
kind of "expected logic" resulting from six hundred years of
chronicling Hell in European art and thought. In fact, Hitler's
victims have nothing to do with Dante's damned, precisely
because of the total absence of "expected logic" in their fate. The
damned—it is almost too obvious to repeat—suffer the
consequences of their sinful actions; cause and effect rule in their
destiny. But the Jews are the victims, not the agents of injustice,
and during the decade of disaster that consumed them and
millions of others, their fate might have been avoided at a dozen
different junctures. There is no logic to their destruction at all,
neither in history, nor in the art that reflects it. Why then do we
depend so often on the false analogy of the camps to a Hell on
earth? Is there some unacknowledged, hidden comfort in the
possibility that an ambiguous logic, whether secular or divine,
was indeed operative in the annihilation of so many millions?
Perverse as it may sound, the image of Hell restores to the
unspeakable, in Steiner's words, "regulated gradations of horror,"
making manageable what otherwise would be intolerable to the
imagination. The dilemma reminds us that the challenge of
writing about the Holocaust is stylistic as well as historical—not

only to tell what one knows, but also to find an idiom and image for what one envisions.

The problem, one cannot repeat too often, is to create a language and imagery that will transform mere knowledge into vision and bear the reader beyond the realm of familiar imagining into the bizarre limbo of atrocity. Vision, however, depends on many variables, not only on one's power to describe the deathcamp experience, but also on one's willingness to risk admitting how that experience may have modified cherished words and values from the pre-Holocaust universe. One way of releasing the Holocaust experience from the bonds of a limiting vocabulary is to change the conventional opposition between living and dying into a more complex relationship between survival and atrocity.[13] "Living" opens out into the future, governed by the expectation of fulfillment; "survival" draws its energy from the past, and is burdened by unforgettable memories that offer little relief to the individual simply because he has survived them. Traditional "dying" also opens out into the future, in the sense that men have invented ceremonies of burial and mourning to create a symbolic continuity for those who are still alive. But death by "atrocity" in the camps permitted no ceremony of continuity; it was no prelude to transcendence, for victim or witness, but the anonymous end of a life of unutterable pain and humiliation.

A failure to distinguish between conventional ideas of living and the singular experience of survival in the deathcamps leads to the misuse of private agony (and hopeful vocabulary) to celebrate the infinitely flexible spirit of that abstract creature called Man. When we use words to make us feel better, we cannot expect them simultaneously to help us *see* better. Consider, for example, the dedication to a book called *Massive Psychic Trauma*, devoted almost entirely to the psychological problems of concentration camp survivors: "This volume is dedicated in honor of the survivors of the Nazi onslaught. They are the living proof of the inviolable dignity of man, the resourcefulness of the human spirit, and inalienability of individual rights." [14] Are those who did *not* survive then the dead proof of the opposite: the "violable" dignity of man, the cravenness of the human spirit, the alienability of individual rights? The lines resound with the rhetoric of hope, consoling our sensibilities while blocking out the memory of despair and ignoring the looming power of meaningless death.

The living dead men (to say nothing of the piles of corpses behind them) who greeted the liberators of Bergen-Belsen and Buchenwald mock, in this context, an expression like "the inviolable dignity of man," which turns insipid in their haunting presence. We cannot celebrate the phoenix while burying the ashes from which it allegedly sprang.

"Man's task," say Robert Jay Lifton and Eric Olson in *Living and Dying*, "is to develop concepts, imagery, and symbols adequate to give a sense of significance to his experience." [15] And, as they point out, most cultures have evolved some way of dealing with death—through gesture, ritual, and verbal formula, through modes of symbolic immortality, whether biological, creative, religious, or experiential. But what culture has evolved a way of dealing with atrocity, particularly with the abnormal dying of the Holocaust? The forms of symbolic immortality are directed toward the future—bearing children, writing books, spiritual rebirth, reincarnation. But we have already had a glimpse of how impoverished are the vocabulary and imagery of renewal when contending with the unmanageable and often unimaginable memories of the camp universe. These memories are irreversibly fused with a kind of death that admits neither rebirth nor renewal—only regret, remorse, and an immobilizing despair over the waste of so much unlived life.

Confusing living and dying in a pre-Holocaust era with the survival and atrocity of the event itself is like dressing up a faded beauty in a splendid gown and presenting her to the public as a great lady a la mode. Trapped by an antique diction, Lifton and Olson establish a connection between death and the continuity of life in a language that has had all threatening sharp edges filed away:

> The winter which makes possible spring, the dark of night followed by the light of day, the suffering which prepares the way for the deepest insight and the greatest ecstasy—these are images of death and rebirth that find universal cultural expression. They suggest a human quest for forms of integrity, movement, and connection that affirms life in the face of death. [16]

We get no help from the serried ranks of these clichés; nothing here inflames the imagination with the challenge of penetrating the strongholds of meaningless death, or with the arduous task of struggling back to a meaningful survival. Phrases like "the dark of night" and "the light of day" limp feebly into these strongholds, only to be smothered by the mounds of corpses they find there. Affirming life in the face of death is more eloquent than relevant to the threat of extermination in the gas chamber, though as long as we think of the Holocaust merely as another kind of dying, we will continue to approach it with such conventional language. Sometimes it seems that the real problem is a failure of intellectual courage, a refusal to pursue the inhuman vision of the Holocaust to its awful, dispiriting end. And this is compounded by the human instinct for form and connection, a too easy faith in the hypnotic power of language to restore integrity to a disintegrating world.

A terminology of order may help us to cope with the experience of chaos, but it does not encourage us to enter its unsettling realm. Coping, for Lifton and Olson, means living in the future, not dying in the past: "The survivor is one for whom having known the end makes possible a new beginning—a beginning freshly unencumbered by the weight of the old and the dead." But this is a dangerously misleading half-truth, the other half of which would define the survivor as one for whom having known the end makes *im*possible a new beginning, *especially* one unencumbered by the dead. To be sure, Lifton and Olson are frank enough to admit that "holocaust is no guarantee of rebirth; having known the end does not ensure that one will make a new beginning." They even concede that for some a new formulation of self may not be attainable. But instead of pursuing the cultural implications of this condition, they *name* it, and by calling it "psychic numbing" they reintroduce (from Lifton's earlier work on Hiroshima) one more formula to make manageable through language a "neurosis" that may actually represent only a more honest if more painful encounter with our heritage of atrocity. Retaining a portion of that heritage, meeting and expressing it imaginatively, accepting the constricted life that confrontation with the Holocaust sometimes imposes, may be a *normal* response to an experience that is mocked by the idea of renewal. The emptiness and despair that accompany what the psychiatrist clinically defines as psychic numbing, a numbing that protects one "from a reality too hard to face and too chaotic to formulate," [17] may not signify a retreat from truth but a simple acknowledgement of how extermination has invaded our lives. It is difficult to understand how anyone acquainted with the details of the Holocaust can *not* remain permanently encumbered—encumbered, not paralyzed—by the burdens they impose.

Who can be blamed for wanting to escape these burdens by turning from the facts of annihilation to the hope for rebirth? This is another kind of normality. But its trustworthiness is impugned unless its vision is built on the kind of death immersion that survivors of the Holocaust were compelled to experience. It is intellectually deceptive and emotionally futile to celebrate a suffering that brought no one salvation, or to twist the physical anguish of the victim into a new form of human grace under pressure. Perhaps all efforts to re-create the climates of the Holocaust should begin by following Stella back to the crematory oven in pursuit of the primal image of atrocity that lay hidden there. Her pouch of ashes is mute testimony to man's doom during that ordeal; if we strew these ashes over our tribute of silence, what voices can we awaken to do justice to *such* evidence? Will they indeed revive a phoenix in the human spirit, or will the creatures who emerge trail inglorious haloes, requiring untraditional brush strokes—and untraditional attitudes—to portray them? A language of rebirth that hurries into the future without paying homage to these ghosts from the past serves neither truth nor the spirits of the dead—who cannot speak for themselves.

Since most students of the Holocaust depend on the voices of others for the seeds of insight, it is worth recalling Benzion Dinur's warning that memoirs on the subject "must be treated in the same way as any other testimony," and must "be properly examined." Two of the most influential "memoirs," which go far beyond the limits of mere recollection, are Viktor Frankl's *Man's Search for Meaning* and Bruno Bettelheim's *The Informed Heart*—works that have inspired and beguiled a generation of readers. Many of these readers assume that the most authoritative sources for understanding the process of survival would come from literal survivors who were also trained psychologists, which of course was the case with both Frankl and Bettelheim. But this is an unwise assumption, since both of these works illustrate forcibly how difficult it is, in Dinur's words, "for the individual to liberate himself from his own personality" when writing about the camp experience. Paradoxically, a much more inclusive and objective account, which achieves greater validity by broadening the base of its sources, is Terrence De Pres's *The Survivor*, though unlike Frankl and Bettelheim the author is neither survivor nor Jew. But even this sensitive study is as much concerned in the end with rescuing the image of man from the chaos of atrocity as it is with the consequences of extermination. Its contradictions are its greatest strength—and its greatest weakness.

Whose voice shall we listen to, and whose shall we trust? Before we can even begin to consider an answer to such a question, we need to examine several investigations of the camp experience, not to discover their "truths" but to evaluate the variety of strategies that have been employed to arrive at them. The diversity of the approaches and the disparity among the conclusions are persuasive evidence that we dare not enter this universe of reconstructed atrocity with uncritical awe. The disarming naiveté of the distinguished psychologist Gordon Allport, in his introduction to Viktor Frankl's *Man's Search for Meaning*, should give us fair warning: "A psychiatrist who personally has faced such extremity," he writes, "is a psychiatrist worth listening to. He, if anyone, should be able to view our human condition wisely and with compassion. Dr. Frankl's words have a profoundly honest ring, for they rest on experiences too deep for deception." Probably no ten consecutive words in that passage would withstand intense critical scrutiny; one is perhaps most surprised by the psychologist's tranquil assumption that *any* experience is too deep for deception. Survivors of Auschwitz like Frankl plunged to different depths of terror in their encounter with extermination; he writes, as all must, with a very partial view, not the authoritative one that Allport attributes to him. Formulas that as recently as twenty years ago captured the innocent imagination in quest of verbal assurances about the coherence of our lives, today resound with an antiquated splendor. Allport identifies Frankl's book with a version of existentialism, thus neatly fitting the Holocaust into a contemporary intellectual niche: "to live is to suffer, to survive is to find meaning in the suffering." [18] The idea of tragedy, and even more, the affirmation of an ancient religious truth (neither of which, let us remember, could anticipate the genocide of the Jews), envelop Frankl's account with a secure perimeter of *purpose*. Frankl clings to it with the pertinacity of a prophet, and this leads to certain verbal and conceptual techniques that dilute the authenticity of his vision for the wary reader, who is not consoled by his astounding conclusion that after Auschwitz man has nothing to fear—except his God.

Viktor Frankl insists that Auschwitz was a scarring death immersion for the victim/survivor only if he permitted it to be. The subtitle of the book's second English edition—*An Introduction to Logotherapy*[19]—betrays Frankl's deeper intention, which is to develop a psychological approach to the deathcamp ordeal that can reclaim hope and the future from even the grimmest encounter with atrocity. Frankl is a leading spokesman for the view that in the deathcamps there was a way to resist the dehumanizing process and to preserve the essential dignity of the human being. One of the most appealing features of his volume, obviously, is that he repeats what many long to hear—that even the Holocaust left an area of freedom, allowing men and women to see themselves, then and later, as more than mere victims of an intolerable fate. Unlike his comrades, says Frankl, whose question was " 'Will we survive the camp? For, if not, all this suffering has no meaning,' " his *own* question was " 'Has all this suffering, this dying around us, a meaning? For, if not, then ultimately there is no meaning to survival; for a life whose meaning depends on such a happenstance—whether one escapes or not—ultimately would not be worth living at all.' " [20]

We are met here by two problems: a way of thinking, and a way of saying, and the two are related. Unwilling to accept the Holocaust as a rent in the apparently seamless web of history and man's spiritual destiny, Frankl is forced to embrace a premise that substitutes statements about reality for the reality itself: survival for its own sake is meaningless; only meaningful suffering makes life worth living. He excludes by verbal fiat the possibility that for thousands in the deathcamps, decimated by the sterile and stagnant time of which Primo Levi wrote, death may have seemed more "worth" dying than life worth living. How can one recapture that state of mind after the event? Frankl chooses not to, but this is because he needs to eliminate ambiguity and contradiction to support his version of survival, not because he wants to develop his vision of it. Somehow, the Holocaust must fit into the old world order (as well as the old *word* order), and in his determination to establish such continuity, Frankl narrows the event to the familiar challenge of finding meaning in suffering. But his language blunts the menacing blade of atrocity and simplifies the threat of extermination into a conventional encounter between the free heroic spirit and human mortality. The horrors of Auschwitz fade behind a wall of rhetoric as vocabulary becomes an instrument to transfigure victim and survivor into potentially noble creatures who have defeated the physical monster of genocide.

The shifting focus of Frankl's narrative, so full of disclaimers, makes illustration difficult. He begins with a curious inexactitude, a dubious humility that distorts the setting of the deathcamp experience. "Most of the events described here," he says, "did not take place in the large and famous camps, but in the small ones where most of the real extermination took place" (p. 3). Since the only locales in Frankl's book are Auschwitz, the main extermination center of Europe, and a subcamp of Dachau, where no large-scale exterminations occurred, one is baffled by this statement. One is equally perplexed by his attempt to dissociate himself from a fictitious band of "heroes and martyrs" whose suffering and death he is *not* describing, and his need to identify himself with the "little man," as if the gas chamber acknowledged distinctions in status to begin with! His book, he insists, "is not so much concerned with the sufferings of the mighty, but with the sacrifices, the crucifixion and the deaths of the great army of unknown and unrecorded victims" (pp. 3–4). The vocabulary of Christian conversion, as we shall see, plays a crucial if enigmatic role in Frankl's efforts to portray the ordeal in a way that would make it psychologically manageable for himself and his readers. "Sacrifice" is a doubtful term for those who did not choose their fate, while "crucifixion," to say the least, is an inappropriate one (both images are fused in the single suggestive word *Passion* of the original German text). Intrinsically, there is nothing objectionable about making the Holocaust more accessible to the imagination of the curious reader. But if it is achieved at the price of transforming the event into only one more difficult spiritual challenge in the history of human suffering—Frankl shows a noticeable aversion to speaking about Jewish genocide—then we have gained little insight into the unprecedented murder—and in such an unspeakable way—of so many millions.

The myth of survival at first coexists in his work with the truths of atrocity, but gradually supersedes it:

In spite of all the enforced physical and mental primitiveness of the life in a concentration camp, it was possible for spiritual life to deepen. Sensitive people who were used to a rich intellectual life may have suffered much pain (they were often of a delicate constitution), but the damage to their inner selves was less. They were able to retreat from their terrible surroundings to a life of inner riches and spiritual freedom. Only in this way can one explain the apparent paradox that some prisoners of a less hardy make-up often seemed to survive camp life better than did those of a robust nature. (pp. 56–57)

How is one to reconcile this dignifying image of inner resistance with Frankl's earlier statement that "the constant necessity of concentrating on the task of staying alive, forced the prisoner's inner life down to a primitive level" (p. 44), or that because of undernourishment "it was natural that the desire for food was the major primitive instinct around which mental life centered" (p. 45)—a detail confirmed by dozens of other accounts? *Man's Search for Meaning* abounds in such contradictions, as if Frankl himself were unconsciously committed to a dual vision, torn between how it really was and how, retrospectively, he would like to believe it had been. In the end, for him, wish virtually cancels out reality, but the casual reader, swept along by the upward momentum of the narrative, finds himself beguiled by strictly verbal persuasions like the following: "Emotion, which is suffering, ceases to be suffering as soon as we form a clear and precise picture of it" (p. 117). The line is a translation from Spinoza's *Ethics*, whose seventeenth-century principles can pay no homage to Auschwitz, the gas chambers, or the Nazi program to exterminate the Jews.

The most persistent premise in Frankl's book, the one without which its structure would collapse into moral confusion, is that a continuity of thought exists between nineteenth-century views of suffering expounded by Dostoevsky, Tolstoy, Nietzsche, and Schopenhauer, to all of whom Frankl alludes, and the unprecedented ordeal of atrocity in the world of the concentration camps. Frankl clings to this belief in continuity partly because he is unable to "form a clear and precise picture" of the difference between *that* suffering and *this* atrocity: to admit the difference is to confess the collapse of values we all share in as heirs of the Holocaust. One is reminded of Emerson's almost irrational

refusal, in his essay on Swedenborg, to accept the independent
existence of devils, since their presence in the universe would
introduce the possibility of absolute evil, and for him that was
equivalent to the madness of atheism. Such a possibility was so
threatening to his own unsystematic constellation of beliefs that
he was intellectually incapable of admitting it into his moral
cosmos, which, he thought, would then be uninhabitable. As
Nelly Sachs will confirm, a universe afflicted by a rough
equivalent of Swedenborg's devils—the experience of the
Holocaust—would be *indescribable* by the alphabet and vocabulary
of transcendence (the one employed by Emerson, Tolstoy,
Dostoevsky, and Viktor Frankl), but uninhabitable only by those
who hid behind the camouflage of outmoded words and attitudes.

To establish a firm connection between suffering in Auschwitz
and general human destiny is a deliberate goal of Frankl's
strategy, embedded in his very diction. The psychological effect
on the reader is not difficult to deduce. Sometimes, says Frankl,
"man may be required to accept his fate, to bear his cross"
(p. 123). This fusion of classical and Christian ideas (*Schicksal* and
Kreuz in the original) lifts the ordeal of the deathcamp out of its
specific context and deludes—no other term seems appropriate—
the reader into accepting Frankl's corollary, offered with
even greater authoritarian fervor: "When a man finds that it
is his destiny to suffer, he will have to accept his suffering as his
task" (p. 123). The effect, if not the intention, of this specious
rhetorical manipulation of concrete terrors like the gas chamber
and crematorium is almost sinister; certainly, it is insensitive.
"Every situation," Frankl observes (and we must shake off the
cobweb of words to recall that he is speaking of deathcamp
inmates), "is distinguished by its uniqueness, and there is always
only one right answer to the problem posed by the situation at
hand" (p. 123). How do we explain this crystalline ethical code to
the young Jewish wife who after searching for five days
through a mound of thousands of murdered Jewish men finally
found her husband's body? "Weary from searching through so
many corpses, am I supposed to be 'happy' to have found his?"
she asks. "Can one clothe such agonies in words?" [21]

In the absence of new vision, responsive to anguished dilemmas
like these, Frankl retreats into old knowledge, and the result is a
barrage of platitudes, bereft of the spiritual agonies of
Dostoevsky's Dmitri Karamazov or Tolstoy's Pierre Bezukhov. "If

there is a meaning in life at all," Frankl echoes his inherited
truths, "then there must be a meaning in suffering. Suffering is an
ineradicable part of life, even as fate and death. Without suffering
and death human life cannot be complete" (p. 106). If we revise
that last line to read "without Auschwitz and extermination in the
gas chamber, human life cannot be complete," we get a more
vivid glimpse of the limitations of Frankl's implicit analogy. The
suffering he alludes to, in the pre-Holocaust era, led in one
direction to the tragic spirit, in another to salvation. Whether we
speak of Oedipus or of Christian man, secular insight or
redemption, human agency is imperative: the sufferer is partially
responsible for his own condition. In choosing an attitude toward
his fate, he is partly governed by the discovery in his present
condition of traces of his own earlier decisions—or
indecisiveness. But at Auschwitz the "selecting" was always done
by someone else; this in one reason why man's fate in the
deathcamps can never be "celebrated" through the traditional
forms of the tragic experience.

Both dramatic tragedy and religious martyrdom are based on
the premise that the individual is free to risk certain choices with
full knowledge that the consequences may lead to extreme
suffering or death. These choices, whether Hamlet's decision to
duel with Laertes, Oedipus's to pursue the truth of his identity
despite Jocasta's pleas, or Sir Thomas More's to adhere to his
Christian principles, are necessary to the individual's vision of
himself as a human being. In the deathcamps, such motives for
choice survived for a time, but the consequences were quickly
removed from the control of the individual, and made so
unpredictable that it was virtually impossible to associate one's
vision of oneself as a human being with the various modes of
punishment and extermination in the surrounding environment.
Certainly "suffering" was inadequate to describe them.

The enduring value of Frankl's book as a guide to
understanding human response to atrocity is virtually
extinguished by his compulsion to transform the ordeal into a
challenge to the potential moral heroism in man. To those (like
Primo Levi) who regard the provisional existence of the
deathcamps as stagnant and sterile, Frankl replies that "often it is
just such an exceptionally difficult external situation which gives
man the opportunity to grow spiritually beyond himself" (p. 114).
Is it an impoverished sense of language or an impoverished

imagination that inspires Frankl to describe the deathcamp trial as "an exceptionally difficult external situation," as if the threat to human life, and the means of executing it, were no different from familiar conflicts in the literature of tragedy and the history of religious persecution? One more example of an actual "difficult external situation" in a deathcamp, recorded by Hermann Langbein, may help us to approach more lucidly Frankl's stubborn refusal (or disappointing inability) to distinguish between living or dying as martyrs, and survival and atrocity in a place like Auschwitz. Langbein tells of a member of the Sonderkommando (which encouraged victims of the gas chamber to enter in an orderly manner) whispering to the doomed the truth of what was about to happen. Whether it was compassion or the need to restore some semblance of self-respect to his battered ego that drove him to this revelation—which was punishable, if discovered, by death—we shall never know. Is this the kind of act of spiritual freedom that, according to Frankl, gives meaning and purpose to one's life? The doomed victims, dismayed and terrified by the "revelation"—and such "loaded" religious terminology, as we see, has its ironic uses too—cried out in fear and disbelief; an SS guard heard the commotion, investigated, quickly discovered the cause, seized the offending Sonderkommando member, and in the presence of his fellow workers, as an exemplary punishment, thrust him *alive* into the crematorium![22]

In the bitter fight for self-preservation, Frankl acknowledges, the prisoner might "forget his human dignity and become no more than an animal" (p. 107). But how are we to view the fate of this wretched anonymous victim, whose human impulse is repaid by a brutal inhumanity, whose act is remembered not for its heroism but for the irreducible horror that results? "Here," Frankl continues (i.e., in the deathcamps), "lies the chance for a man either to make use of or to forego the opportunities of attaining the values that a difficult situation may afford him. And this decides whether he is worthy of his sufferings or not" (p. 107). Was the man thrust alive into the crematorium worthy of his sufferings? What *were* his sufferings, and what have they to do with "attaining the values" that Frankl speaks of? As one wades through the rigidly ethical and Christian vocabulary of Frankl's book—he speaks of the man who "takes up his cross," of "salvation," of "eternal life"—one feels assaulted by the undertow of conversion, as if Frankl secretly yearned for a transfiguration of Auschwitz into nothing more than a test of the religious sensibility, a division of men into the unredeemed and the redeemable. As a Jew, he can hardly (like Dostoevsky) invoke the image of an archetypal Christian sufferer; but he comes perilously close when, after admitting the difficulty of achieving the spiritual commitment he celebrates, he suggests that "even one such example is sufficient proof that man's inner strength may raise him above his outward fate" (p. 107). It can hardly be accidental that two paragraphs later Frankl cites Tolstoy's *Resurrection* as a work in which man meets death "in a courageous and dignified way" (p. 108).

The speculation that either Tolstoy or Christianity might provide a model of suffering to illuminate the agony of men and women exterminated in a gas chamber haunts Frankl, until he adopts it as a verifiable truth. For every Father Maximilian Kolbe, who *chose* to enter the gas chamber in place of a Polish prisoner (with a wife and children outside the camp),[23] there were literally millions of victims too paralyzed by the unprecedented ordeal before them to exercise Frankl's last spiritual freedom of controlling their *attitude* toward their fate. Among the values that the Holocaust has forced us to surrender—or at least to revise—is reliance on the role of fate in men's lives. What "attitude" can we discover that would include the gas chamber as an acceptable alternative in the scheme of human destiny? To identify extermination as a possible equivalent of man's fate is to grace it with a meaning it neither merits nor can sustain. One awful dilemma for the victim of the deathcamp was that he was left without a conception of fate commensurate with the kind of death that confronted him.

With one exception—though Frankl mentions it nowhere. Speaking of the revolutionary hero in Andre Malraux's *Man's Fate*, Irving Howe says that "he confronts his fate despite a foreknowledge of doom, he believes that in the twentieth century death can take on heroic dimensions only if it is the necessary consequence of revolt and revolt is an act of *choice*." Revolution, Howe continues, is "a deliberate engagement with death as a means for measuring the possibilities of freedom." [24] Later we will have to examine some of the deliberate engagements with death that erupted in several ghettos and extermination camps, to see whether these revolts resemble the acts of choice Howe mentions, and whether they achieve the heroic dimensions Frankl longs for. Since options for "doing" were virtually eliminated in the restrictive life of the camps, Frankl substitutes options for "thinking," those inner or attitudinal choices that liberate the individual from what Frankl casually describes as "the sufferings of the moment" (p. 117). But the liberating attitudes he calls for are so often shaped by what is done *to* one, the foreknowledge of doom to which Howe alludes is so closely allied in the camps to a specific kind of *unimaginable* doom—not "merely" death—that it is impossible to separate the two, attitude from fate. They interact, they go into solution, as it were, but are so transformed by the chemistry of atrocity that though we still call them "attitude" and "fate" after the event, this is more a habit of expression than an expression of insight.

Frankl cannot surrender the impulse to consider everything that happens to man as part of his fate. Survival for him becomes not a struggle but an acquiescence, a miracle of will that mitigates the ruthlessness of the marauder, extermination, by invoking human agency (attitude) as a defense against its assaults on the physical self. If he were to accept the deathcamp as a *violation* of man's fate, its oppression would become indefinable and Frankl would be deprived of an idiom to make it manageable. As long as he pretends that suffering in Auschwitz was a condition of mind more than a distress of body, hence (according to his reasoning) a state of limited rather than total vulnerability—as long as he assumes this posture, he can declare that existence in the concentration camp "was an opportunity and a challenge" (p. 115). By circumventing the death encounter in favor of spiritual heroism, Frankl avoids the difficulty of altering his reader's consciousness so that it can contend with the moral uncertainties of the Holocaust. His own moral view is clear-cut, precise, almost self-congratulatory: "One could make a victory of those experiences, turning life into an inner triumph, or one could ignore the challenge and simply vegetate, as did a majority of the prisoners" (p. 115). It comes as no surprise to the reader, as he closes the volume, that the real hero of *Man's Search for Meaning* is not man, but Viktor Frankl.

The view proposed by Frankl—that when man finds it is his destiny to suffer, he will have to accept his suffering as his task—has pernicious implications. It sets the Holocaust solidly into the bedrock of spiritual history, and deflects our response from protest, outrage, and the need for reorientation in an

outmoded or discredited moral universe to a stoic determination
to transmute the gas chamber into an aftermath of Calvary, with
its victims "suffering proudly—not miserably—knowing how to
die" (p. 132). No quotation could more vigorously demonstrate
atrocity's need for its own vocabulary, an idiom to evoke the
event instead of forcing it into a train of associations with dubious
relevance to the explicit cruelties of the deathcamp. In the absence
of such an idiom, the voice is led up winding corridors of rhetoric,
often immune, as is Frankl, to the dissonance of its verbal vision.
Consider the following example, perhaps the most gruesome
illustration of misplaced simile in all of concentration camp
literature. The perversion of grim image by conventional spiritual
language results from Frankl's refusal to concede to the Holocaust
the slightest quality of an unmanageable event. Speaking about
coping with the extremity of Auschwitz, he says:

> The attempt to develop a sense of humor and to see things in
> a humorous light is some kind of trick learned while
> mastering the art of living (*Lebenskunst*). Yet it is possible to
> practice the art of living even in a concentration camp,
> although suffering is omnipresent. To draw an analogy: a
> man's suffering is similar to the behavior of gas. If a certain
> quantity of gas is pumped into an empty chamber, it will fill
> the chamber completely and evenly, no matter how big the
> chamber. Thus suffering completely fills the human soul and
> conscious mind, no matter whether the suffering is great or
> little. Therefore the "size" of human suffering is absolutely
> relative. (pp. 69–70)

Unfortunately, the gas in the chambers of Auschwitz completely
filled the human *lungs*, not the human soul and conscious mind;
one cannot imagine how Frankl's conscious mind could remain
blind to his sinister analogy, though it confirms the danger,
everywhere evident in his book, of permitting the word or phrase
to take precedence over the fact. The quintessential feature of the
victim's existence in Auschwitz, the reason why that ordeal
continues to haunt and perplex us decades after the event, is that
it drifts in a realm beyond analogy, while we struggle to find a
language to bring it back to our recognizable earth.

The customary use of metaphor is to clarify through image an
abstract idea; as Susan Sontag has shown in *Illness as Metaphor*,

metaphor can just as easily be used, whether by choice or habit, to distort or manipulate an ideal. Frankl's allusion to gas pumped into a chamber, considering the subject of his book, abstracts a concrete and overwhelming event, making apparently innocuous through the infinite expansiveness of human suffering, the real terror of the concentration camp—the extermination of human beings. Hiding behind a consoling phrase like "the art of living" is the horror not merely of dying, but of *such* dying, what I have called atrocity. Something might be said in defense of an "art of survival," but this was practiced by men and women to *escape* suffering, not to absorb and transcend it. Indeed, much has been said, as we shall see in a later chapter, about the "art" of survival by Tadeusz Borowski, but Frankl would not be enchanted by the ironic and cynical tone of his stories, or by the English title of the book in which they appear: *This Way for the Gas, Ladies and Gentlemen.*

Intoxicated by his therapeutic view of human experience, including the Holocaust, Frankl makes physical survival a matter of mental health. Implicit in much of what he says is a paternal chastising of prisoner disillusionment, not because it was an unjustifiable response, but a useless one, a condition to be cured rather than a distress to be comprehended. Psychiatrists have always perceived man ideally as a creature who copes, but few have been as content as Frankl to transcend the terrors of annihilation with such superficial rhetorical ease. To the shivering victim, about to surrender his most precious possession without understanding why, his words offer a mystifyingly irrelevant counsel: "One should not search for an abstract meaning of life. Everyone has his own specific vocation or mission in life; everyone must carry out a concrete assignment that demands fulfillment" (p. 172). So nonsensically unspecific is this universal principle of being that one can even imagine Heinrich Himmler announcing it to his SS men, or Joseph Goebbels sardonically applying it to the genocide of the Jews!

Although his publishers like to stress that Frankl developed his theory of logotherapy, or the need for meaning, *after* his concentration camp experience, Frankl himself insists that he formulated its principles prior to his ordeal.[25] This corrective explains much of the strategy of his book, which has expanded through two English editions to include larger and larger sections on the will to meaning and its role in human endeavor. If man, as

logotherapy assumes, is a self-determining creature, then
Auschwitz must somehow be squeezed into the mold of theory,
instead of adjusting theory to the experience of men. Not the gas
chamber itself can threaten the ultimate freedom to choose one's
attitude toward one's life—and one's death. How one suffers
proudly as he suffocates, or contemplates that fate for spouse or
children, parents, friends, or relatives, Frankl does not
tell—because he does not ask. Such questions are the scourge of
the future Frankl cherishes, a contagion threatening the health of
the spirit that knows how to "suffer bravely" and feel ennobled,
not degraded, by destruction in gas chamber and crematorium.
Eventually, a tone of parody begins to contaminate the vocabulary
of transcendence, as one hungers for more than verbal
confirmation of Frankl's conviction that suffering "ceases to be
suffering in some way at the moment it finds a meaning, such as
the meaning of a sacrifice" (p. 179).

Language alone cannot give meaning to Auschwitz. In the
jungle world of atrocity, one could as easily argue that the
deathcamps deprived sacrifice of meaning, that the depth and
uncontained scope of Nazi ruthlessness poisoned both Jewish and
Christian precedents and left millions of victims without potent
metaphors to imagine, not to say justify, their fate. Frankl's
recollected account of his tranquil demeanor in the midst of
catastrophe creates so many specious effects, whatever his
intentions, that his linking of survival with "healthy" attitude
appears to celebrate theory more than fact. By the end, Frankl
seems totally oblivious to his own early assertion that on the
average "only those prisoners could keep alive who, after years of
trekking from camp to camp, had lost all scruples in their fight for
existence . . . the best of us did not return" (p. 7).

Herman Langbein estimates that 60,000 former Auschwitz
inmates were still alive in other European camps or elsewhere
when the war ended in May 1945. Did these represent the "best"
or the "worst"? The question, like the terms, is outmoded.
Concepts like "justice," "sacrifice," and "the dignity of dying"
cannot encompass the reality of extermination because in the
deathcamps the Nazis created a system that did not acknowledge
the meaning of such a vocabulary. Father Kolbe's act was a
genuine sacrifice, but this inspiring moment in the history of
Auschwitz was an exception, tolerated by the Nazis though
certainly not through reverence for the gesture. It could not serve

as a model for future victims because the men and the system that were destroying them forbade it. But the human imagination has been nourished for so long on such abstractions that it continues to relish them and prefer them to the less savory options of moral confusion or despair, or to the more indigestible diet of learning to live with a double vision and to speak with two voices—the voice of Auschwitz and the voice of civilization. Although a survivor himself, Frankl cannot concede a separate voice to the deathcamp universe; he speaks with the authority of a civilization uncontaminated by atrocity. He writes as a healer, not as a historian, a psychiatrist whose professional task is to reconcile man with his moments of utter desolation and create a way of liberating the future in spite of them. The human goal is admirable, but the approach gives a very provincial view of survival, and the student of the Holocaust must not be misled by it. The fact that 60,000 human beings—though their appearance at liberation belied this description—survived Auschwitz is less a triumph of the will than an accident of the body, combined with so many gratuitous and fortuitous circumstances that we will probably never be able to disentangle chance from choice, or relate effect to discernible cause.

Thirty years later, as a recent interveiw confirms, Frankl was still determined to view events like the Holocaust as mere challenging aberrations in the uninterrupted flow of man's spiritual destiny, not as ruptures in a tradition that no longer seemed viable: "Even if you are caught as a helpless victim in a hopeless situation, you may transcend that situation and turn a tragedy into a triumph on a human level by the attitude that you adopt and bear it with." [26] If this doctrine had been more succinctly worded, the Nazis might have substituted it for the cruel mockery of *Arbeit Macht Frei* (Work Brings Freedom) that greeted victims at the entrance to Auschwitz and other camps. The leaders of the Warsaw ghetto uprising knew better; Frankl's "wisdom" was an invitation to Treblinka. Resistance also led to extinction, for all but a lucky few, but they at least learned, together with their less fortunate companions, that in the realm of atrocity what a man thought or felt was less vital than what he did. In the camps themselves, few were free to *do* even what they thought or felt; they did what they must, to stay alive, with a vague sense that the most crucial choices were not theirs at all.

If after the personal experience of Auschwitz Frankl can still expound such theories, is it any wonder that we continue to wrestle with the question of survival, and of interpreting the behavior of victims under the shadow of annihilation? Imagining that shadow, reimagining it, living uneasily beneath it and its implications, understanding those implications (for the past *and* the future)—our natural instincts are to avoid the whole enterprise, or to generate rays of sunlight that will radiate through its darkness. Greater minds than Frankl's have failed—or refused—to pursue the Holocaust to its nullifying end, for the similar reason that it was not consistent with their vision of man's spiritual destiny. Several weeks after *Kristallnacht* in November 1938, Mahatma Gandhi published a statement in response to letters asking him to comment on "the Arab-Jew question in Palestine and the persecution of the Jews in Germany." [27] Only the latter subject need occupy us here. Like so many of his contemporaries, Gandhi acknowledges Hilter's ferocity but underestimates its power, scope, and single-minded determination by virtually dismissing Hitler as "an obviously mad but intrepid youth" (p. 41). Like Frankl, Gandhi devotes most of his energy to the attitude and behavior of the potential victims, ignoring the attitude and behavior of the persecutors, on which the response of the victims depend. Gandhi's conviction that "no person who has faith in a living God need feel helpless or forlorn" (p. 41) is probably an accurate reflection of what many devout Jews of the period believed, but it reverberates with a wan echo in the ears of a post-Holocaust generation. His main advice—that the Jews invoke Indian *satyagraha* or "strength of the soul" to oppose Nazi violence—reads today like a swan song to a world that could not imagine the unimaginable doom of extermination.

Gandhi's inability to penetrate the true threat in Germany (and later in the occupied countries) may first be seen as an indirect tribute to the civilized humanity of the victims, who refuse to ascribe to the enemy inhuman motives they cannot perceive in themselves. He writes:

> If I were a Jew and were born in Germany and earned my livelihood here, I would claim Germany as my home even as the tallest gentile German may, and challenge him to shoot me or cast me in the dungeon; I would refuse to be expelled

or to submit to discriminating treatment. And for doing this I should not wait for the fellow Jews to join me in civil resistance, but would have confidence that in the end the rest are bound to follow my example. If one Jew or all the Jews were to accept the prescription here offered, he or they cannot be worse off than now [!]. And suffering voluntarily undergone will bring them an inner strength and joy which no number of resolutions of sympathy passed in the world outside Germany can. (p. 42)

Imagine with what hilarity Joseph Goebbels, himself no mean manipulator of language in behalf of specific goals, would have digested this invitation to Jewish "suffering voluntarily undergone." Martin Buber, who replied to Gandhi's open letter three months later, found its general principles praiseworthy, but reproached its author because he "has cast not a single glance at the situation of him whom he is addressing," and "sees not him nor does he know him and the straits under which he labours" (p. 1). Buber's foresight, considering that the extermination camps had not yet been built, nor the war even begun, is prophetic; he understands that the Nazis, both in their character and their philosophy, are invincible to the appeal of Gandhi's *satyagraha*.

   Although Gandhi (together with millions of his contemporaries) suffered from a failure of imagination, this does not completely explain his position. In the letter he shows unlimited willingness to tolerate slaughter for the sake of his principles, revealing even more clearly than Frankl the hypnotic power of words to convert an inhuman ordeal (whose concrete details still floated vaguely in the future) into a rhetorical glory:

   The calculated violence of Hitler may even result in the general massacre of the Jews by way of his first answer to the declaration of such hostilities [i.e., civil resistance]. But if the Jewish mind could be prepared for voluntary suffering, even the massacre I have imagined could be turned into a day of thanksgiving and joy that Jehovah had wrought deliverance of the race even at the hands of the tyrant. For the God-fearing, death has no terror. (p. 42)

One might be forgiven for hoping to be spared such a deliverance, as well as wondering who would be left to celebrate it. If Jonathan

Swift had written those words, we would have applauded the irony and implicit parody; but Gandhi was serious. Buber's piercing rejoinder (in 1939!) reverberates with somber irony through succeeding generations: "Now do you know or do you not know, Mahatma, what a concentration camp is like and what goes on there?" (p. 4). But the question was not sufficient to modify Gandhi's certitude; nor does it appear to have altered Viktor Frankl's devotion to the value of suffering, although *he* could have answered Buber's inquiry in the affirmative.

When voices as universally prestigious as Gandhi's declared that there was still a decent and morally acceptable manner of averting Jewish catastrophe, who can blame the rest of the world, to say nothing of the potential victims themselves, for disbelieving in the approaching disaster? A way of viewing reality that had nothing to do with passivity or cowardice, that grew out of centuries of faith by Jews and Christians alike in the power of suffering to transfigure pain into spiritual triumph, persuaded men that the impending Holocaust could be contained (and borne) by the exertion of an inward and outward moral pressure. By applying the language of transcendence to the experience of atrocity, Gandhi hopes to change the situation, but only ends by misreading the threat:

> I am convinced that if someone with courage and vision can arise among them to lead them in non-violent action, the winter of their despair can in the twinckling [*sic*] of an eye be turned into the summer of hope. And what has today become a degrading man-hunt can be turned into a calm and determined stand offered by unarmed men and women possessing the strength of suffering given to them by Jehovah. It will be then a truly religious resistance offered against the godless fury of dehumanized man. The German Jews will score a lasting victory over the German Gentiles in the sense that they will have converted the latter to an appreciation of human dignity. (pp. 43–44)

Few passages better illustrate the impotence of this arsenal of words, which proved so futile against the fatal weapons of atrocity. "Courage," "vision," "despair," "hope," "suffering," "religious," "godless," and of course the omnipresent "human dignity"—they represent a last effort of traditional vocabulary to forestall a genocide it could not conceive. How much more ineffectual is the identical vocabulary *after* our knowledge of the event!

The pursuit of martyrdom was an integral part, perhaps even a desirable part, of Gandhi's possible fate. He knew from years of self-denial that his actions *and* his words had the power to affect the British authorities in India and sear the conscience of the world. But the Jews of Germany and later of Eastern Europe did not share Gandhi's international renown, nor had their collective history (unlike Gandhi's private conduct) won the admiration of the human race. When the last act of their drama drew near, few cared to attend it, while even fewer members of the small audience were curious—or indignant—enough to peer behind the final curtain to face the waning light of their existence. Because they were actors on the stage of atrocity, the idiom of their performance was too unfamiliar to shock the witnesses into a vivid sense of the reality that their drama represented. The witnesses preferred the safer diction of a Gandhi, even though Buber tried to teach them a crucial lesson in semantic distinctions:

> The word "Satyagraha" signifies testimony. Testimony without acknowledgement, ineffective, unobserved martyrdom, a martyrdom cast to the winds—this is the fate of innumerable Jews in Germany. God alone accepts their testimony, God "seals" it, as is said in our prayers. But no maxim for suitable behaviour can be deduced therefrom. Such martyrdom is a deed—but who would venture to demand it? (p. 5)

Apparently more would venture than Buber cared to believe, including some who would survive the Holocaust themselves. Gandhi lived a life (and died a death) of testimony *with* acknowledgement; many maxims for suitable behavior could be deduced therefrom. But if Buber considered the persecution of the Jews in Germany in 1938 and 1939, which the world chose to ignore, as "martyrdom cast to the winds," how are we to regard today that even more deafening testimony *without* acknowledgement of extermination in the gas chambers? Surely we must begin by recognizing what Buber was already hinting, that such a fate, which the Nazi murderers indeed "demanded," cannot be defined by a term like "martyrdom," which we reserve for less shattering testimonies like Gandhi's. Orthodox verbal and spiritual scaffolding cannot support the unorthodox destinies of these victims.

At first it seems that Bruno Bettelheim, in *The Informed Heart*, is prepared to confront the implications of this viewpoint. A trained psychoanalyst who was imprisoned for a year in Dachau and Buchenwald from 1938 to 1939, Bettelheim was shrewd enough to realize that his professional expertise offered little help "toward the solution of how to survive and survive halfway decently in the camps." [28] Unlike Frankl, he concedes the overwhelming influence of environment on the prisoner's capacity to survive, although because he never observed life in a deathcamp, he sometimes forgets that the purpose of Dachau and Buchenwald when he was there was punishment, not extermination. He often blurs the difference between the two, confusing an extreme situation with a terminal one. Bettelheim writes of his experience (as he endured it) with the psychology of hope, and with good reason: partly through the intervention of prominent Americans, he was released after a year and eventually emigrated to America. The title of his book, *The Informed Heart*, provides an enticing image and attractive sanctuary for those determined to resist the dehumanizing influence of a totalitarian atmosphere.

For those who abandoned hope at the gates of Auschwitz because they knew there was no possibility of intervention from beyond the barbed wire, another image might be more appropriate; but Bettelheim is quicker to blame than to understand the *transformed* heart that often resulted from daily proximity to the gas chambers. If depth psychology alone, as he argues, could not adequately explain changes in character in the camps, some other theoretical framework would have to be developed. Because he is determined to see the concentration camp ordeal as an outgrowth of the shift toward modern mass society and rapid technological change, his explanations try to adapt or adjust that ordeal to the more comprehensive question of living "the good life" in the second half of the twentieth century. The camps are a laboratory for Bettelheim, a place where one can observe human behavior and learn—the most important lesson of the camps, apparently, for him—that "man must be better protected, through education or otherwise, against [society's] potentially destructive influence. He must be better equipped to change society so that it will not be an obstacle to living the good life, but a setting that facilitates and encourages it" (p. 44). But how does this help us to understand the Holocaust, which was often engineered by highly educated men who believed in selective rather than universal autonomy, and whose conception of "the good life" simply differed from Bettelheim's? Once more we encounter a faith in human control over atrocity, an unwavering conviction that the key to understanding human response in the concentration camp universe was the individual's ability or failure to exercise choice in behalf of his own survival.

Bettelheim is less concerned with how the inhumanity of the murderers eroded the humanity of their victims than with the "saving" detail that "some persons managed to retain their humanity in the German concentration camps even after ten years or more" (p. 48). One wonders whether the "persons" of whom he speaks, upon their liberation, would have celebrated this (unelaborated) fact with the same enthusiasm. Such a fact cannot be isolated from the fate of those less fortunate. Bettelheim seems unequipped to contend with Buber's mournful formulation, "testimony without acknowledgement," though he is honest enough to pay passing homage to the idea. Confessing the difficulty of decision making, he adds that "however restrictive or oppressive an environment may be, even then the individual still retains the freedom to evaluate it. On the basis of this evaluation he is also free to decide on his inner approval or resistance to what is forced upon him" (p. 72). This resembles some of Frankl's notions, though the association is more specifically ethical than vaguely spiritual. Aside from its rhetorical splendor, does this mean that the Jew was inwardly free to assent to or repudiate his arrest, deportation, beating, torture, selection for the gas chamber? "True," Bettelheim graciously admits, "in an extremely oppressive environment these inner decisions can lead to little or no practical consequences" (p. 72). Buber would have understood this; but what would he have made of the subsequent non sequitur: "Therefore the more man is geared toward achieving 'practical' results, the more he may view the making of inner decisions that lead to no practical end as a total waste of energy, and hence avoid making them" (p. 72).

Bettelheim would probably be astounded to find this conclusion applauded as a clear-sighted defense of the "learned" helplessness that afflicted so many deathcamp inmates, whose inner selves were deflated not through cowardice or weakness of will, but because of the perceived hopelessness of their situation. He clings valiantly to the notion that the "consciousness of freedom," so vital to the individual threatened by the encroachments of modern mass society, could also operate fruitfully in the concentration camp environment (p. 104). Because he knows that when human affairs are managed by others, whether parents or "society," the spirit of autonomy withers away and the individual loses his identity, he cannot surrender his devotion to "man's inner ability to govern himself," and to the "conscientious search for meaning despite the realization that, as far as we know, there is no purpose to one's life" (p. 75). But there is an immense difference between a search for meaning and the discovery that a "purpose" has been established by one's persecutors—extermination. Bettelheim's crucial vocabulary—"identity," "self-respect," "inner freedom," and "autonomy"—swells that catalogue of terms that try to impose an assumed coherence on a trial that eludes familiar categories. The effect once more is to bring the Holocaust into line with familiar experience by making it verbally manageable, rather than approaching it as a fundamental violation of all disciplined thought and orderly action, lacking a convenient niche in contemporary interpretations of the human dilemma.

As long as we can believe that some men, including of course Bettelheim, were able to mount intellectual defenses against atrocity, we need not grant that the Holocaust was a totally dehumanizing experience or that the genocide of the Jews represented a contempt for human life unparalleled in the history of civilization. Although Bettelheim distinguishes verbally between concentration camps and extermination camps, although he admits that his personal observations were limited, he nevertheless undertakes an elaborate classification of behavior in what he calls "extreme situations" which he intends as an authoritative analysis of the Holocaust ordeal. The greatest danger about his work is that the reader may be persuaded too easily by its dogmatic tone. He presents many of his premises as if they were intrinsically valid, whereas actually they merely serve his determination to approach the "truth" through generalization rather than ambiguity or contradiction. In order to understand the role of the German concentration camps in the history of man, he insists, "any emphasis on atrocities as such or on individual fates will not do" (p. 109). Only a certain kind of imagination could argue that the camps' "social meaning is what makes them important as an example of the very nature of the coercive mass state" (p. 109). Reminded of Benedict Kautsky's warning that even "when you're talking about the same period of time, prisoners in the same camp lived as if on different planets," one wonders how trustworthy the simplest of Bettelheim's conclusions can be. They reflect a mind with a message, unwilling to surrender its faith in the future or its belief that even the Holocaust can be explained in morally and psychologically meaningful terms.

One pays a price for such belief, and that is to substitute attitude for event. Bettelheim ends the first paragraph of his famous 1943 article on "Individual and Mass Behavior in Extreme Situations," one of the germs of *The Informed Heart*, with a curious demurral: "It is not the intention of this presentation to recount once more [in 1943!] the horror story of the German concentration camp for political prisoners." [29] Is it a chance conjunction of temperaments that led Viktor Frankl to include in the first paragraph of *Man's Search for Meaning* (in 1947 one of the first accounts of Auschwitz in any language) a virtually identical denial: "This tale is not concerned with the great horrors, which have already been described often enough . . ."? Can *any* story of the camps, *any* history of the period, *any* attempt to confront the enigma of the Holocaust evade the horrors and still speak with authority about their implications? By shelving emphasis on "atrocities as such," by declaring that attention to "individual fates" will not do, Bettelheim excludes the most exasperating questions for those who are still struggling to find a place for the Holocaust in the spiritual chronology of the twentieth century.

Bettelheim comments with satisfaction on the strange relief some of his readers felt upon encountering his initial interpretations of the concentration camps (presumably he means his 1943 article): "It seemed that even when dealing with the most gruesome aspects of an oppressive mass society, the intellectual defense through understanding was still the most effective assurance that one was not altogether helpless and might even safeguard one's personality in the face of extreme threat" (p. 106). If the Holocaust were merely a threat to personality integration, one might comprehend such feelings of relief; but once we admit that the threat of atrocity is physical disintegration, the mutilation of the body far more than the soul, we recognize that Bettelheim's strategy is to emphasize reassurance in spite of the facts. His conviction that the Hitler mass state was only a passing phenomenon (an oddly casual phrase for an event that cost the world over thirty million lives) exudes the inveterate optimism of an earlier century. Confronting his words in an age when terrorism and torture have grown commonplace, one can only marvel at the audacious confidence of an old-fashioned mind: "Despite temporary setbacks, including the fall of the antique world, every new development in man has soon challenged him to reach a higher integration and a deeper consciousness of freedom. These alone can change technical advances into truly human progress" (pp. 106–107). What dimensions must an event achieve before it ceases to represent a temporary setback and rouses the specter of permanence?

The need to believe that despite what is done to us, a direct connection exists between inner nurture and outer fate, is the clearest current running through *The Informed Heart*:

> Those prisoners who blocked out neither heart nor reason, neither feelings nor perception, but kept informed of their inner attitudes even when they could hardly ever afford to act on them, those prisoners survived and came to understand the conditions they lived under. They also came to realize what they had not perceived before; that they still retained the last, if not the greatest, of the human freedoms: to choose their own attitude in any given circumstance.
> (p. 158)

The waters of such thought are muddied considerably by Bettelheim's own damaging admission later on that most of the time "concern for personal integration and integrity had to be sacrificed to preserve life" (p. 200), or that "in the end most prisoners chose to be sure of their bread rather than their self esteem" (p. 201), but he seems undismayed and unchastened by the conflicting points of view. Lurking behind the "sacrifice" and the "choice" lies an unrecognizable world of moral chaos that Bettelheim is compelled to ignore in order to avoid the stagnation of his theme.

What comfort would the young Elie Wiesel have felt, as he watched helplessly while an SS man beat his father, to know that he was free to choose his own attitude toward this humiliating episode? Or the Jewish prisoner assigned to send "selected" inmates into a room one by one to receive fatal phenol injections, when he encountered his own father as the next victim? Bettelheim's reason for ignoring such crucial experiences illuminates with an unholy glow the crude and often cruel limitations of scientific detachment when confronting this theme: "The analysis of behavior inside the extermination camps, while more horrid, offers less of psychological interest, since prisoners there had not time or occasion to change much psychologically" (p. 243). This sweeping dismissal of the psychological importance of the terrifying universe of extermination reveals little of value, as we shall see, about the victims, but much concerning the author, whose premises about "resistance," "heroism," "attitude," and "choice" are so diluted by human behavior in the deathcamps that he is forced to retreat from their threat to his theories. By applying what I have called the terminology of transcendence to the encounter with inappropriate and meaningless death, Bettelheim sidesteps the deeper challenge of the Holocaust: acknowledging the diversity of human response to a singular and unpredictable event, and finding an idiom and vision to incorporate it into a description of man's fate in the twentieth century.

In Bettelheim, theory and interpretation have a way of displacing direct rendering of the experience of atrocity, deflecting our attention from the event itself and manipulating our response in favor of some startlingly affirmative conclusions, considering the horror to which the victim is exposed. Bettelheim describes the episode that held nothing but terror for the defenseless prisoners in *all* camps: prolonged roll call in winter. On a cold night during a snowstorm, hungry and scantily clad inmates were forced to stand at attention in the open after a twelve-hour working day. Many died of exposure. Although elsewhere in his volume Bettelheim harshly criticizes Jews for not rebelling in a hopeless situation, here he more charitably concedes that "open resistance was impossible, as impossible as it was to do anything definite to safeguard oneself" (p. 137). The only defense is for the individual to disappear into the mass, though Bettelheim fails to explain how this process occurs. His theory of a split "between the figure to whom things happened and the prisoner himself" assumes that the mind can detach itself from the suffering body, and that surrendering individual existence to become part of the

"group" while standing motionless in the freezing cold is
meaningful as both concept and action. Exactly whose attitude
(other than his own recollections) Bettelheim has explored in
order to reach the following remarkable conclusions, he does not
say; but the reader is left perplexed by how they are to be
reconciled with his vigorous defense elsewhere of the connection
between survival and autonomy in a mass age:

> Unfortunate as the situation was, the prisoners then felt free
> from fear as individuals and powerful as a mass because "not
> even the Gestapo can kill us all tonight." Therefore, they
> were actually happier than at most other times of the camp
> experience. They did not care whether the guards shot them.
> They were indifferent to acts of torture. The guards no
> longer held authority, the spell of fear and death was broken.
> When this stage was reached, a quasi-orgiastic happiness
> spread among the prisoners who by forming a mass had
> defeated the Gestapo's effort to break them. (pp. 137–138)

Some peculiar changes between the account of this episode in his
1943 article and the 1960 book version add to our sense of the
untrustworthiness of this excursion into memory and
interpretation. "After more than 80 prisoners had died," says the
article, "and several hundred had their extremities so badly frozen
that they had later to be amputated, the prisoners were permitted
to return to the barracks." [30] Since such figures could hardly
support his theory that "group survival" had defeated the
Gestapo's efforts to break them, Bettelheim modified this in *The
Informed Heart* to read "because by then more than fifty prisoners
had died, the men were allowed to go back to the barracks." [31]
The mortality rate has dropped forty percent, while the mention
of frostbite has disappeared. Not so curiously, the phrase about
the "quasi-orgiastic happiness" of the prisoners has been *added* to
the book version, reflecting Bettelheim's impulse in selected
episodes to transform atrocity into some form of heroic resistance.

Another survivor of a similar roll call, this time in Auschwitz,
confirms one of the ideas we have been exploring—our way of
"seeing" the Holocaust depends almost entirely on someone else's
way of "saying," not on abstract principles that we apply
externally to the ordeal of atrocity. Against Bettelheim's internal

interpretation we can measure Charlotte Delbo's external presentation, to compare how the "voice" of the author can sharpen or blunt our response to the reality:

> With her neck retracted into her shoulders, her chest pulled in, each woman puts her hands under the arms of the woman in front of her. In the first row, they cannot do this, and they are rotated. Chest to back, we stand huddled together and although we thus set up a common circulation for all, a common circulatory system, we are all frozen. Annihilated by the cold. Our feet which remain distant, cut-off extremities, cease to exist. Our shoes were still damp from yesterday's snow or slush, from all the yesterdays. They never dry out.
>
> We must stand motionless for hours in the cold and in the wind. We do not speak. The words freeze on our lips. The cold throws a whole nation of women who stand motionless into a stupor. In the night. In the cold. In the wind.
>
> We stand motionless and the amazing thing is that we are still standing. Why? No one thinks "What is the use" or else does not say it. With our last bit of strength, we stand.[32]

Can we ever pierce the inner world of resistance, so vital to Frankl and Bettelheim, before we appreciate the outer universe of assault, the sheer physical threat that no one could enter the concentration camp prepared to meet? Charlotte Delbo's image of "a common circulatory system" may have the *force* of a metaphor, but she is speaking literally of freezing, not of friendship. Bettelheim's interest in "the mental attitude of most prisoners" lifts the ordeal into an intellectual sphere, where we can comfortably substitute explanation for immersion.

Unfortunately, short of questioning them all (which obviously was impossible), there was no way to determine a clear picture of the mental life of most prisoners. Generalizations about human behavior in "normal" society are not so easy to project or validate in the unpredictable environment of atrocity. "To survive," says Bettelheim, "not as a shadow of the SS but as a man, one had to find some life experience that mattered, over which one was still in command" (p. 147). In Bettelheim's camps before the war, where many prisoners received letters and money from home, could buy small necessities and food at a canteen, and according to Bettelheim often used toothbrushes and slept on pillows, surviving "as a man" could be identified with items of familiar civilization, even though access to them was limited and sometimes arbitrary. But if the same individuals could freeze to death or die from exhaustion at a roll call, does not the concept of surviving "as a man" require redefinition? Surrounded by a death experience so uncommon, how much inner insulation can be provided by reliance on a common "life experience," so radically alienated from one's present circumstances? Viktor Frankl argued that thinking of his wife's love for him, and his for her, helped keep him alive. But since she died in the gas chamber, and his presence in Auschwitz made apparent to him that this was the fate of most Jews in the camp, was his dependence on this life experience to support survival a realistic and meaningful choice or a form of self-deception, designed to protect one from confronting catastrophe?

When prisoners stopped acting, Bettelheim insists, they soon stopped living, and there is much evidence to support this, especially for the *Muselmänner*, whose glazed indifference to their surroundings quickly marked them for extermination. But the reverse of this principle—that is, that a direct connection existed between action and survival—plunges us back into a world of moral terminology that obscures more than it illuminates. "What seemed to make the critical difference," says Bettelheim, "was whether or not the environment—extreme as it was—permitted (or promised) some minimal choices, some leeway, some positive rewards, insignificant as they seem now, when viewed objectively against the tremendous deprivation" (p. 148). He speaks of this "area of freedom" as if it were identical with the kind of moral challenge facing men daily in precamp society, where survival is not such a crucial issue, and certain kinds of conduct simply unthinkable, for the majority of individuals. We get a clearer glimpse of options available in this "area of freedom" from Olga Lengyel, a Jewish doctor who survived Auschwitz and was willing to be more specific than Bettelheim:

> The entire policy was to reduce us to the lowest moral level. And they could boast of results: men who had been lifetime friends ended up by hating each other with real repugnance; brothers fought each other for a crust of bread; men of formerly unimpeachable integrity stole whatever they could;

and often it was the Jewish capo who beat his fellow Jewish sufferer. . . . Power alone prevailed. The feeble and the aged could not dare to hope for pity.[33]

These were actions, and they had purposes, and indeed they aided survival. Extreme environments may still tolerate minimal choices, but words like "choice" and "freedom" are so modified by the threat of atrocity that they acquire an unfamiliar resonance in the world of the camps.

As a physician, Lengyel attended women prisoners during childbirth, then killed the newborn infants and pretended that they had been stillborn. "And so," she concludes, "the Germans succeeded in making murderers of even us. . . . The only meager consolation is that by these murders we saved the mothers. Without our intervention they would have endured worse sufferings, for they would have been thrown into the crematory ovens while still alive." Is this choice between two horrors any choice at all? Lengyel admits that the opportunity to practice her profession at Auschwitz helped keep her alive (though having cleaner living quarters and access to better food were far more important than any inner area of freedom resulting from her position); but what satisfaction can one derive from such "practice," and what generalizations about survival can one equate with it? The very efforts Lengyel employed to retain what Bettelheim would have called "personality intergration" led to her "murdering" babies. Are we to apply standard medical ethics to this situation? Compare Lengyel's honest (but hardly triumphant) outburst—"I marvel to what depths these Germans made us descend!"—with Bettelheim's feeble attempt to navigate the shoals of atrocity, whose details quiver menacingly behind the looming rocks of his phraseology:

> What supports self-esteem and true independence is not fixed and unchanging, but depends on the vagaries of the environment. Each environment requires different mechanisms for safeguarding autonomy, those that are germane to success in living, according to one's values in the particular environment.[34]

But killing normal infants is never a "value," only a necessity, the lesser of two unacceptable evils. It may have been "germane" to Lengyel's (and the mothers') success in living, but—to repeat

Buber's sober rejoinder to Gandhi—"no maxim for suitable behaviour can be deduced therefrom."

Even when Bettelheim ceases to cloak reality behind phrases like "the vagaries of the environment" and presents concrete instances of what he considers to be "integrative responses" to the death threat, he imagines them as forms of heroic resistance that others might emulate. He repeats a story (not based on personal observation) of a woman prisoner (who had been a dancer) ordered by an SS officer to dance for him before she entered the gas chamber. Complying, she seized his revolver as she danced, shot the officer, and was herself immediately shot to death. Ignoring the vicious contempt for human dignity that such SS conduct illustrates, Bettelheim uses this impulsive gesture to support the unlikely proposition that "in an instant the old personality can be regained, its destruction undone, once we decide on our own that we wish to cease being units in a system." [35] His theories require him to dismiss despair or temporary madness as equally possible motives for this desperate act, which for him illustrates the victim's willingness "to risk her life to achieve autonomy once more" (p. 259). The temptation to deduce maxims for suitable behavior from such actions is irresistible to persons like Bettelheim, whose approach to the Holocaust sometimes seems to be inspired by nostalgia for the heroic spirit of a vanished romantic age. He ends his account of this episode with a stirring celebration of that spirit: "if we cannot live, at least we die as men" (p. 259).

How much credence can one allow to a theory of resistance built on one unwitnessed gesture that is open to various interpretations? Olga Lengyel reports a similar incident, but her response leads us in a different direction:

> One day a selectee wrested a revolver from an S.S. and started to beat him with it. Desperate courage certainly inspired this gesture, but it had no effect except to bring mass reprisals. The Germans held us all "guilty"; "collective responsibility" they called it. The beatings and the gas chambers explain, in part, why the history of the camp includes few open revolts, even when mothers were forced to surrender their children to death.[36]

Fear of torture and terror of extermination are great demoralizers. From the remembered perspective of Auschwitz, Lengyel knows that imagined effects cannot efface the physical reality of "beatings and gas chambers." The contradiction between the two, the tragic defiance Bettelheim longs for to support his theory of the informed heart and the fate of extinction that atrocity imposed on debilitated victims, surfaces in his book periodically but is never reconciled. In a moment of clarity (or forgetfulness?) he appears to concede the defeat of the autonomous self: "It seems that an institution like the concentration camp permits of no really successful defense—the only way not to submit to it in some measure would have been to destroy it." [37] But one senses that a voice of deeper conviction speaks some pages later in the following inconsistent observation: "the story of the extermination camps shows that even in such an overpowering environment, certain defenses do offer some protection, most important of which is understanding what goes on in oneself, and why" (p. 257). The more one gropes through Bettelheim's own gropings to bring light out of the shadowy realm of the concentration camp experience, the more one suspects that the process of logical inference he depends on may be inadequate to conjure up a sufficiently complex vision of that ordeal.

Heedless of Buber's repudiation of a martyrdom "thrown to the winds," indifferent to how the prospect of "testimony without acknowledgement" may paralyze the will, Bettelheim transforms Jewish genocide into a form of Jewish suicide, thus diminishing the role of the agents of atrocity and transferring the major responsibility for their extermination to the victims: "Millions of Jews of Europe who did not or could not escape in time or go underground as many thousands did, could at least have marched as free men against the SS, rather than to first grovel, then wait to be rounded up for their own extermination, and finally walk themselves to the gas chambers." This version of Jewish compliance, not invented by Bettelheim but eagerly espoused by him, heaps scorn on the passive victim and virtually ignores the murderer, who organizes and executes the deed. It is a comfortable view because it confronts the reader only with a rational cowardice, not an irrational racist hatred, and protects Bettelheim (and the reader) from having to face a vision of atrocity that eliminates familiar ideas of cause and effect from the ordeal of the Jews. Indeed, both Frankl and Bettelheim suppress emphasis on the raison d'être of the Nazi racial policy—the genocide of the Jews. If annihilation rather than "depersonaliza-

tion"—one of Bettelheim's favorite words—was
the inspiration for this policy, then the value of "personal
autonomy" in controlling one's fate is considerably weakened,
while Frankl's dependence on a proper attitude to ensure survival
grows irrelevant. When the death sentence has been pronounced
in advance by someone else, as it had been for all Jews, many
Gypsies, and most Soviet prisoners of war, at the very least, then
the future becomes, in Primo Levi's words, an "invincible barrier"
and history stops.

Is there a difference between the knowledge that one is
"destined to die" (p. 248) (Bettelheim's words) and the
consciousness that one is doomed to be murdered for no reason,
cremated, have one's ashes strewn anonymously across a mute
and alien earth, vanish from humanity and be forgotten? I choose
to be dramatic deliberately, to distinguish between the "destined
to die" that describes the general fate of men, and a unique
atrocity that improves in appearance only when camouflaged by a
traditional vocabulary. Jacob Robinson, whose pamphlet on
Bettelheim demolishes the accuracy of numerous details in *The
Informed Heart*, offers some judicious commentary on the question
we have been examining: "The attempt to submerge the
extermination of the Jews into some larger context and to present
it not as murder of the Jewish people but as one of many victims
of totalitarianism is in line with widely used terminology of
concealing the specific nature of the Holocaust during and after
the war." Certainly the Jews were not the only victims of the
Holocaust; Robinson estimates that more than four million Soviet
prisoners of war died in concentration camps.[38] Few of them
"marched as free men against the SS" before their execution
either, though Bettelheim, as Robinson mentions, does not charge
them with passivity or cowardice. But only the Jews had been
chosen in advance for a total program of genocide; thus somehow,
Bettelheim must incorporate his theory of personal autonomy into
the failure of so many millions to survive. Random brutal
execution—and executioners—would reduce such a theory to
intellectual rubble.

Bettelheim's previously quoted observation that the "analysis
of behavior inside the extermination camps, while more horrid,
offers less of psychological interest" now is seen to confirm not a
truth but a disjunction between an unprecedented horror and the
psychological premises that Bettelheim depends on. Any analysis

of such behavior, including speculations about what might or
might not reinforce the chances for survival, must begin with an
understanding of that horror. Equally essential is that the
investigator be flexible enough—as Bettelheim is not—to
surrender every vestige of value inherited from the pre-Holocaust
universe, *provided* the evidence warrants such abandonment. By
viewing the Holocaust simply as an expression of twentieth-
century totalitarian oppression of the autonomous
spirit, Bettelheim is able to advocate the renewal of that spirit
without asking how a heart informed by atrocity—by this
particular atrocity—may also have been deformed by it.

Fifteen years after the appearance of *The Informed Heart*,
Bettelheim entered the lists of survivorship once again, this time
to tilt against two works whose assumptions and conclusions
contradict many of his own. In a long review of Lina Wertmüller's
film *Seven Beauties* and those published excerpts from Terrence
Des Pres's *The Survivor* that he had read, Bettelheim resumes the
role of scourge of those who would "interpret survivorship
falsely." [39] Unaware that many of the charges he directs against
the film and the book are equally appropriate to his own earlier
work, he writes with even less specific authority here; he identifies
himself as "an inmate of concentration camps and one of the all
too few fortunate survivors" (p. 33), though Wertmüller and Des
Pres are in no way concerned with the prewar punishment camps
that he knew from personal experience. They confront the
concrete challenge of surviving atrocity, of how the human being
behaves when the threat is the trauma of extermination. At first it
seems as if Bettelheim may finally have found an idiom for
entering this unfamiliar world, which he describes in his review
(in language absent from *The Informed Heart*) as "the unimaginable
abomination—the unspeakable horror of yesteryear" (p. 31), but
he soon lapses into the recognizable vocabulary of the earlier
work, whose moral orientation is simply baffled by the
contradictions and ambiguities of Wertmüller's essentially visual
art. By trying to apply the "truth" of history to the shifting vision
of cinema, Bettelheim does justice to neither, merely proving that
we must embrace various and often contradictory viewpoints in
our efforts to understand the event we call the Holocaust.

By accusing *Seven Beauties* of "falsifying what survival was all
about" (p. 43), Bettelheim narrows the range of possible
interpretations and continues to insist that there is a quality we

call "human dignity" that must assert itself in extreme situations if survival is to be meaningful. The idea that under certain circumstances "survival is not worth having" (p. 46) is easily uttered by one not immersed in those circumstances, though indeed in the camps and ghettos some individuals acted on that principle and took their own lives. Rather than concede that the concentration camp experience tested resources beyond the capacity of most men—certainly beyond the capacity of Wertmüller's protagonist, Pasqualino—Bettelheim censures both her and her character for falsifying the reality of the camps. The crucial episode of the film, according to Bettelheim, confirms (to Bettelheim's discredit) his extraordinary conviction that the "extreme conditions of the camps brought out in often exaggerated form the values by which prisoners had lived, but rarely changed them" (p. 47). One is not surprised to learn that amoral persons acted as amorally as before, since Auschwitz was not designed to reform criminals. But what are we to do with the evasive assertion that "decent ones tried to remain decent—at least, as much as possible" (p. 47)? Who determines the limitations of that possibility?

Pasqualino is certainly not one of the decent ones, but his friend Francesco and the anarchist Pedro are, and their fates are bound up with Pasqualino's behavior in the crucial episode. The camp commandant appoints Pasqualino barrack leader and orders him to select six of its inmates for execution. If he refuses, she will execute them all. Although he does not agree with great glee, he makes the selection (to the dismay of his friends) because six victims are fewer than all. Bettelheim finds his behavior offensive, and uses it as evidence that Wertmüller herself believes that the will to survive justified any action—though why a petty criminal like Pasqualino should be expected to behave otherwise Bettelheim does not make clear. But by focusing his moral searchlight on Pasqualino and his creator, Bettelheim deflects our attention from the real source of evil in the deathcamp universe, the initiator of the command to select six for execution, the malicious and cynical commandant, who enjoys seeing prisoners squirm. By imposing such options on human beings morally unarmed for such debasement, the Nazi mind created a world where meaningful choice disappeared and the hope for survival was made to depend on equally impossible alternatives. Pasqualino's acquiescence is not so alien from the dilemma facing members of the Jewish councils, ghetto police, and certain barrack "elders" in the camps, all of whom were *ordered* to measure one set of lives against another, with their own always hanging in the balance. If Pasqualino accedes with less anguish than they, it is simply becuase he is less sensitive to the moral issues, which were virtually nonexistent for him in precamp life. But such sensitivity, had he possessed it, would have complicated, not simplified, his ordeal.

Adam Cierniakow, head of the Jewish council in the Warsaw ghetto, could resolve his personal difficulty by committing suicide, thereby retaining a tiny fragment of freedom and dignity—though the gesture saved none of his fellow Jews. But in the camp, according to Wertmüller's vision of the world created not by the prisoners but by their murderers, even this small area of "dignified" choice vanished. Pedro, the anarchist, no longer able to tolerate an existence where some men have the power to impose such choices on others, leaps into the cesspool and suffocates or is shot to death. Unaccountably, Bettelheim finds such action comic and morbid, though as Des Pres will stress, "shit" became both metaphor and emblem of the level to which men were reduced in the deathcamps. What else could describe such a life—and such a death? Pedro's end is consistent with the atmosphere that has been created *for* him—not *by* him—by Nazi cruelty. If man's fate has been transfigured—or disfigured—into such an image by the new reality of the camps, then surely honesty requires us to adjust our expectations of survival to include this image. But then we must suspend our nostalgia for more dignified images.

The second half of this crucial episode requires even more dramatic adjustments to our traditional notions of moral man. Bettelheim is offended by the film's suggestion that dignified human protest such as Pedro's can culminate in such a "ridiculous" death. Certainly such an episode is offensive, but the fault is not Wertmüller's; debasement of life was so total in the camps that no civilized gesture could be sure of promoting a civilized response. One is preplexed by Bettelheim's objection that *Seven Beauties* equates genocide with the practices of everyday life, since the focal moment of the film, when Pasqualino is ordered by the camp commandant to shoot his friend Francesco for inciting an uprising, is unlike any other episode from his trivial, precamp existence. He is paralyzed by a situation without possible human options—a drama played out repeatedly in the real camps—and he cannot imagine how to respond to the impossible ones. Wertmüller uses her lens to capture this classic instant of atrocity when the camera pauses on Pasqualino's hesitating arm with the gun pointed at his friend's head. Viewers like Bettelheim who insist on direct moral response to such unanticipated crises—he would have simply turned the gun on the SS guard—reveal a limited understanding of the distressed human will when faced with the prospect of such meaningless death, for oneself or one's friend. We have just seen the consequences of heroic gesture in Pedro's sordid demise. Perhaps Pedro's past experience as an anarchist had trained him to accept futility as his fate. Pasqualino is struggling with a morality he has never encountered before, and its drama is intensified because *we* have never been forced to participate in this particular malice of the Nazi mind either. It belongs only to victim and potential survivor, whereas we are merely present at its birth.

The confrontation is not between a former hoodlum and a fixed ethical principle, as Bettelheim implies, but between two human creatures, Pasqualino and Francesco, who try to work out their destiny in a hopeless predicament while retaining some shred of human dignity. "Be brave and shoot," says Francesco; "If you don't, someone else will, and I'd rather a friend did it. . . ." *"Francesco lifts up his head and looks at his friend pleadingly,"* read the directions in the printed text. *"Pasqualino isn't able to pull the trigger."* "This is torture," cries Francesco; "come on, hurry, I can't play the hero much longer." [40] And this is the point: the Holocaust has little to do with playing the hero, for victim or survivor. The Nazi mentality creates the scene, but the "actors" must suffer their own doom, and tradition offers no analogy to help them. Imposing heroic expectations misinterprets the moment; no triumphant gesture exists. This sort of dying imprisons the human spirit in a physical humiliation from which there is no escape. "If you wait any longer," exclaims Francesco, "I'll pee in my pants" (in the printed translation; the English subtitles of the film speak of defecation); Pasqualino finally shoots, perhaps to prevent this final degradation, a vain attempt to limit the unbearable for his friend in the absence of any means to affirm his humanity in the last instant of his life.

Art requires interpretation, but Bettelheim reduces this scene to the simple objection that it is "completely untrue to the reality of

the camps." [41] But we know that some SS enjoyed forcing
prisoners to torment and even to kill each other (Bettelheim cites
an example of this himself in *The Informed Heart*). No single reality
will ever be found to fit the miasma of the deathcamps. Here,
however, the belief in the necessity of heroic defiance compels
Bettelheim to conclude that a prisoner given a gun by an SS man
to shoot his friend "would have known that he could not survive"
and would have shot the SS man instead. Perhaps in literature,
which so often idealizes human behavior; but in life, hundreds of
members of the Sonderkommandos working in the gas chambers
and crematoriums of Auschwitz (leading men to their deaths)
knew they would not survive, and with the exception of one
large-scale recorded rebellion shortly before the installations were
dismantled, and a handful of minor episodes, they displayed little
inclination for heroic defiance. The mournful fact is there; the
explanation, if we ever discover a satisfactory one, can only be
attributed to lack of heroism by those who have never served in a
Sonderkommando.

According to Bettelheim, Pedro's leaping into the shit and
Pasqualino's shooting of his friend transform "tragic assertions of
human dignity" into "jumping into feces and a comic avoidance
of a pants accident." [42] But somewhere before comedy and
beyond tragedy lies an abnormal realm where atrocity provokes
meaningless deaths like the ones we have just witnessed. And
anyone who looks closely at Pasqualino's ravaged face, as he
stares blankly at his reflection in the mirror after his return home
to "normal" postwar reality, will encounter an equally futile
survival. Together with Bettelheim we may not *favor* this
conclusion; but if the deathcamp does not change a petty criminal
like Pasqualino into a spirit purified by his anguish, perhaps we
should blame our expectations, not the art of Lina Wertmüller. As
a diminished human creature, Pasqualino reminds us of the
urgency of reexploring the implications of survival in a
post-Holocaust era.

It may be unpalatable—Bettelheim certainly finds it so—that
those who wish to act with dignity are destroyed in a ridiculous
way. But ridiculing the victim's life was built into the Nazi
program of genocide. What could be more ludicrous than finding
Brausebad or "shower" painted over the entrance to the gas
chamber; or clothing prisoners in garments much too big or too
small for their frames; or handing out soap and towels to people

who are about to perish in the gas chambers? In *Seven Beauties*, complains Bettelheim, "we are made to feel that human dignity is a sham." What else *was* human dignity to those millions of victims whose fate was placed beyond their power to intervene, who realized too late how they had been betrayed (and unsuspectingly *permitted* themselves to be betrayed) by the inherited belief that human nature everywhere shared a fundamental core of humanitarian principles that could not be eroded even by a totalitarian state? Perhaps the SS themselves were surprised at how easily both agents and victims of genocide adapted to their encounter with such erosion. But their surprise did not dissuade them from adopting atrocity as an acceptable mode of behavior. Nor did it furnish the victims with a useful weapon against the force determined to destroy them.

Bettelheim's principal stricture against Lina Wertmüller's portrait of a survivor is that Pasqualino "is not a person whose experiences have added to his depth" (p. 34). Like Frankl, he embraces the formula that suffering must lead to moral growth, among whose components Bettelheim includes "understanding, compassion, and the ability to feel guilty" (p. 34). No one would dispute that survivors of the deathcamps were *altered* by their ordeal, though it is not clear why confusion, resentment, and a frustrating sense of wronged innocence should not be equally adequate responses. A vocabulary of nonvalue is needed to balance the fusion of values sacred to an earlier era that is implicit in Bettelheim's language. What is the source of guilt attributed to survivors, sometimes by their own words: their own survival, or the deaths of others? What they have done, or failed to do? In the pre-Holocaust moral universe, where atrocity did not prevail, deeds made a difference and guilt could be the consequence of choice exercised or withheld. But as the bleak memory of the camp atmosphere lingers in Pasqualino's eyes, and in our minds, is it meaningful to say that he must feel "guilty" of his friend's death (when the friend himself pleaded with him to shoot)?

The tangled moral situation of the deathcamp universe drags the analyst of survivorship into contradictions despite his allegiance to clear-sighted consistency. Eventually one realizes that the elusive nature of the reality, not the wavering vision of the analyst, is responsible. Driven by his determination to develop a unified theory of survival, Bettelheim can insist that those who had the best chance to survive continued to live by the compulsions of culture, "to exercise some small moral restraint over the body's cruder demands" (p. 40), to avoid sacrificing the lives of others to gain advantages for themselves. But simultaneously, impelled by the desire to thwart the versions presented by Wertmüller and Des Pres, he can conclude that the "harsh and unpleasant fact of the concentration camp is that survival had little to do with what the prisoner does or does not do" (p. 40). This is an enormous concession, though all it means, in the broadest sense, is that the survivor was one who was still alive—for whatever reason, and in whatever condition—when the Allies liberated the camps. Corollary to this position is the truth that if the Germans had won the war, *all* Jews in the camps, together with millions of others on their death list, would have perished, despite the compulsions of culture or any other inner or outer resources. No behavior or attitude, in other words, *ensures* survival; Bettelheim is certainly correct when he warns that "any discussion of survivorship is dangerously misleading if it gives the impression that the main question is what the prisoner can do" rather than the need to defeat those who maintain the camps (p. 41).

This being so, Bettelheim's implicit contempt in *The Informed Heart* for Jews who waited "to be rounded up for their own extermination, and finally walk themselves to the gas chambers" disintegrates, though in his review he fails to acknowledge the perversity of his earlier position. Instead, he assails Des Pres for ignoring the serious problem of "man's behavior when his will to resist has been completely broken" (p. 43). This is precisely the question that Bettelheim neglected when he charged the Jews with passive complicity in their own annihilation. Pursuing it would reveal that the patterns of behavior men develop under conditions of atrocity to protect that will often violate all premises about culture, moral restraint, and self-sacrifice that we have learned to cherish in a world before and beyond the Holocaust. *Within* the Holocaust universe, as we search for valid feelings toward its events and the conduct of its victims, our human need to find a fixed center of moral being confronts a dark world of nonvalue where the means of "staying alive" are too alien to support the simple options of approval or disapproval that Bettelheim imposes on them. If a minimal form of "virtue" assisted survival in some instances, the opposite was true often enough to cast serious doubt on the value of such categories to assess the consequences of human behavior in the concentration camps.

The stance of moral superiority, the one adopted by Frankl and Bettelheim, was supposedly tested by the situation of atrocity that each experienced, though neither considers reconstructing the horrors, different as they were, to be of primary importance in their narratives. Their emphasis as psychologists is on a healthy future; hence they cannot afford to be burdened by too much grisly ballast from the past. The most serious deficiency of their work is that it is based on a presumed knowledge by their readers of the concrete details of the worst that happened in the camps. Their theories about survival, *as one reads them*, do not seem to be generated by the experience of atrocity; we are asked to accept on faith their conclusions about the effect of events that many still have difficulty accepting in fact. Jacob Katz's warning to historians of the Holocaust is relevant here: "moral judgment can only be pronounced on individuals when we have fully imagined the plight they were in, and that is why any such moral judgment has to be preceded by a reconstruction of the situation as exact as historical sources will permit." [43] Since most studies of survivorship involve moral judgment, in the sense that a particular kind of behavior is said to have made possible a certain desirable result, one test of their value is their commitment to fully imagining the plight of the victims before assessing the consequences of their conduct.

By this measure, Terrence Des Pres's *The Survivor* is a work of singular strength. Whatever the validity of his ultimate theory of survival—for he has one too—it is based not on categories of behavior but on an unflinching presentation of the unthinkable. One of the disturbing paradoxes of his book is that the overwhelming defilement of man latent in his presentation (much of it direct quotation from survivor accounts) dilutes the power of the talent for life that, he alleges, enables some victims to endure their ordeal. His attempt to reconcile defilement with dignity raises the question of a need for totally fresh verbal designations to fuse the two into new if tentative images of what it means to be human in a post-Holocaust era. If, as Des Pres argues, "survival is an experience with a definite structure," what constitutes the "language of ultimate concern" [44] that we should use to describe it? Does the "archaic, quasi-religious vocabulary" that he employs enlarge or restrict our vision of the unspeakable, and of man's attempt to remain human within its perimeter? Although he intends to separate himself from the spiritual/religious dogmatism of a Frankl and the ethical/psychological dogmatism of a Bettelheim, does a passage like the following really liberate him from the language of transcendence that they depend on: "There is a power at the center of our being, at the heart of all things living. But only in man does it assume a spiritual character. And only through spirit does life continue by decision" (p. 94)? Such vocabulary, even when used in behalf of "life itself" (p. 94), cannot free the imagination from associations with religious content, whether Des Pres intends this or not. A word like "power" inevitably implies choice or control, a force that directs some men toward survival while others, who have it not, drift or careen toward death or extermination. And even though Des Pres speaks of a biological impulse, he uses specifically moral terms, "as if the decision to survive were an inner fate expressing itself through a conscious assent of the will" (pp. 87–88).

Despite Des Pres's frank disclaimer that "speculation about the relation between survival behavior and basic life processes is speculation only" (p. vii), so strong is our need (and his) to establish a system of cause and effect at work in the deathcamps that we discern in such speculation—what indeed it gradually comes to possess—the passion of conviction. Although he insists that the experience itself is what counts—a premise that his predecessors do not seem to share—his assumptions about what it means to "stay human" do not encourage the exploration of the melancholy fact that staying alive in the camps sometimes required the practice of being less than human. To his credit, he rejects the charge, implicit in much of Frankl and Bettelheim, that failure to survive is somehow related to the character of the victim rather than the destructive quality of his experience (which includes the character of his *murderers*). Nevertheless, he shares with them the belief that "survival behavior reveals typical forms of response to extremity" (p. vii), though he supports his theory with a base of testimony immensely broader than what they chose to avail themselves of. But when we consider that less than two percent of survivors have ever written about or testified to their ordeal, and that except for a handful of buried notes and diaries none of the millions who perished have left any account at all, we realize how precarious is any theory that tries to organize so few private agonies into a typology of survival.

Symbolic manipulations of consciousness, Des Pres suggests, once helped the human imagination through its encounters with dying; but the terrors of extermination prohibit symbolization. There is no analogy to the gas chamber, no image to convey its nullification of man while simultaneously affirming the spiritual dignity of the victim. Confrontation with the ultimate atrocity must be concrete, not metaphorical: "the essence of survival," Des Pres insists, "is passage through death." He does not mean the epic descents of a Dante, an Aeneas, or an Odysseus. Holocaust survivors do not return from a symbolic encounter, but a literal one; they are not strengthened for a journey through purgatory to paradise, or armed with a vision for founding a new empire, or warned that their homeland is awaiting their heroic return. Their death immersion (and ours, if we can follow them stripped of symbolic insulation) is strictly physical: typhus, dysentery, malnutrition, torture, extermination. But unlike one of Charlotte Delbo's survivors, who exclaims "I'm not living. I died at Auschwitz and no one sees it," Des Pres's prototypical survivor seems unwilling to accept the totality of the death immersion. Overtly, he says, "the survivor defers to death, covertly he or she defies it" (p. 100). This double momentum runs through his volume, as the victim negotiates the fatal rapids of annihilation, trying to keep the fragile craft of his life afloat. Closer to death, Des Pres argues, "survivors are rooted more urgently in life than most of us. Their will to survive is one with the thrust of life itself, a strength beyond hope, as stubborn as the upsurge of spring" (p. 21). Whether this is poetry or truth we can never determine, partly because of its celebratory tone, partly because the affirmative force of the diction raises the specter of the opposite position, one Des Pres himself would certainly not care to defend: that those who for whatever reason did not qualify for survival somehow lacked the "thrust of life" and "strength beyond hope," were not "stubborn as the upsurge of spring" but victims of the autumn of despair.

Whether these victims wanted to live or not made absolutely no difference to their murderers; and even for those who avoided initial selection, the will to survive had little relation to their fate, *provided* their Nazi persecutors had already made the decision to liquidate them. Des Pres quotes as established psychological fact the *retrospective* sentiment of a survivor that there was an inner connection between his determination and his destiny: " 'It was then, faced with this spectacle of physical decay, with death rising like a tide on all sides, that I decided in my mind that I must live' " (p. 88). How many men and women who now say they made this decision *then*, actually survived because of it? How many who abandoned "choice of life" as futile and trusted luck or advantage, survived? We will never know. Yet even as he argues for connection—this is one of the challenging enigmas of his book—Des Pres acknowledges that a deeper principle than the strength beyond hope was at work in the deathcamps: "once the will to live had been regained it was constantly undermined by chance and despair. Prisoners survived by chance, they died by chance, and they *knew* it" (p. 90). How does the victim tolerate this psychological tug-of-war between the inner determination to live and the external accident of survival? Unless we are prepared to abandon the Holocaust to psychological chaos—and Des Pres is not—we must invent a version of unified response. The danger is always that we adapt the event to the version, thereby simplifying and even falsifying the event. The heroic notion that "survivors may be killed, but as long as they live they will not be afraid" (p. 21) could only have been invented by a nonsurvivor.

Indeed, that statement appears early in *The Survivor* in a discussion of Solzhenitsyn's novels, and raises the question of whether judgments on literary characters are transferable to literal ones. In concentration camp literature, when the writer creates a vision distinct from the survivor's (less coherent) version, does the order of art distort the disorder of experience? The dignity available to Camus's Dr. Rieux and Solzhenitsyn's Nerzhin, Kostoglotov, and Shukhov belongs to the illusion of art. The "dignity" available to Des Pres's survivor cannot escape the disillusionment of life in the deathcamps. Des Pres defines this dignity with the familiar vocabulary of transcendence: "a sense of innocence and worth, something felt to be inviolate, autonomous and untouchable . . . one of the irreducible elements of selfhood" (p. 65–66). But if I stand by and watch the members of my family marched off to the gas chamber (or discover a few days later that this is where they had been driven), and am conscious of not having done anything to protest, how can I after this consider my dignity "inviolate, autonomous and untouchable"? Even if the

members of someone *else's* family are marched off to
extermination, and whether through fear or impossible
circumstances I do nothing—am I not violated in the irreducible
core of my self, touched to the quick by the very deaths I have
been unable to prevent? Do I still inhabit a world where dignity
can assert itself as though untouched by what I have seen, what I
have failed to do? One survived in the deathcamps, one survived
the Holocaust, but to pretend that the idea of dignity remains
intact after the event, for the literal survivor or for the others, is to
perpetuate an illusion of continuity in the human spirit that does
not exist, because *such* an experience allows no opportunity for
growth and purification. We return to the image of those ashes,
that cannot transcend themselves.

Of course men go on living, even though some stains on the
soul of history are indelible. But what do those stains imply for
the moral environment we inhabit after atrocity subsides? Des
Pres is thoroughly aware of the demands (not the temptations)
that the extremity of deathcamp existence imposes on the prior
values of prisoners. He knows (what Bettelheim and Frankl were
reluctant to admit) that sacrifice "is meaningless in a world where
any person's death only contributes to the success of evil"
(p. 100). But he is less inclined to pursue the corollary principle
that in the camps any person's *survival* might also contribute to
the success of evil, because the Nazi system of genocide corrupted
the very springs of moral existence. Although prisoners at
Auschwitz might delude themselves that in stealing valuables and
food from "Canada" (where the belongings of exterminated
deportees were stored) they were asserting an irreducible
life-force, they knew that the source of their provisions was
victims, chiefly Jews, less fortunate than themselves. This vicious
irony was inherent in their situation, and though they can be
blamed neither for their conduct nor for its occasion, it is difficult
to see how their dilemma can be explained by Des Pres's
conviction that in the deathcamps "to choose life means to come
to terms with, but also to resist, the forces of destruction"
(p. 100). A life that thrives on the death of others represents a
bizarre form of resistance. Des Pres's concession that "survivors
had to choose life at the cost of moral injury," that "they had to
sustain spiritual damage and still keep going without losing sight
of the difference between strategic compromise and
demoralization" (p. 131), is one more example of a vocabulary

bravely but vainly trying to describe a human ordeal that traditional language is powerless to evoke. Since no code existed (nor would have been enforceable if it had) to define the lower limits of "strategic compromise," beneath which the essence of selfhood loses the name of dignity, we are left with the option—the one Des Pres chooses—of studying the upper limits of survivor behavior, those life-affirming efforts that might restore, in Buber's words, acknowledgement to the testimony of such anguish.

Men "condemned" to live by codes most of them would shrink from in normal society enact a drama of moral alteration that cannot merely be celebrated as an attempt "to preserve a basis of trust and community" in the camps (p. 141), as if a clear-cut choice between right and wrong made any difference to a man dying of starvation. Although Des Pres insists that the "bread law" (you don't steal another man's bread) was the one law "all prisoners knew and accepted" (p. 140), his own citations contradict this view. True, when such "thieves" were caught by other prisoners, they were beaten and sometimes killed. But killing a starving man who from desperation (not contempt) takes another man's bread cannot so easily be described as an affirmation of moral order. To support his view, Des Pres quotes the following passage from Jorge Semprun's *The Long Voyage* (which is not a survivor account, incidentally, but a novel): "I saw people grow pale and collapse when they realized that a piece of their bread had been stolen. And it was not only a wrong that had been done to them directly. It was an irreparable wrong that had been done to all of us. For suspicion settled in, and distrust and hate." [45] But the principle of selective quotation, when one is discussing survivorship, can be used to serve many masters. Earlier in this passage, Semprun had said that "to steal this piece of black bread is to send a comrade to his death . . . to choose another man's death to insure your own life" (p. 60), and though he does not imply approval of this action, neither does he use it to evolve a theory of survival behavior. He is drawn to the inconsistency rather than the unity of human response in the camps. In the lines succeeding those quoted by Des Pres, Semprun's narrator introduces a less sanguine view of human nature under the pressure of atrocity: "Any one of us could have stolen that piece of bread, we were all guilty. Every theft of bread made each of us a potential bread thief. In the camps, man becomes that animal capable of stealing a mate's bread, of propelling him toward death" (p. 60). From *this* point of view, murdering the thief (though we call it punishment) is a form of moral suicide for the executioners, despite our attempt to transform it into a harsh but necessary justice. It may be, as Des Pres argues, that one's life depended on such measures, but to add that one's "humanness" depended on it too (p. 141) is to forget momentarily—what Des Pres himself has presented so powerfully in the chapter on "Excremental Assault"—how thoroughly the camps and their rulers purged the possibility of the human from the natures of their victims.

Semprun's narrator has a dual vision, one recognizing that the circumstances of atrocity intensify latent impulses that might never be expressed in normal society (just as Elie Wiesel described a father and son throttling each other for a piece of bread, ignoring the social bonding that usually supports the family tie). If every starving man is a potential bread thief, Semprun says, depending not on the limits of his morality but on the limits of his belly, "in the camps man also becomes that invincible being capable of sharing his last cigarette butt, his last piece of bread, his last breath, to sustain his fellow man" (p. 60). His narrator's conclusion that "we didn't need the camps to understand that man is a being capable of the most noble as well as the basest acts" (p. 60) suggests that one of the deepest mysteries of the camps is not why some men survived and others did not, but how the contradictory demands of external reality tempted, cajoled, corrupted, or repulsed the already tangled inclinations of the victim. If some versions of survivorship cheer us with the disclosure of what men can achieve in extremity, other versions disturb us with their revelation of what they cannot. Our way of seeing is tied as much to the "truth" as to someone else's way of saying.

The greatest contribution of Des Pres's *The Survivor* may be an unwitting one—its own dual vision is at odds with a countervailing impulse toward a unified moral view of the Holocaust, and this very tension reenacts the tormenting challenge of the event itself. Was the survival experience a gradual but irreversible movement from defilement to decency, an eventual (redeeming) discovery of "a fabric of discernible goodness amid that evil" (p. 88), or was it a continuous vibration between the two, an uncharitable, unpredictable, uncontrollable wavering between suffering without value and hope without confirmation? Virtually every statement about the deathcamps contains the seeds of its own contradiction, so that truth often depends on the source of one's authority rather than on literal moments of atrocity to provide a basis for generalizable results. It may be, as Des Pres insists, that survivor accounts furnish evidence "that the moral self can resurrect itself from the inhuman depths through which it must pass" (p. 50). But this is true only if we regard testimony as a heroic deed, not as an act of remorse or commemoration. Every survivor, says Des Pres, carries with him the dead he left behind; for some—Elie Wiesel and Nelly Sachs in particular, as we shall see—they represent a powerful obstacle to the resurrection of the moral self. The dispute between these dead and the survivors who bear them on their memories if not their consciences charges the imaginative worlds of both novelist and poet with an energy that compels one to qualify and perhaps modify Des Pres's interpretation of "the moral emotion which horror provokes" (p. 46).

One can speak, as Des Pres does, of "the ethical content of an experience" (p. 47); one can scarcely disagree with his conclusion that "moral judgment depends on knowledge of what took place" (p. 47). But when future generations read that in a suburb of Berlin called Wannsee some men sat around a conference table to discuss ways of exterminating European Jewry, and as a result, European Jewry was virtually exterminated, how will they acknowledge the ethical implication of this historical testimony, to say nothing of judging it? And what consolation, ethical or not, do we derive from the assertion that "a mangled body reveals a mangled soul," or that torture and extermination have spiritual consequences? Des Pres himself has mounted overwhelming evidence for those moments in the deathcamps when the mangled body appeared to reveal nothing but the mangled body: prisoners forced to urinate into one another's mouths, or suffocating in excrement (Bettelheim notwithstanding) after having been thrown into manure pits by SS men. Once more the spirit of Jonathan Swift would marvel at the ingenious irony of the situation, of a mind that records these details and almost in the same breath adds that life itself "depends on keeping dignity intact," and "on the daily, never finished battle to remain *visibly* human" (p. 64).

If symbols tend to actualize in extremity, if atrocity transforms life into concrete forms of existence like "actual pain and actual defilement" (p. 69), how do we translate into significant meaning the notion that physical experience, the ordeal of the body, becomes "the medium of moral and spiritual being" (p. 69)? Is Des Pres's assertion—an admirable and inspiring tribute to the victims who endured such agonies—of a "sense of something inwardly inviolate" (p. 71) demonstrable fact or necessary hope? It leads to the dubious argument, more charitable than Bettelheim's, but perhaps no more persuasive, that some prisoners, unable to endure these agonies, could die of "moral disgust" (p. 80). Certainly the initial horror of Auschwitz affected the will to live, as inordinate grief, terror, and brutality darken the horizon of any man's life. But to argue that "vast numbers of men and women died because they did not have time, the blessing of sheer time, to recover" (p. 81), suggests once more that normal choice, control of attitude, played a disproportionate role in determining the possibilities of survival. It deflects our attention from the unalterable circumstance that those who died in Auschwitz were killed there, by actions and conditions so murderous that even the healthiest and strongest-willed could not survive without concrete physical supports to nourish their rapidly debilitating bodies. If they managed to escape selections and elude SS rage, bakers and cooks, whatever the power at the center of their being, had better chances of survival than almost any other prisoner in Auschwitz (except perhaps for German criminals, who were given positions of power by the Nazis). And if they were neither Jewish nor Russian, their chances of surviving tripled and quadrupled.

The paradoxical quality of *The Survivor* is that Des Pres is oblivious to none of this. Practical morality—"To preserve life survivors had to use the means at their disposal" (p. 115)—vies with intrinsic morality—"There was in all the camps a significant drive toward decency" (p. 111)—and as a result we perceive the survival experience through several lenses, convinced by the spectacle illuminated by each one until we begin to wonder about the contradictory visions they bring into focus. If solidarity supported survival in some instances, in others survival absolutely prohibited mutual support. Prisoners who had private access to extra food or clothing usually could not disclose their secret without drying up the sources of their personal benefit, because these sources were limited. In other words, we are left with the enigma that collective action was more effective than individual effort only when individual effort was not more effective than collective action. But we cannot build a consistent principle of survival on such uncertainties.

Realistically viewed, resistance was not always the life-affirming gesture that Des Pres speaks of. Members of the Polish underground in Auschwitz working in the camp "hospital" bred typhus-infected lice and spread them on expensive sweaters that they then gave as gifts to especially brutal SS men. One of the most feared apparently gave the sweater to his wife, who contracted typhus and died. Des Pres knows that episodes like this one occurred in the camps; he admits that "life goes on by using the methods of the enemy" (p. 129). Of course, death goes on by using these methods too, and though it is difficult to avoid acknowledging this fact, and impossible to blame the agents, it is not clear why one should be cheered by a survival impulse that is forced to devise such ingenious methods of destruction to express itself. The survivor of Auschwitz who recounted the above episode is not in a celebratory mood when he describes it:

> The fight against informers and the attempts to infect SS-men with typhus are a graphic illustration of what Auschwitz was like and what methods were used there to win the battle of life and to combat the inhuman lawlessness of the SS-men. It is impossible for people living in safety today to judge, thirty years later, these desperate struggles.[46]

When resistance takes such a macabre form, one can only mourn the effects of atrocity on our "humanness," so distorted by the necessities of existence in a deathcamp. One is scarcely consoled by Des Pres's observation that for survivors "what counts is life and the sharing of life" (p. 166). In Auschwitz, the sharing of life could not be separated from the fearing of death, and the "special grace" (p. 169) of the survivor—that he or she was glad to be alive—could not possibly cancel the "archetypes of doom" (p. 177), entrenched in memory, that cost the lives of those millions deprived of such grace.

Despite his contention that survival is an unmetaphorical experience, even Des Pres cannot escape the limitations of particular language when seeking an appropriate diction for his version of survival. What else is "grace" if not a religious metaphor? The human type he is concerned with could not emerge from the page without a throng of images, which in a passage like the following nearly drowns its identity: "Survivors return from the grave, they come through Hell, and some, after descent into darkness and the defiling filth of underground sewers, rise again into the common world of sun and simple life" (p. 177).

Language here controls our response, but does it accurately (and objectively) define the survivor experience? With this fusion of Dante, Dostoevsky, Christianity, and perhaps the democratic spirit, we come perilously close to losing sight of the distinctive features of the deathcamp survivor. Does one emerge from the pit of Auschwitz to mere sun and simple life, as if the common world—to say nothing of one's own personality—has been unaffected by what one has left behind? Can we present an authentic portrait of unaccommodated man if we use a language of accommodation to paint it? Indeed, can we speak of unaccommodated "man" when Auschwitz was crowded with unaccommodated *men*, of whom Benedict Kautsky could write, as we have heard: "Even when you're talking about the same period of time, prisoners in the same camp lived as if on different planets, depending on the work they had to do."? [47] Only if we simplify the Holocaust into a collective trauma, only if we consent to Des Pres's theory that survivors share "a past identical for everyone who came through the common catastrophe" (p. 184), can we begin to accept the phenomenon that he describes as *"the"* survivor. But do we serve the complexity of the ordeal by eliminating private agonies and substituting a single historical fate? The many voices of *The Survivor* speak not from specific pasts but toward a specific future, the eventual delineation of a talent for life "which enables men and women to act spontaneously and correctly during times of protracted stress and danger" (p. 192). Instinct and ethics unite here in the improbable idea that there was a trustworthy response to the gas chamber, or a controllable means of surviving such an extremity.

We have seen some examples, and we will see more, of the shifting implications of "humanness" in the deathcamp environment. Until we explore its variations, how can we attribute significant meaning to Des Pres's conclusion: "Something innate—let us think of it as a sort of biological gyroscope—keeps men and women steady in their humanness despite inhuman pressure" (p. 199)? The human face alone was so unrecognizable

on the day of liberation that one must instinctively proceed with
caution before redefining the quality of the "human" after
Auschwitz. The Holocaust bursts its verbal boundaries, though
language tries to contain it within definable perimeters. If, as Des
Pres says, dignity "in its human context presupposes
self-awareness and a deliberate resistance to determination by
external forces" (p. 201) (which is not so different from
Bettelheim's position in *The Informed Heart*), what are we to say of
the victims? Is their surrender to external forces, their collapse of
will "undignified," lacking in the human? *Their* pain spills over in
such variety and abundance that words cannot confine it to a
manageable theory of behavior. Like Bettelheim, Des Pres
believes that survivors "strive to keep themselves *fundamentally*
unchanged by the pressures to which they respond" (p. 202).
Charlotte Delbo would have called this asking the impossible of a
heart that could bear no more. Why should the test be whether
the self is fundamentally unchanged by the experience of atrocity,
by the historical presence of Auschwitz in our lives? Do we cling
to the possibility because the implications of an irreversibly
altered idea of the human are so unsettling that we hesitate to
grant them admission to our perception of twentieth-century
reality? In recent centuries men cherished faiths that preached
that we were more than we appeared; one of the sorrowful truths
of the Holocaust (and other mass atrocities in our time) is that we
are less than we believed. It is an unflattering conclusion, but not
necessarily a ruinous one, provided our view of the diminished
future includes not only vestiges of human promise, but the
shattered decencies from the past.

Shall we really find cause for joy in Olga Lengyel's conclusion
to her account of Auschwitz that if "even in the jungle of
Birkenau, all were not necessarily inhuman to their fellow men,
then there is hope indeed"? [48] This is meager nourishment for the
hungry moral appetite, starved by the sordid spectacle of the
deathcamps. And how consoling is Des Pres's speculation that
some "magic will" or "imperishable power" in the survivor
enabled men and women "under dehumanizing pressure . . . to
preserve themselves in ways recognizably human" (p. 193)?
George Steiner's alternate view commands attention here: that in
the deathcamps, the only choice available (as determined by the
circumstances imposed by the SS men) was between being more
or less inhuman. Gratitude that some tens of thousands survived

while millions died should not be mistaken for a principle of
redemptive meaning. The losses so far exceed the "gains" that it
seems irreverent to assess the significance of survival without
feeling burdened by the weight of the dead. Frankl and
Bettelheim, by consolidating their responses to the Holocaust into
phrases like "the will to meaning" and "the informed heart,"
flinch at the possibility of a suffering so despiritualized by atrocity
that it can never rise above the heavy drag of a maimed mortality.
Des Pres is less averse to flinching, but his "biological wisdom"
that if the soul lives after Auschwitz, it resides *in* the flesh, and
does not transcend it, offers very fragile support to the theory that
men can remain fundamentally unchanged by the experience of
atrocity. We flee the harsher conclusion that Auschwitz and other
camps were totally consecrated to death and extermination, and
that survival was a violation of their goal (nearly achieved), not a
triumph over it. To some, the testimony of survivors may seem a
tribute to the life-force and written proof that moral heroism is
redemptive even in Nazi deathcamps; but to others, bearing
witness means simply homage to the dead, a recognition that
during the period of history we call the Holocaust the human
spirit faltered, and the human body, bereft of support, succumbed
to an annihilation it no longer had the power to prevent.

TWO

Auschwitz: THE DEATH OF CHOICE

Suppose Dante's pilgrim in the *Divine Comedy* had arrived at the exit from the Inferno to find the way barred by an electrified barbed-wire fence, posted with warnings reading "No trespassing: Violators will be annihilated." When the spiritual and psychological equivalents of Purgatory and Paradise are excluded from human possibility, to be replaced by the daily threat of death in the gas chamber, then we have a glimpse of the *negative* implications of survival, especially for the Jews, in the Nazi extermination camps. After we peel the veneer of respectable behavior, cooperation, hope, mutual support, and inner determination from the surface of the survivor ordeal, we find beneath a raw and quivering anatomy of human existence resembling no society we have ever encountered before. When deathcamp necessity congeals the ordinary life instinct and forces men and women who would stay alive to suspend the golden rule and embrace in its place the iron one of "do unto others before they do unto you," we must expect some moral rust to flake from the individual soul. We are left with a spectacle of reality that few would choose to celebrate, a world where Nazi brutality eliminated most of the human supports that sustain the meaning of words like "future" and "dignity" and "love." But such a world so threatens our sense of spiritual continuity—understandably— that it is agonizing to consent to or even imagine its features without introducing some affirmative values to mitigate the gloom.

If we pursue the proposition that some stains on the soul of history are indelible, where will it lead us? It will lead us certainly to an unfamiliar version of survival, to the conclusion that after Auschwitz, after the Holocaust, the idea of human dignity could never be the same again. It will force us to reexamine the language of value that we used before the event, and to admit that at least when describing the Holocaust, if not its consequences, such language may betray the spirit and the facts of the ordeal. Perhaps this is what Primo Levi, himself a survivor, was trying to say in *Survival in Auschwitz* when he wrote:

> Just as our hunger is not that feeling of missing a meal, so our way of being cold has need of a new word. We say "hunger," we say "tiredness," "fear," "pain," we say "winter" and they are different things. They are free words, created and used by free men who lived in comfort and suffering in their homes. If the Lagers [camps] had lasted longer a new, harsh language would have been born; and only this language could express what it means to toil the whole day in the wind, with the temperature below freezing, wearing only a shirt, underpants, cloth jacket and trousers, and in one's body nothing but weakness, hunger and knowledge of the end drawing near.[1]

This crucial observation leaves us with a profound dilemma, since no one has yet invented a vocabulary of annihilation, though the Nazis created a long list of euphemisms to deflect the imagination from their brutal purposes. For this reason we must bring to every "reading" of the Holocaust experience a wary consciousness of the way in which "free words" and euphemisms can distort the facts or alter them into more manageable events.

If a vocabulary of annihilation really existed, it would offer us a darker vision of Jewish destiny than the one evoked by Gandhi, Frankl, and Bettelheim. Unlike them, Levi concedes that survival in a place like Auschwitz "without renunciation of any part of one's own moral world" (p. 84) was impossible for all but a few superior individuals—and when we are speaking of the fate of millions, the behavior of those few appears almost irrelevant. For example, Levi describes the preparation for a "selection," that incomparable moment of terrified anticipation when the victim, deprived of choice, saw his doom—death in the gas chamber—depend on the whim or hatred of an enemy he was powerless to resist. Surely this moment tests the value and meaning of that "inner freedom" which Frankl and the others celebrate so strenuously, while rejoicing in the principle that even in extremity one still controls one's attitude toward one's fate. Refusing to graft a language of value onto the fragile branch of chance, Levi speaks of self-deception, not inner freedom. "Whoever is unable to prepare for it materially," he says, "seeks defense elsewhere." Each tries to convince the other that the danger is less than it seems. "I brazenly lied to old Wertheimer," Levi reports, telling him that "he need have no fears, and in any case it was by no means certain that it was a selection for the gas chamber" (p. 114). Although it is absurd to hope, Levi hopes too, but does not succumb to the illusion afterward that his absurd hope had any connection with his equally absurd and threatening fate. "On this slender basis," he admits, "I lived through the great selection of October 1944 with inconceivable tranquillity. I was tranquil because I managed to lie to myself sufficiently. The fact that I was not selected depended above all on chance and does not prove that my faith was well-founded" (p. 114).

After the selection, as those who have escaped this time and those who will die in a few days in the gas chamber lie beside each other in their bunks reflecting on the episode, Levi hears an old prisoner named Kuhn praying aloud and "thanking God because he has not been chosen" (p. 118). Levi reacts with an indignation that would be inexplicable, were we not sensitive to how such language of value may distort the facts of extermination. To Levi, Kuhn's prayer is a self-serving attempt to reawaken a vital principle of cause and effect in the miserable lives of the prisoners, a desperate, blind clinging to connection between choice and fate that ignores the truncated destinies of his fellow inmates:

> Kuhn is out of his senses. Does he not see Beppo the Greek in the bunk next to him, Beppo who is twenty years old and is going to the gas chamber the day after tomorrow and knows it and lies there looking fixedly at the light without

saying anything and without even thinking anymore? Can
Kuhn fail to realize that next time it will be his turn? Does
Kuhn not understand that what has happened today is an
abomination, which no propitiatory prayer, no pardon, no
expiation by the guilty, which nothing at all in the power of
man can ever clean again.

If I was God, I would spit at Kuhn's prayer. (p. 118)

Every survivor has his Beppo the Greek, as his burden if not as
his blame; the abomination of extermination cannot be diminished
or obliterated by laudatory verbal formulas about the task of
suffering, the power of inner freedom, the opportunity for choice,
or the spiritual or biological triumph of survival. It is for Levi a
gloomy truth that we must accept as our heritage from the age of
Auschwitz, an unredeemable bond that continues to draw interest
from the human spirit as the excessive price the world must pay
because once the Nazi mind invested in a program for the
genocide of the Jews.

Theories of survival that exalt human dignity despite the ordeal
of atrocity do not contend with the possibility of man being
totally reduced—even temporarily—to a nullity. By shifting the
angle of vision, Levi exposes a view of the deathcamps where
traditional ideas of human worth simply vanish. Describing the
initial humiliation of the members of his convoy who escaped
immediate gassing, as they stood about with cropped hair in
soiled, ill-fitting garments, he says:

> Then for the first time we became aware that our language
> lacks words to express this offense, the demolition of a man.
> In a moment, with almost prophetic intuition, the reality was
> revealed to us: we had reached the bottom. It is not possible
> to sink lower than this; no human condition is more
> miserable than this, nor could it conceivably be so. (p. 22)

The irony is that Levi has encountered the beginning, not the end
of his nullification as a man. He speaks not of creatures of rare
inner strength, the Frankls and Bettelheims who are in no way
representative of the victims or survivors, but of the common men
who depend, who have been taught and have learned to depend
for their humanity on an external world with which they can
identify. He draws a compassionate portrait of the progressive

"extermination" of these men while they are still alive, and it is clear that for them, at any rate, normal sources of dignity are completely beyond their control:

> Imagine now a man who is deprived of everyone he loves, and at the same time of his house, his habits, his clothes, in short, of everything he possesses: he will be a hollow man, reduced to suffering and needs, forgetful of dignity and restraint, for he who loses all often easily loses himself. He will be a man whose life or death can be lightly decided with no sense of human affinity, in the most fortunate of cases, on the basis of a pure judgment of utility. It is in this way that one can understand the double sense of the term "extermination camp," and it is now clear what we seek to express with the phrase: "to lie on the bottom." (p. 23)

Survival for this individual, whose "life or death can be lightly decided [by others] with no sense of human affinity," is not simply a matter of turning one's attitude toward the future, or of clinging to a hypothetical inner freedom as if all men had nurtured their lives prior to deportation on the kind of ethical imperatives implicit in nineteenth-century religious and secular culture. Can a man so degraded be blamed for suspending his sense of "dignity" and "restraint," as we normally understand these terms? A certain external support within the environment of extermination is necessary to keep them alive; but in the morally denuding atmosphere of the deathcamps, this external support rapidly deteriorated, leaving most victims clinging to anything that reduced their suffering and satisfied their needs.

Levi is not oblivious to the importance of trying to internalize some of those external supports in order to create an inner world of value as ballast against the chaos outside. He articulates, but does not necessarily endorse, an attitude we have met before: "In this place it is practically pointless to wash every day in the turbid water of the filthy washbasins for purposes of cleanliness and health; but it is most important as a sympton of remaining vitality, and necessary as an instrument of moral survival" (p. 35). The concept of "moral survival' is too deeply embedded in the imagination to be surrendered without a struggle, and Levi's reluctance is symptomatic of man's efforts in the deathcamps to retain a reality that was systematically undermined by the

concrete situation in which he found himself. Levi acknowledges
the dilemma with rare honesty:

> The more I think about it, the more washing one's face in
> our condition seems a stupid feat, even frivolous: a
> mechanical habit, or worse, a dismal repetition of an extinct
> rite. We will all die, we are all about to die: if they give me
> ten minutes between the reveille and work, I want to
> dedicate them to something else, to draw into myself, to
> weigh up things, or merely to look at the sky . . ." (p. 35)

If we marvel at the hope of some who clung to extinct rites in the
very shadow of the gas chambers, must we not mourn the despair,
and seek to understand the behavior that grew from it, of others
who had to endure without the solace of those rites?

The consequences of this predicament may seem morally
intolerable to the contemporary mind, but they are nonetheless
unavoidable. They illuminate a version of survival less flattering
to the human creature than the one we examined in the previous
chapter, but their spokesmen—and spokeswomen—deserve a
hearing if only to clarify our vision of how utterly the Nazi
mentality corrupted moral reality for the victims. Moreover, this
complementary vision may enable us to comprehend better how
little discredit falls to these victims, who were plunged into a
crisis of what we might call "choiceless choice," where crucial
decisions did not reflect options between life and death, but
between one form of abnormal response and another, both
imposed by a situation that was in no way of the victim's own
choosing. Consider this brief episode narrated by Judith Sternberg
Newman, a nurse by profession, who was deported to Auschwitz
from Breslau with 197 other Jewish women; three weeks later,
only eighteen of them were still alive:

> Two days after Christmas, a Jewish child was born on our
> block. How happy I was when I saw this tiny baby. It was a
> boy, and the mother had been told that he would be taken
> care of. Three hours later, I saw a small package wrapped in
> cheese cloth lying on a wooden bench. Suddenly it moved. A
> Jewish girl employed as a clerk came over, carrying a pan of
> cold water. She whispered to me, "Hush! Quiet! Go away!"
> But I remained, for I could not understand what she had in
> mind. She picked up the little package—it was the baby, of

course—and it started to cry with a thin little voice. She took
the infant and submerged its little body in the cold water.
My heart beat wildly in agitation. I wanted to shout
"Murderess!" but I had to keep quiet and could not tell
anyone. The baby swallowed and gurgled, its little voice
chittering like a small bird, until its breath became shorter
and shorter. The woman held its head in the water. After
about eight minutes the breathing stopped. The woman
picked it up, wrapped it up again, and put it with the other
corpses. Then she said to me, "We had to save the mother;
otherwise she would have gone to the gas chamber." This
girl had learned well from the SS and had become a
murderess herself.[2]

How is one to pass judgment on such an episode, or relate it to
the inner freedom celebrated by other commentators on the
deathcamp experience? Does moral choice have any meaning
here? The drama involves the helpless infant, whose fate is
entirely in someone else's hands (and the fate of the equally
helpless infant Oedipus only reminds us how far life in
Auschwitz had drifted from the moral order, and even the moral
ironies, of art); the absent mother, who may or may not have
approved of the action; the "agent" of death, who coolly sacrifices
one life to preserve another, as a deed of naked necessity, without
appeal, not of moral choice; and the author, sole witness to a
crime that is simultaneously an act of charity and perhaps of
literal secular salvation to the mother. Vocabulary once more
limps through a situation that allows no heroic response, no
acceptable gesture of protest, no mode of action to permit *any* of
the participants, including the absent mother, to retain a core of
human dignity. The *situation* itself forbids it, together with the
Nazi "law" stating that mothers who refuse to surrender their
newborn infants to death must accompany them to the gas
chamber. This predatory profile of survival, when fear of such
death, not affirmation of a basic human dignity, drives men and
women to behavior they would not consider under normal
circumstances, confirms another moment when reality defeats a
language of judgment: "I wanted to shout 'Murderess!' but I had
to keep quiet and could not tell anyone."

In the absence of humanly significant alternatives—that is,
alternatives enabling an individual to make a decision, act on it,
and accept the consequences, all within a framework that

supports personal integrity and self-esteem—one is plunged into a moral turmoil that may silence judgment, as in the above example, but cannot paralyze all action, if one still wishes to remain alive. Ella Lingens-Reiner, another Auschwitz survivor, offers a crude but critical instance of how effectively the optionless anguish of the deathcamp could alienate dignity from choice. In her barracks there was a single limited source of water for washing and for draining excrement from the latrine. If the women took the water for washing, the primitive sewage system would be blocked, creating an intolerably offensive (and unhealthy) situation. Lingens-Reiner lucidly sums up the condition of choiceless choice, where the only alternatives are between two indignities: "It is dreadful to be without water; it is impossible to let people take away all the water while faeces are piling up in the ditches!" [3] As one wavers between the "dreadful" and the "impossible," one begins to glimpse a deeper level of reality in the deathcamps, where moral choice as we know it was superfluous, and inmates were left with the futile task of redefining decency in an atmosphere that could not support it.

In contradiction to those who argue that the only way of surviving was to cling to the values of civilized living despite the corrupting influence of the deathcamps, Lingens-Reiner insists that those who tried to salvage such moral luggage imposed fatal burdens on themselves. She tells of her own difficulty in ridding herself of such inclinations: shortly after arriving, she says,

> I was still under the impression that it was advisable for people in our situation to behave with exemplary correctness. To the very last I could not get rid of this notion, although it was quite absurd. In reality only those prisoners had a chance to survive in the camp—if they were not privileged on account of their profession, beauty, or other specially favorable circumstances—who were determined to do the exact opposite of what they were told to do, on principle to break every rule governing civilian life. (p. 22)

This harshly practical view flatters no one, neither the author, nor her companions, nor the reader, all of whom are confronted by conditions that with very few exceptions *prohibit* the exercise of uncontaminated moral freedom and hence the achievement of a tragic dignity to temper the austerity of human doom in Auschwitz.

Lingens-Reiner, who as an Austrian, non-Jewish physician held a triply privileged position in the camp, was able to save one woman selected for gassing by reporting to the Political Division that an SS man needed her particular skill in his work. But her success was tainted by the response from that department: "We'll have to take another in her place." By her own confession, a memorable act of courage and human concern for one victim was *simultaneously* perverted by the dilemma of choiceless choice into extermination for another:

> by facing a great risk I had achieved nothing. If I rescued one woman, I pushed another to her doom, another who also wanted to live and had an equal right to live. "We'll have to take another in her place." And for this I risked never seeing my child again! Was there any sense in trying to behave decently? It was difficult not to despair. (p. 82)

It was equally difficult, if not impossible, to generate a widely applicable ethics of survival from such an unpredictable existence, when "saving" and "condemning" were so tightly intertwined. Prisoner physicians like Lingens-Reiner were often forced to accompany SS men on their "selections" in the infirmary, and sometimes to save the healthier patients they would deliberately point out the hopeless cases. "In fact," concludes Lingens-Reiner explicitly, "in our situation normal principles of human and professional ethics broke down, because the problems we had to face were previously non-existent, and in dealing with them we did not know what to do" (p. 83).

Just as Primo Levi felt the absence of a language of annihilation to kindle the experience of extermination, so Lingens-Reiner is sensitive to the absence of a viable moral vocabulary to *describe* (if not to judge) the "previously non-existent" human dilemmas of survival in a deathcamp. For example, when total theft and sabotage of everything belonging to the SS was a generally approved rule of conduct, how was one to enforce internal decency among the prisoners? She tells the story of a young girl who was found by other prisoners eating from the food parcel of a bunkmate who had just died of typhus. These prisoners, perhaps jealous, reported the incident to the camp elder, a German Communist and long-term inmate. She in turn decided as a disciplinary measure that the offender (though weakened by a recent ordeal with typhus herself) should join the barracks cleaning detail—heavy work for such a fragile creature. Within a week, she was dead—from exhaustion and malnutrition. One death among ten thousand, Lingens-Reiner calls it, as she struggles to assess the event, which weighed upon her even though it could not "count." Her confusion is evident as she tries to discover a relevant principle of justice in a situation inherently unjust in origin: "she had died because of the human and moral failure of somebody [the woman camp elder] who desired to be a champion of a new ethic and was neither amoral, nor dominated by selfish motives, nor made callous by her long imprisonment" (p. 92). But when someone who is not amoral, or selfish, or callous, is nevertheless declared guilty of human and moral failure, then we detect the distinct outlines of a system of behavior that cannot be contained within a conventional moral frame.

"The Camp Senior," Lingens-Reiner reflects, "had acted from a conscious moral principle. She wanted to keep the flag flying in the middle of chaos and total moral collapse. She wanted to uphold the law of decency. But in her rigid, meagre, cramped determination she could not find the way to simple human tolerance and kindness" (p. 93). When the abstract notion of prisoner justice is translated into the concrete instance of a starving woman eating food that "belonged" to a dead fellow inmate, what "law" has been violated, and by whom (except the SS, who were beyond the reach of justice)? Is one finally forced to concede that human dignity is a luxury mainly for those who still retain some means of appeal—for members of normal society who even when starving may try to work, buy, borrow, beg before they are driven to steal, or camp prisoners who through their privileged positions had extra sources of nourishment and hence were not forced to become scavengers to stay alive? Those who applaud the triumph of an "inviolable dignity" in the deathcamps cannot explain the fate of this woman, a sacrifice to a system of destruction that encouraged, that often *required* prisoners to prey on each other in the continuing struggle for survival. The luxury of dignity was so often tainted by utter humiliation that it was virtually impossible to find generally applicable principles of behavior to favor survival or even the retention of self-respect in the deathcamps. Even Lingens-Reiner is forced to conclude her analysis of this episode in a spirit of uncertainty: "Or did I misread the case? Had the Camp Senior thought out what she was doing? Had she deliberately risked the girl's life so as to maintain the correctness and the authority of our self-administration? One was as possible as the other" (p. 92).

Primo Levi, who admitted the idea of "moral survival" into his vocabulary only to doubt its relevance to Auschwitz, nevertheless presents an eloquent statement in its behalf, though he is very careful to offer it as the conviction of his German friend Steinlauf, not his own. Steinlauf believes:

> that precisely because the Lager was a great machine to reduce us to beasts, we must not become beasts; that even in this place one can survive, and therefore one must want to survive, to tell the story, to bear witness; and that to survive we must force ourselves to save at least the skeleton, the scaffolding, the form of civilization. We are slaves, deprived of every right, exposed to every insult, condemned to certain death, but we still possess one power, and we must defend it with all our strength for it is the last—the power to refuse our consent. So we must certainly wash our faces without soap in dirty water and dry ourselves on our jackets. We must polish our shoes, not because the regulation states it, but for dignity and propriety. We must walk erect, without dragging our feet, not in homage to Prussian discipline but to remain alive, not to begin to die.[4]

On the basis of this passage, Levi would seem to be on the side of Frankl and Bettelheim; but no one who reads the rest of his volume could make this mistake.[5] Levi's experience in Auschwitz has taught him to be suspicious of all systems of survival; his southern temperament has inculcated "a more flexible and blander doctrine," according to which "nothing is of greater vanity than to force oneself to swallow whole a moral system elaborated by others, under another sky. No," he concludes, "the wisdom and virtue of Steinlauf, certainly good for him, is not enough for me. In the face of this complicated world my ideas of damnation are confused; is it really necessary to elaborate a system and put it into practice? Or would it not be better to acknowledge one's lack of a system?" (p. 36). But if Steinlauf's need is Levi's nemesis, if one man's veracity is another's

self-delusion, then no single theory of survival is totally
trustworthy, and perhaps the only valid test one can apply is
empirical rather than absolute.

Levi's vision of the Lager law is more pitiless than the
comforting variations we encountered in the previous chapter,
and it makes the challenge of survival infinitely more ambiguous.
He believes that "in the face of driving necessity and physical
disabilities many social habits and instincts are reduced to
silence" (p. 79). He sees little evidence of the kind of community
celebrated by Frankl and Des Pres: "in the Lager things are
different: here the struggle to survive is without respite, because
everyone is desperately and ferociously alone" (p. 80). Such an
axiom would have paralyzed Frankl's theory about the will to
meaning, as it threatens Des Pres's belief in something "inviolate,
autonomous and untouchable, . . . which is most vigorous when
most threatened." If someone vacillates in his drive to survive,
says Levi,

> he will find no one to extend a helping hand; on the contrary,
> someone will knock him aside, because it is in no one's
> interest that there be one more "mussulman" dragging
> himself to work every day; and if someone, by a miracle of
> savage patience and cunning, finds a new method of
> avoiding the hardest work, a new art which yields him an
> ounce of bread, he will try to keep his method secret, and he
> will be esteemed and respected for this, and will derive from
> it an exclusive, personal benefit; he will become stronger and
> so will be feared, and who is feared is, ipso facto, a candidate
> for survival.

Selfishness as a source of respect, a community of fear rather than
love, disregard of the physically defeated—is it any wonder that
Levi invites his readers to judge, with some bitterness, "how much
of our ordinary moral world could survive on this side of the
barbed wire" (p. 78)?

The sharing that represents an ideal of community in normal
society, and for which some commentators find evidence in the
camps, was not necessarily the most effective, and certainly not
always the most possible form of behavior. It had its counterpart
in the privacy of some survival strategies, which lose their value
when divulged to other victims. One sort of survivor is forced by
circumstances to act counter to his (and our) ideal of conduct, not

because the deathcamp has awakened hidden brutal instincts, but because such tactics appear normal and reasonable in the abnormal atmosphere of atrocity. A certain kind of charity simply ceases to motivate behavior in the camps:

> with the mussulmans, the men in decay, it is not even worth speaking, because one knows already that they will complain and will speak about what they used to eat at home. Even less worthwhile is it to make friends with them, because they have no distinguished acquaintances in camp, they do not gain any extra rations, they do not work in profitable Kommandos [work details] and they know no secret method of organizing. (p. 81)

What would appear cruel and insensitive in normal society sounds like practical common sense in Auschwitz, where different and unorganized values prevailed, inspired by a constant death threat that is totally alien to our world and resembles nothing that we can imagine.

Suppose we suspend our need to discover an ethics of survival, whether based on moral values or social or biological imperatives, and approach the camp ordeal as one from which no familiar or acceptable system of cause-and-effect behavior can be derived. The implications reach far beyond moral ideology to the role of time and history in human destiny, to the structure of character and the very unity of our lives in the twentieth century. History assures us that man is superior to time when retrospectively he can explain the unexpected, account, in this instance, for the extermination of a people, uncover a system for surviving and thus reduce the event to a partial intellectual order that somehow theoretically balances the price in human lives paid for that order. But from the perspective of the victims, who of course far outnumbered the survivors, the disorder of meaningless death contradicts the ordering impulses of time. Those who died for nothing during the Holocaust left the living with the paralyzing dilemma of facing a perpetually present grief. To the puzzled inquiry why interest in the Holocaust seems to grow as the event recedes into the past, one answer may be that there is no inner space or time to bury it in.

The fault lies not in our own deficient vision, but in the nature of the experience, which challenges our imagination with a nearly impossible task. Confrontation with the springs of conduct in the deathcamps represents less a recollection of times past (with the observer imposing a Proustian order on familiar materials) than a collection of past moments, whose intrinsic chaos urges us to invent a new moral and temporal dimension for its victims to inhabit. Levi describes with precision the source of the tension:

> For living men, the units of time always have a value, which increases in ratio to the strength of the internal resources of the person living through them; but for us, hours, days, months spilled out sluggishly from the future into the past, always too slowly, a valueless and superfluous material, of which we sought to rid ourselves as soon as possible. With the end of the season when the days chased each other, vivacious, precious and irrecoverable, the future stood in front of us, grey and inarticulate, like an invincible barrier. For us, history had stopped. (p. 107)

Now the "future" stands behind him, as it were, *and* us, still an invincible barrier between the way it was and our manner of perceiving it, separating two different ideas of time and value. An imperious need to revive "normal" feelings for space, time, and value rivals an irrepressible solicitation from that hermetic "moment" of the deathcamp universe to achieve expression in an unfamiliar idiom.

Ella Lingens-Reiner comments on the effect of this rivalry. As time passed, she says, the sense of the world outside (*our* world still) blurred, and the inner life of people who endured months and years in the camps atrophied. Such people

> transferred their ambitions and emotions to the life inside the camp. Therefore they would fight for positions not only because they intended to survive, but also for their own sake, because it satisfied their need to win power, recognition and a following within the precincts. Some of them invested their whole being in these matters, and so lost much of their intellectual and even moral standards.[6]

She writes not with contempt, but with compassion, with an effort to convey how subtly a deathcamp-inspired behavior could infiltrate a common sense of dignity and triumph over the victim's vision of decency. After praising the tremendous achievement of some women in preserving "their personal integrity in spite of everything," she adds with utter frankness: "the truly frightening thing was that women who had striven for that integrity, who still took life and ethics seriously, proved in the end too small for their overwhelming destiny, and never noticed when they acted on principles which were in reality those of National Socialism" (p. 91). She speaks not of habitual criminals or self-serving collaborators, but of individual women who believe in integrity but find their response to reality determined by a "destiny" that admits no meaningful moral opposition: the threat of death in Auschwitz.

Evidence can probably be found in one document or another to support almost any interpretation of inmate behavior in the deathcamps; hence those who speak of "the" survivor as if he or she were a representative type falsify the experience by the very (literal) singularity of their view. In an extermination camp like Belzec almost no one survived, and in Treblinka and Chelmno very few,[7] because the purpose of these places was to exterminate Jews, and the conditions that supported survival in a complex camp like Auschwitz simply did not exist there. In Auschwitz, with its main camp (chiefly for "political" prisoners), its gas chambers and crematoriums at Birkenau, and its factories at Buna-Monowitz, to say nothing of its smaller scattered subcamps, the sheer size of the operation created numerous posts that had to be filled by inmates—in the kitchens, in the crude infirmaries, in the various building Kommandos that were needed to support constant expansion. Those lucky enough to obtain (and keep) these posts—through chance, through influence, through the accident of their professional or vocational training—were in a better position to endure the hardships of camp life than those who were assigned to exhausting labor details, whose members quickly grew vulnerable to disease and malnutrition, and hence to selection for the gas chamber. The attrition of humane feelings and the waning sense of choice in one's own destiny should come as no surprise to those who can imagine what it must be like to lose the ability to mobilize hope and to lapse into a state of what some psychologists call learned helplessness.

One can perhaps imagine it, one can even try to describe it, but how faithful to the experience of victims are our attempts to reconstruct from the psychological rubble of despair those attitudes and actions that presumably support survival? "As the solitary hunted creature," says Lingens-Reiner, "felt the threat come nearer to her and had to fight more strenuously, day after day, to stave it off, she would consider it increasingly as a personal, individual fate which she tried to evade, and would become more and more indifferent to the anguish of others" (p. 117). This is a world we do not like to recognize, because we do not want it to be established as a precedent for the one we inhabit now. But the "solitary hunted creature" in Auschwitz longed to survive until the next day, not until the world of normal expectations was restored. Primo Levi is not the only survivor to insist that those who behaved in the camps as they had behaved outside, by following orders, eating only their own rations, and observing the discipline of work, rarely lasted more than three months. According to his darker vision, which, he says, is a result of observation, not cynicism, there was always someone who would agree to betray a natural solidarity with his comrades in exchange for a position of privilege. Discounting the romanticism of oppression inherited from an earlier age, Levi argues that the phenomenon of totalitarianism, which reached its supreme form of expression in the deathcamps, liberates in the individual asocial impulses too fragmentary and destructive to be harmonized into a unified theory of survival:

> We are aware that this is very distant from the picture that is usually given of the oppressed who unite, if not in resistance, at least in suffering. We do not deny that this may be possible when oppression does not pass a certain limit, or perhaps when the oppressor, through inexperience or magnanimity, tolerates or favours it. But we state that in our days, in all countries in which a foreign people have set foot as invaders, an analogous position of rivalry and hatred among the subjected has been brought about; and this, like many other human characteristics, could be experienced in the Lager in the light of particularly cruel evidence. (p. 83)

Any theory of survival that ignores this evidence is too abstract to merit unqualified endorsement.

Even more problematic for anyone attempting to establish a valid version of survival is the specific fate of the Jews. The Jews were not in Auschwitz to work; they were there to die. Beneath the illusion of hope lay the daily and sometimes hourly possibility of selection for the gas chamber. "Human beings," says Lingens-Reiner, "who have this fate constantly before their eyes, as an immediate menace to every individual, live under conditions so abnormal that it is almost pointless to subject their behavior to an analysis" (p. 117). If we were to acquiesce totally to this position, the works of Frankl, Bettelheim, and even Des Pres would become superfluous and perhaps irrelevant. Their conviction that "normal" impulses can and indeed must flourish especially in the midst of abnormality if the individual is to survive is at best qualified and at worst discredited by the view that traditional moral choices simply did not exist in Auschwitz. If, as Lingens-Reiner suggests, the "worst" survived as often as the "best," the morally callous as often as the spiritually vital, then the development of a survivor prototype exhibiting qualities favoring survival—whether judgmental in intent or not—would seem to be a vain endeavor.

Indeed, celebrating survival as a triumph of the human spirit, or of the will to resist, or of man's inflexibly moral nature, deflects our attention from one of the most melancholy bequests of the Holocaust—that survival may not be a supreme blessing after all. Alongside the version that affirms new lives stands the version that merely attests to living on. Dr. Joost Meerloo, a psychiatrist who worked with Dutch survivors after their liberation, reported that for many of them every "future is denied, any gratification is forsaken, and a withdrawal into persistent unhappiness takes place. . . . There are certain psychic wounds that prevent the utilization of the new-found freedom. These victims continue to live under the enemy's death verdict." [8] Although this can hardly be embraced as a universal principle, it leads to a vision of the Holocaust experience that mocks the image of the phoenix and the solemn joy of rebirth. It reminds us that those who were left "behind" still possess the power to summon survivors back into the realm of night, to hear what Nelly Sachs will call the mutilated music of their lives. Listen to the voice of an adolescent survivor of the deathcamps, trapped between a knowledge of the intolerable and the desire to disbelieve: "One cannot forget what one has lost. I don't believe that my parents were shoved into the oven, although I saw it with my own eyes. When the war was over, I went back home hoping to find them." [9] On the one hand, the experience of unspeakable atrocity; on the other, the instinctive longing for reconciliation and renewal, the desperate hope that total disruption of human life has been only an illusion. There is simply no place in familiar moral reality for a line like that—"my parents were shoved into the oven"; where then in the traditional landscape of death is the reader to locate it?

The human need *outside* the deathcamps to see the Holocaust as some kind of continuum in the spiritual (if not the physical) history of man repeatedly stumbles over the limits of language. An entire vocabulary, which for generations furnished a sanctuary for motive and character, no matter how terrible the external details, has been corrupted by the facts of *this* event. How after Auschwitz are we to conceive of the individual in conflict with his environment and his society? We think of Hamlet, wrestling with the awful responsibility of vengeance, meditating on death (then recall the members of the Sonderkommandos in Auschwitz, drowned in corpses but lacking the leisure of a Hamlet); of Oedipus, resolutely pursuing his identity, gaining insight though the price is high (then consider those victims who faced the consequences of *their* identity—being Jewish—and knew how minimal was an "insight" that would soon be transformed into smoke); of Anna Karenina, whose miserable fate does not destroy the sublimity of the grand passion that preceded it (then compare the futile love of that adolescent for parents who were "shoved into the oven"). We listen to another child's voice, contemplating her destiny with a confusion that admits no resolution, and wonder what conventional motives like "vengeance," "insight," and "passion" could possibly have to do with her:

> Maybe it would have been real lucky if I had gone toward the left with my mother and the others when the Nazis in the camp separated the prisoners for gassing and for working. They are at peace, they have no struggles. Is it lucky to have had to live in concentration camps and D.P. camps like I did? Not to know whether I would live or die from day to day? And to come out of it alone, and not be with my family? I have often wondered if I would not have been better to have been taken care of by the Nazis, as my mother was. But, here I am and I have to live; what for? [10]

Viktor Frankl might argue that a few sessions of logotherapy would greatly enhance this child's will to meaning. But such a superficial response to her despair demeans responder, victim, and the experience itself, one reflecting a world where men and women are divided into those "for gassing" and those "for working." Such bizarre options now constitute the reality that orphaned the child, and we are silent partners to her vain attempt to rescue from oblivion the uncompleted life of an exterminated parent—or to return to oblivion her own arrested existence.

How is it possible, without violating the complex and contradictory truths of Auschwitz and the other deathcamps, to create out of such unpromising material a literature celebrating the growth of the human spirit? An epic of genocide would seem to be a contradiction in terms. Testimonies to the strength of the spirit during the Holocaust must face the fact of how little nourishment humiliation of the body left that spirit to feed on. The implications of this confrontation cannot fail to influence our response to various versions of survival. Ever since the time of classical antiquity, the tragic vision has left us room to balance physical suffering with moral grandeur. The hero has a voice, up to the moment of his death, and through noble resignation or defiance can transcend the limits of his mortality. Hamlet's dying words to Horatio assure him of a future:

> *If thou didst ever hold me in thy heart;*
> *Absent thee from felicity awhile,*
> *And in this harsh world draw thy breath in pain,*
> *To tell my story.*

And indeed, we still have Hamlet's noble story before us. But what narrative can tell the story of six million anonymous victims, who left no voice behind? And how is a child, who saw his parents "shoved into the oven," to play Horatio in a world far harsher than any dreamt of in Horatio's philosophy?

Heroic defiance, growing into tragic insight, needs a vision of moral order to nourish it, and this is precisely what the Holocaust universe lacks. The Holocaust is a saga without a controlling myth, opening out into an unending vista of chaos. Sporadic gestures of compassion or support within the deathcamps, which—as we have seen—often saved one life at the cost of another, cannot change this. Clearly the usual notion of tragedy, with the hero or heroine caught between difficult choices, but free to embrace an attitude toward the consequences, and hence to preserve his or her moral stature, does not apply to men and women dying in gas chambers—or clinging to life in their vicinity. Agamemnon's dilemma as father and warrior, Clytemnestra's grief and later her rage, Iphigenia's very helplessness as the victim of a greater struggle, all achieve grandeur by the controlling myth that lifts them into a timeless statement about human destiny and divine will. But how are we to portray that mother of three children who reputedly was told by the Nazis that she might save *one* of them from execution? She was free to "choose," but what civilized mind could consider this an example of moral choice, or discover in modern history or Jewish tradition a myth to dignify her dilemma? The alternatives are not difficult, they are *impossible*, and we are left with the revelation of a terrifying question posed by a universe that lacks a vision to contain it. How is a character to survive *any* decision in such a situation, and retain a semblance of human dignity? What can one do but echo the weary refrain of the young girl who survived her family: "But, here I am and I have to live; what for?"

There are many answers to *this* question, but none of them transfigures the victim or survivor of the Holocaust into a creature of heroic dimensions, despite our longing for a moral miracle to ease the pain of our perceptions. Such a transfiguration would link fate with choice by restoring to the victims a significant moral agency in their own survival. Despite scattered instances where this may have been true, there is overwhelming evidence to suggest the contrary. Of the "older" Jewish prisoners in Auschwitz with tattoo numbers below 150,000, reports Primo Levi, only a few hundred were left by 1944:

> not one was an ordinary Häftling [prisoner], vegetating in the ordinary Kommandos, and subsisting on the normal ration. There remained only the doctors, tailors, shoemakers, musicians, cooks, young attractive homosexuals, friends or compatriots of some authority in the camp; or they were particularly pitiless, vigorous and inhuman individuals, installed (following an investiture by the SS command, which showed itself in such choices to possess satanic knowledge of human beings) in the post of Kapos, *Blockältester*, etc.; or finally, those who, without fulfilling particular functions, had always succeeded through their astuteness and energy in successfully organizing, gaining in this way, besides material advantages and reputation, the indulgence and esteem of the powerful people in the camp.

> Whosoever does not know how to become an "organisator,"
> "Kombinator," "Prominent" (the savage eloquence of these
> words!) soon becomes a "mussulman." In life, a third way
> exists, and in fact is the rule; it does not exist in the
> concentration camp. (p. 81)

The fortunate Jews mentioned here bear no resemblance to
prototypes of spiritual strength; they survive (and only up to this
point) because they have been in a position to organize their lives
around a sustaining physical environment, meager as it may have
been. Nothing in their combination of luck, shrewdness, and
energy betrays spiritual inspiration or a source of moral vitality.
The mingling of charity and aggression, of the golden with the
iron rule that drives men in normal surroundings—the "third
way"—quickly made one vulnerable in the morally stifling
atmosphere of the deathcamps.

Our perception of that atmosphere, our need to see a shining
clarity beyond its ambiguous smoke, may help to explain why
some commentators, retreating from the theories of heroic
spiritual resistance, adopt an opposite position, much more
gloomy but equally comforting—the argument that the Jews were
weak and helpless creatures who collaborated in their own
extermination.[11] Since responsibility is directly related to choice,
one can make this charge only by ignoring or denying how
radically the Holocaust disrupted the equilibrium of our moral
and spiritual universe. If no logic can be found in the Nazi
program of genocide, shall we turn in our desperate search for
explanations to a supposed passive "logic" in the Jewish mind,
which led inevitably from the ghettos of Europe to the gas
chambers of Auschwitz? If this were true, then we *would* have a
myth, unflattering but durable, to shore up our faltering vision of
order in historical time: an ancient tradition of Jewish acceptance
of suffering made possible the slaughter of millions. But when the
need for intellectual order causes one to minimize how the Nazis
barbarized the moral premises by which civilized men try to live,
and to shift some of the blame for the atrocities of the Holocaust
onto the victims themselves, then perhaps we should abandon the
quest for order and approach the event with the frank admission
that the search for guilty victims cannot adequately illuminate it.

At another level of perception, which ignores the convenient
distinction between victims and survivors but acknowledges the
persisting influence of one on the other, survival is not a triumph

at all, but another form of defeat. In her account of the
Frenchwomen who were deported with her to Auschwitz, *Le
Convoi du 24 Janvier*, Charlotte Delbo speaks of one survivor who
twenty years later still suffers from the indifference, ignorance,
and lack of understanding that she meets among those who had
not been deported. Who still thinks, she asks, of the 40,000 Jewish
children from Paris who were burned in Auschwitz? And how, we
might add, is one to think of them? The situation of choiceless
choice that dominated existence in Auschwitz forbids her to
forget but offers her no proper form of commemoration, while her
frustration is intensified by the gulf separating her from those
who did not share her past. She formulates her own theory about
survivors, but it provides us with nothing to celebrate:

> From what I've observed among numerous camp survivors,
> there are two categories: those who left, and those who are
> still there. I'm one of the latter. So on September 24, 1952,
> when I was giving birth, I didn't think of the joy that a child
> would bring me; I was thinking—and had been for days and
> months and years—I was thinking of the women of my age
> (32) who had died in degradation without knowing that
> joy.[12]

The women who died in degradation, the 40,000 Jewish children
of Auschwitz, all those, in Martin Buber's words, whose deaths
represent testimony without acknowledgement and who continue
to assault memory and imagination for that very reason—these
exemplify a different version of survival, one that summons us
back into the circumference of their past instead of liberating us
into a boundless future. And they continue to hover precisely
because we have no ceremony—including a ceremony of
language—to pacify their ghosts.

The challenge before us is to move behind the heroic
enhancement of survival theories to the unheroic diminishment of
men and women who are soiled by the situation they find
themselves in, whether they live *or* die. The survivor does not
travel a road from the normal to the bizarre back to the normal,
but from the normal to the bizarre back to a normalcy so
permeated by the bizarre encounter with atrocity that it can never
be purified again. The two worlds haunt each other, as the
memory of her dead comrades pollutes the joy of expectant

motherhood for Charlotte Delbo's companion from Auschwitz. It
is impossible to determine exactly when the potential victim
began to perceive—if he ever did at all—how the universe he was
about to enter differed from the one he had left behind, but we as
readers have the opportunity to assess that difference and to
respond to its implications. We have a dramatic portrait of this
moment from Salmen Gradowski, a member of the last Auschwitz
Sonderkommando, whose notes were dug up in a canteen near
one of the crematoriums about a month after Soviet troops
liberated the camp:

> Have a look at this, my friend. Here goes a group composed
> of over two hundred men selected from among that large
> human mass, recently arrived. They are walking with their
> heads bowed low, full of heavy worry. Their arms are
> drooping, despair has seized them. There were thousands of
> them and now only a minute group has been left. They
> arrived with their wives and children, with parents, brothers
> and sisters, and now they remain lonely and foresaken,
> bereft of wives, children, father and mother, brothers and
> sisters. Everywhere they were together. They had left the
> ghetto together, they had left the [transit] camp together and
> in the train they were shut in together. And now, at the last
> stage, when the culminating point, so horrifying and awful,
> had been finally reached, they got separated. What will
> happen in these moments when [wives and children] will not
> be able to manage by themselves?[13]

Husbands, fathers, sons, and brothers should help to protect the
members of their family, and all their inner energy at this
moment must be concentrated on that desire. But their outward
situation frustrates the inward drive, as a paralyzing sense of
physical helplessness atrophies the will to action that cannot find
any normal form of expression.

As for *abnormal* forms of expression—rushing, unarmed, against
the enemy's machine guns or into the electrified barbed wire for a
quick death, only those who observe these wretched men from a
distance and not from within the perimeters of atrocity can
continue to be baffled by the absence of spontaneous revolt.
Leaderless men, tormented by the fate of their families, trapped
between memory of misery and an uncertain future, caught in a

momentum they regret but now cannot easily escape, drift toward a disaster that in its very essence allows no human gesture against it. Few men are prepared to die when they sense in advance that their "testimony" will remain forever unacknowledged. One cannot repeat too often that the value of a human gesture depends not only on the motive of the gesturer, but on the humanity of the world in whose presence it is made. The Nazi-dominated world inside the deathcamps was designed to make such gestures virtually impossible. One of the most vivid illustrations of this painful truth comes from an account of evidence offered at the twenty-month trial of Auschwitz guards in Frankfurt in 1964 and 1965:

> The witness in the stand is Jean Weiss. One asks oneself under what burden this man still lives, how he can go on living at all, what nightmares haunt him at night. He was an expediter of death at Auschwitz—stretcher bearer and corpse packer; his freight was corpses; everything was done promptly. From the Black Wall [against which prisoners were shot] to the spot where blood was running out of still-warm bodies into the drain back to where the next batch of victims had just collapsed, covered with blood: "We looked like butchers," says Jean Weiss. And in the room in which Klehr [one of the defendants] manipulated his phenol hypodermic, Weiss and another prisoner held the selectees whose lives the "medical orderly" was about to end.
>
> "We had to stand behind them, hold their left arm horizontally and put their right arm over their eyes. The other bearer then stepped in front of them, took them by the feet, and carried them out."
>
> Jean Weiss's cup is not yet empty. He cries, and then he goes on:
>
> "It happened on September 28, 1942. I don't know how many were lined up ahead of my father. The door opened and my father came in with [another] prisoner. Klehr talked to my father and told him: 'You will get an anti-typhus injection.' Then I cried and had to carry out my father myself. Klehr was in a hurry. He injected two prisoners at a time because he wanted to get back to his rabbits."
>
> The next day Klehr asked him why he had cried. "I would

have let him live," Klehr said after hearing the reason. Why hadn't Weiss told him?

Judge Hofmeyer: "Why didn't you?"

The Witness: "I was afraid that Klehr would make me sit down next to him."[14]

What legend of "fathers and sons," from ancient myth to modern fiction, furnishes a precedent for this "confrontation" between generations? From such moments of truth is the chaos of Auschwitz born. Do we call Weiss's fear "cowardice," blame him for not protesting against his father's "fate," even at the risk of his own life, and thus ease the situation back into a bearable tradition of normalcy, where the tragic figure is always called upon to make such difficult choices, accepting the consequences with moral strength? The very idea of moral strength falters in the presence of a Klehr as the "antagonist," and a fatal phenol injection in the heart, followed by annihilation in the crematorium, as the physical destiny of the protagonist. Hamlet might have thought twice about his mortal fate, had he been pinned helplessly against the wall by Laertes' poisoned foil, with no weapon to take up his own defense, and no means of obtaining one.

Moments of truth like Jean Weiss's must be measured against our longing for a Moment of Truth in the deathcamps, when the human will asserted itself and a reborn dignity prevailed. Versions of survival are modified by visions of extermination like the following, recorded in his diary by Sonderkommando member Salmen Lewental of Auschwitz:

A mother was sitting with her daughter, they both spoke in Polish. She sat helplessly, spoke so softly that she could hardly be heard. She was clasping the head of her daughter with her hands and hugging her tightly. [She spoke:] "In an hour we both shall die. What tragedy. My dearest, my last hope will die with you." She sat . . . immersed in thought, with wide open, dimmed eyes. . . . After some minutes she came to and continued to speak. "On account of you my pain is so great that I am dying when I think of it." She let down her stiff arms and her daughter's head sank down upon her mother's knees. A shiver passed through the body of the young girl, she called desperately, "Mama!" And she spoke no more, those were her last words. The order was given to conduct them all into the road leading to the crematorium. . . . I quickly vanished from that place, I did not see the further course of events.[15]

Nor do we need to. The imagination of disaster takes over at this point, together with a stiff courage to enable us to accompany these victims to the portals of annihilation. Mothers and daughters, like fathers and sons, search in vain for a language or gesture to dignify their extinction. A millenium of culture cannot soothe the harsh circumstances of their death, circumstances that confirm the utter contempt for the human that lay at the heart of the Nazi final solution. Heroism perishes in the presence of such contempt.

But the language of heroism does not. If we return for a moment now to what George Steiner in another context calls the "blackmail of transcendence," [16] we will see how a particular vocabulary, inherited from a culture irrelevant to Auschwitz, can nevertheless transform our response to the desolate episodes we have just examined. Viktor Frankl introduces an entirely different voice into the atmosphere of Auschwitz when he tries to cheer up some of his fellow inmates who have grown disheartened about their fate:

> I spoke of our sacrifice, which had meaning in every case. It was in the nature of this sacrifice that it should appear to be pointless in the normal world, the world of material success. But in reality our sacrifice did have a meaning. Those of us who had any religious faith, I said frankly, could understand without difficulty. I told them of a comrade who on his arrival in camp had tried to make a pact with Heaven that his suffering and death should save the human being he loved from a painful end. For this man, suffering and death were meaningful; his was a sacrifice of the deepest significance. He did not want to die for nothing. None of us wanted that.[17]

Frankl tactfully fails to comment on the results of these pacts, invented by men on their sole initiative. Imagine delivering this saccharine speech to the mother about to enter the gas chamber with her daughter. Or consoling Jean Weiss with Bruno Bettelheim's rhetorical flourish that "however restrictive or oppressive an environment may be," man is still free "to decide on his inner approval or resistance to what is forced upon him."

The irrelevance of Bettelheim's language is illustrated by two further moments of truth from Auschwitz, recorded by Hermann Langbein. One describes the end of Meilech Herschkowitz, a former theater director. Selected for death in the gas chamber, Herschkowitz turned to an SS man whom he knew casually from Sunday performances in the camp, and the following exchange occurred:

> "I've been 'selected' for the gas chamber and am due to be burned. Can't you help me?"
> The SS man replied: "There's nothing I can do."
> "Don't you think, Herr Unterscharführer [corporal]"—Herschkowitz continued—"that if I have to die, at least I've earned a bullet?"
> "You're right," was the answer of the Unterscharführer, who drew his revolver and shot Herschkowitz.[18]

Herschkowitz's attempt to control what is "forced upon him" by hoping for the "dignity" of execution by firing squad once more confirms how alien such expectations were in the SS universe. We witness the summary obliteration not only of a life, but of the idea that one still had options in choosing an "honorable" manner of death.

The other "moment" Langbein reports from David Rousset, who described a group of "selectees" being escorted to the gas chamber:

> An old man, who could hardly move his legs any more, sat down along the way. An accompanying guard roared at him: "Get moving, or I'll beat you within an inch of your life!" Quickly the old man exclaimed: "No, don't kill me, I'm going, I'm going!" and rejoined the procession to the gas chamber.[19]

Once again the choice is not between life and death, resistance and submission, courage and cowardice, but between two forms of total humiliation, in this instance each leading to the extinction of a life. By shielding himself instinctively from an immediate threat, the victim inadvertently consigns himself to a consequent one; once one's ultimate fate had been decided by the murderers—and for the Jews, extermination was their fate from the moment they entered the camps—the freedom of moral decision vanished because the antagonist was in total control of the means of supporting life and the manner of imposing death. One could not escape one's enfolding doom, even temporarily, by pretending that responses from the normal world would be heard with sympathetic ears. Langbein's examples dramatically ratify that. Perhaps this is what one survivor meant when he wrote bitterly: "Only to survive, to survive, everything consists in that, and the forms of survival are extreme and loathsome [*ekelhaft*], they are not worth the price of life." [20]

To celebrate the mutual support that in exceptional cases aided survival in the deathcamps is to misrepresent the restraining influence of impending atrocity on the natures of even well-intentioned men. In Auschwitz, caution was the better part of valor, not because men feared to die—though most did—but because of the sense of futility with which the Nazi atmosphere clouded *all* gestures of protest, physical or spiritual. Hermann Langbein, a non-Jewish Austrian Communist, a political prisoner in Auschwitz with a favored position and hence with a good possibility of surviving, makes a painful confession about his own underground organization's failure to aid Jews threatened with the gas chamber. He tells of the plea of Dr. Alfred Klahr, a high-ranking Austrian Jewish Communist, to the underground leadership in the camp to initiate an uprising in opposition to the recently reinstituted policy of gassing the Jews (the policy had been suspended briefly when Liebehenschel replaced Höss as camp commandant):

> Although Klahr's opinion carried weight with us, we rejected his suggestion. A general revolt would have had no chance of success, since the Russian front [in January 1944] was still far away at that time, and the Polish partisan groups in the surrounding mountains were weak. To be sure, it would have been possible to take some SS men with us, but without a doubt we would have to reckon with a horrible destruction of all prisoners, including those who had no idea of any uprising and would not have taken part in it. We could not accept the responsibility for such consequences. Since in the end 60,000 human beings, including Jews, survived their

confinement in Auschwitz, the results subsequently
confirmed the correctness of our decision.[21]

Langbein is honest enough to add that he did not have a good
conscience about the decision either then or later, and to admit
that he neglected to mention this episode, which made a strong
impression on him, in his official postwar report about his
experience in Auschwitz.

"Conscience" is simply an insufficient monitor of human
behavior in the deathcamps, though Langbein would be the first
to acknowledge that between January 1944, when his group
refused to organize an uprising, and October 1944, when a few
hundred desperate Russians and Jews in the last Sonderkommando blew up one of the crematoriums (thus disabling it)
in a vain attempt to break out of the camp, hundreds of thousands of Jews were exterminated. In assessing the conduct of
individuals in Auschwitz, we must face the paradox that *in*-
action increased the possibility for survival among non-Jews, as
the Russian front slowly drew closer, while simultaneously it
ensured the death of the Jews, particularly those from Hungary,
who began arriving in huge numbers in the late spring of 1944.
Powerless men, virtually unarmed, were forced by circumstances
and the egoism of the survival impulse to choose uncertain life
over certain death. Their "choice" certified the continuing doom
of the Jews. Who can blame them? Who can praise them?
"Choice," "blame," and "praise" join that expanding list of free
words that died in Auschwitz, leaving no successors.

When decisions determined by the desire to continue *being* are
described with a vocabulary of value, the quality of that being is
inevitably distorted. The leaders of Langbein's underground
group made their choice from the relative security of their
knowledge that non-Jews were not destined for the gas chamber.
The world of those who *were* so destined was more harrowing, the
options available to them far more circumscribed, so that the
version of survival implicit in Langbein's situation (and he freely
admits this) is totally alien from the dilemma facing the Jews. This
is another reason why we must pluralize all efforts at analyzing
survival. Among a surplus of untenable positions it may seem
irreverent to pursue the "worst," but surely one of the worst was
the ordeal of Sonderkommando members in Auschwitz-Birkenau,
whose task was to burn the bodies of the gassed (including at

times members of their own families). Salmen Lewenthal was one
of them, and in his diary, literally unearthed at Auschwitz in 1962,
he tried to capture the mental state of the prisoner while he was
engaged in his gruesome work:

> we were running under the threat of the clubs of the SS men
> who supervised us. We were lost to such a degree that none
> of us knew what he was doing and how, and whatever was
> happening to him. We lost ourselves so much that we were
> as if lifeless. Driven on we ran like automatons, not knowing
> whither we were running, what for and what we were doing.
> One did not turn to look at one another. I know that not one
> of us was fully conscious, did not think, did not reflect. They
> reduced us to such a state that we became like . . . when we
> came to our senses somewhat [we saw] who was being
> dragged to be burnt and what was going on around us. The
> work was soon over. All persons were already dragged out
> from the gas bunker, were thrown upon a truck and were
> taken to [the pyre?], where people were burning, gassed
> yesterday and the day before yesterday; [all] bodies were
> thrown into the fire. After the work, when people had
> returned to their blocks, they lay down to rest and then the
> tragedy began.[22]

What he means is that then the men could think about their
situation, and *we* realize, even if they cannot, that the real tragedy
is the *absence* of the truly tragic in their experience. They have no
significant choices, since refusal to cooperate is only another form
of suicide, and anonymous death at this moment, they know, will
add no dignity to their refusal and do nothing to stop the
slaughter of the Jews. Other men will continue. There is a singular
but almost providential irony in the missing simile from the
passage just quoted, where Lewental's manuscript was decayed by
its burial in the earth—a dramatic if accidental tribute to the
futility of analogies when we seek to evoke the unthinkable:
"They reduced us to such a state that we became like . . ."

Lewental struggles toward an understanding of what being in
the Sonderkommando implies for his humanity and the humanity
of his comrades, as the "spiritual will to live" gradually filters
through his numbed consciousness and is transformed into a
desire to remain alive void of any associations other than its own

insistent force. Somehow the fragmentary phrases of his damaged manuscript seem appropriate to this confrontation between concrete atrocity and a man's sense of how one ought to behave. Moral authority meets loathsome fact, and what emerges is that most men prefer not to die in such a way, and will do anything, including burning the bodies of other men, to stay alive a little longer—*even when they suspect, as Lewenthal and his comrades must have, that their doom is sealed anyway.* The history of Auschwitz has made this an empirical truth, and no theory of survival can rescue it from its dismal fate. We reserve judgment for the authors of that fate, not its victims. The circularity of Lewental's style attests not to a poverty of words but to the utter simplicity of his vision:

> the only thing in which they [people] do not differ is the fact that everyone is subconsciously mastered by the spiritual will to live, by the aspiration to live [at] any cost, one wants to live because the whole [world?] does not care for his own life or for his own person but for the public welfare only. He would like to survive for the one or the other reason and for the sake of this or that and so he finds hundreds of quibbles. But the truth is that one wants to live at any cost, one wants to live because one lives, because the whole world lives. And all that one wishes, all with what one is, if only slightly, bound . . . is bound with life first of all, without life . . . such is the real truth. And so, briefly and clearly . . . [if] anyone asks why . . . I shall answer . . . that is . . . and later for . . . let them state: I am too weak, I was formerly . . . under the pressure of the will to live, so that I should be able to estimate rightly . . . the will to live, but not . . . is at stake. (p. 139)

The habit of filling in ellipses might tempt one to embellish Lewental's elementary statement about how men behave in the vicinity of the gas chamber when unlike their less fortunate fellow Jews they are still "under the pressure of the will to live," but his own prose gives no hint of moral motive other than the naked desire to remain among the living. When the option is between one form of ignominious death or another, do we add to our understanding of the event by deducing "exemplary" models of behavior for men existing between such choiceless choices? By imposing a pattern for ordered conduct on moments when men could not think or reflect, as Lewental says, do we enter into the reality of the event or attempt to reconstruct it in a light less displeasing to our besieged eyes?

The illusion that under the worst of circumstances—and in Auschwitz, for the Jews in particular, all but a very few circumstances were of the "worst"—men and women could meaningfully distinguish between what they did (or suffered) and the attitude they adopted toward their deeds is supported more easily by language than by events. The relation between deed and motive, fate and intent, collapsed so often in the deathcamps that it ceased to represent an ethical bulwark for the victims. "I lived better in Auschwitz than many of my comrades," confessed one of the prisoner functionaries, "without feeling that it was immoral. In the concentration camp, no one has the right to judge himself according to moral rules that would be valid in normal times." [23] This survivor is not *proud* of his behavior, nor is he particularly happy about the suspension of values that dominated the general struggle to survive in the world of Auschwitz. And he managed to live comparatively "well." Imagine the desolation of Salmen Lewental, as he tries to describe what the will to survive has done to men who were forced to live "ill" beyond conception by the daily routine of destruction:

> Why do you do such ignoble work, what do you live for, what is your aim in life, what do you desire . . . what would you like to achieve living this kind of life. . . . And here is the crux . . . of our Kommando, which I have no intention to defend as a whole. I must speak the truth here, that some of that group have in the course of time so entirely lost themselves that we ourselves were simply ashamed. They simply forgot what they were doing . . . and with time . . . they got so used to it that it was even strange [that one wanted] to weep and complain; that . . . such normal, average . . . simple and unassuming men . . . of necessity get used to everything so that these happenings make no more any impression on them. Day after day they stand and look on how tens of thousands of people are perishing and [do] nothing. (p. 139)

This is description, not judgment: man is a creature who adapts. Lewental's shame does not presume blame, nor do his questions about purpose and goal exact replies. He had already answered his questions: "one wants to live because one lives, because the whole world lives." Members of the Sonderkommando did not choose degradation, any more than the luckier kitchen workers or medical orderlies "chose" decency. "Do you think, perhaps, that I *volunteered* for this work?" rings out the desperate voice of another Sonderkommando member, who like Lewental did not survive. "What should I have done? To be sure, I could have run into the [electrified] barbed wire, like many of my other comrades. But I want to survive! Maybe a miracle will happen! Today or tomorrow we can be liberated." He asks whether those who work in the munitions factory at Monowitz have a nobler occupation, or the women who sort out the clothing and valuables of those already gassed, for shipment back to Germany? "We all work for them at their command," he insists, defining precisely the situation in Auschwitz, where one side had all the power over life and death and the other none at all, including the very important power of martyrdom, of dying as an example—since "running into the wire," followed by cremation, was a testimony without acknowledgement that inspired neither physical nor spiritual resistance among the forlorn victims of the deathcamps. "You think the members of the Sonderkommando are monsters?" that wretched voice exclaims in despair; "I tell you, they're like the others, only more unfortunate." [24]

It is impossible to determine today whether bitterness, anguish, or fidelity to truth inspired Lewental to reach out beyond the grave (though even such conventional images fail here) to soil the satisfaction of those survivors who seek respect for having suffered so much "during that time":

> it is understandable that they will not recall deeds done in the camp, when for a bread ration every most insignificant foreman used to kill a man so that he would be able at his [cost?] and at the cost of tens [of thousands of men?] to survive in the camp. . . . There was a time in this camp, in the years 1941–1942, when each man, really each one, who lived longer than two weeks, lived at the cost of other victims, at the cost of lives of other people or on what he had taken from them. (p. 147)

Although this is not the whole truth of survival in the deathcamps, it represents a darker version, leading to a more somber vision of the Holocaust universe, one we can hardly ignore in our search for insight into that realm. We acknowledge it not to the discredit of victim or survivor, but as a comment on a way of existing that cannot be measured by the standards of ordinary society, where cooperation is welcomed as the desired goal of social behavior, and violation of it is considered an inherently destructive act. Fortune, in the form of the Nazi system of atrocity, created a challenge to the moral imagination that was neither "moral" in any acceptable sense nor easy to imagine. The gravity and confusion of the final solution for the survivors was not that only a few were able to exercise charity and compassion despite its nihilistic force, but that so many were driven— "normal, average . . . simple and unassuming men," as Lewental concedes—by life-threatening circumstances not of their own devising to engage in life-supporting activities that would make dignity blush and would mark the human image with a permanent moral scar.

Despite his bitterness and gloom, despite his overwhelming sense of despair, even Lewental is not immune to the vocabulary of transcendence when events offer him the slightest justification for describing human nature with familiar moral terminology. As a member of the Sonderkommando working in Crematorium III he was not an eyewitness to the spontaneous rebellion on October 7, 1944 in Crematorium II or to the destruction on the same day of Crematorium IV, but these futile efforts—no one escaped[25]— temporarily restore to his imagination a sense of normal moral tradition, and he lapses easily into a language of celebration. He speaks of the few men who stayed behind to blow up the crematorium and to cut the wires—apparently not electrified at the time—surrounding the women's compound,[26] and it is dramatically clear to us how vital even in the last days of his life was this *exceptional* illustration of an escape from the choiceless choice that imprisoned the will of most men and women in Auschwitz:

> They gave up everything sacrificing their own selves. Is it not a sacrifice of their own lives laid down on the altar? Laid down to full consciousness, with complete self-denial? Why, nobody forced them to do so at that moment. They could have tried to escape together with all the others and yet they renounced it for the good of the cause. And therefore who is

able to gauge the courage of our comrades and the heroism of their deed? Yes, yes, there the best, truly the best and the most worthy men perished who were capable of living and dying with dignity. (p. 170)

The tribute may be doubly deserved since, contrary to Lewental's statement here, the possibility of mass escape in broad daylight with the SS guards immediately alerted was virtually nonexistent. The uprising was a desperate response to the certainty that the Sonderkommando was about to be liquidated; it was carried out with full knowledge that the larger non-Jewish underground movement in the main camp would not support it. Whether the hundreds of victims, shot down by the SS or burned alive in a barn where a number of "escapees" were discovered hiding, felt that they lived and died their last moments with dignity is impossible to ascertain; what the few who remained behind to certain doom must have felt is even more speculative. What *is* clear is Lewental's need to create for himself and for posterity a favorable image of human nature in extremity, one reestablishing the ruptured connection between choice and destiny. Revolt, even when futile, gives Lewental access to an idiom—"sacrifice," "self-denial," "courage," "heroism," and "dignity"—that allows him to shore up the hopeless ruin of lives in the Sonderkommando with a verbal scaffold. Whether the resultant human edifice represents illusion or reality, Lewental's hope or genuine transformation, we can never know. But we do know that whenever Lewental salutes those who are about to die with their *own* voices, not with the rhetoric of inspiration, his tone is steadily mournful, a sad countermelody to that solitary moment of revolt in the Sonderkommando when men were briefly reacquainted with choice, if only the choice to die.

The countermelody resounds from the anteroom of the gas chamber, where young Jewish girls are awaiting their end:

Many girls stood and sat around, their heads bowed and preserved a stubborn silence, looked with deep revulsion at this base world and particularly at us. One of them spoke, "I am still so young, I have really not experienced anything in my life, why should death of this kind fall to my lot? Why?" She spoke very slowly in a faltering voice. She sighed heavily and proceeded, "And one should like so much to live

a little bit longer." Having finished she fell into a state of
melancholy reverie and fixed her gaze on some distant point;
fear of death emanated from her wildly shining eyes.
(pp. 144–145)

The problem for the vast majority of Holocaust victims was not
how to survive, but *why* such death, and in such a way. This
unanswered and perhaps unanswerable question keeps their
spirits hovering restlessly, like Hamlet's father's ghost, in our
memory. The problem for the contemporary mind, beyond the
"happier" one of explaining survival, is how to incorporate this
heritage of meaningless death into our vision of the present.

   That vision is dual: it includes what Primo Levi calls the
"uniform internal desolation" that afflicted prisoners in the
deathcamps when they contemplated the buried humanity of their
persecutors (to say nothing of their own apparent doom), and the
occasional intrusion of that other world of normality, which cast
some dim light on the dark shadows of desolation. Neither has
meaning without the other. Levi's firm vision of Auschwitz is
modified by his personal contact in Buna-Monowitz with an
Italian civilian worker named Lorenzo, who befriends him and
brings him bread and other rations every day for a month. Levi
attributes his survival to this man,

> not so much for his material aid, as for his having constantly
> reminded me by his presence, by his natural and plain
> manner of being good, that there still existed a just world
> outside our own, something and someone still pure and
> whole, not corrupt, not savage, extraneous to hatred and
> terror; something difficult to define, a remote possibility of
> good, but for which it was worth surviving.

But how many victims (or potential survivors) had a Lorenzo to
balance the ordeal of moral chaos, someone whose "humanity
was pure and uncontaminated" because "he was outside this
world of negation"? [27] With few exceptions, as we have seen, to *be*
in Auschwitz was to be polluted *by* Auschwitz, because daily
existence under what Lewental called "the pressure of the will to
live" required it; Levi's lucky contact with Lorenzo was neither
model nor rule for behavior in the deathcamps. It does not ease
the dilemma of choiceless choice.

This dilemma is complicated by the unavoidable necessity of writing about the world of negation inside the deathcamps while remaining conscious of a world of potential affirmation, Lorenzo's world, that coexists with it beyond the barbed-wire barriers. Understandably, as we try to recreate the Holocaust universe, we are more inclined to bring affirmation inside than to let negation escape. We have verbal and conceptual tools for imposing order on chaos; we have greater difficulty containing the chaos that spills over the rims of Auschwitz onto the surrounding "peaceful" terrain. The logic of the deathcamp slogan—*Des einen Tod ist des anderen Brot* (one man's death is another man's bread)—eludes neat distinctions between villainy and heroism and introduces a way of being that is without familiar literary or historical precedent. "Under the conditions of Auschwitz," Hermann Langbein suggests, "only too often both character and intellect broke down." [28]

One of the most effective attempts to chronicle the nature of this breakdown, and certainly one of the most devastating literary treatments of the very "conditions of Auschwitz" we have been examining, is the group of stories written by Tadeusz Borowski, himself a survivor, some of which were published under the title *This Way for the Gas, Ladies and Gentlemen.* Borowski's strategy is to fuse techniques of fiction with details of fact in a way that obliterates usual sources of tension in literature and introduces us dramatically to the atmosphere of what I have abstractly called the world of choiceless choice. He draws us not into an imaginative (and imagined) world, but into the daily routines of Auschwitz itself, then takes us beyond history by manipulating tone and point of view and enfolding the narrated events with an insulating irony to try to salvage some of the reader's disintegrating admiration for human nature. Slowly it becomes clear that his own disintegrating admiration is at stake too, as he struggles, in his own words, "to tell the truth about mankind to those who do not know it." [29]

For Borowski, the concepts of heroism and villainy died with the first deportations to the deathcamps. In a searching exposition of the theoretical basis of Borowski's literary achievement, Andrzej Wirth examines the original idea of tragedy that evolved in his work following his dismissal of those two concepts. New crimes, Wirth assumes, call for a new literature, for a sense of tragedy that has nothing to do with the classical conception based on the necessity of choice between two systems of value. The hero of Borowski's stories is a hero *deprived of all choice*. He finds himself in a situation without choice because every choice is base. The tragedy lies not in the necessity of choosing but in the impossibility of making a choice.

Borowski, perhaps more powerfully than any other writer on the subject, discredits the argument that an exemplary individual attitude or act could be pitted against a system of mass extermination. "Death in the oven was tragic [though not in the customary sense] irrespective of whether a genius or the average man was being burnt," writes Wirth. Hence the victim could not transform himself, like Melville's Ahab, into a unique hero or, again like Ahab, create a unique antagonist from machinery of destruction that was deliberately designed to reduce all its victims to interchangeable ash. "The de-individualization of the hero," says Wirth, "was accompanied by a *de-individualization of the situation*." [30] As a consequence, both the nature of good and the source of evil were blurred, as was the traditional relationship between hero and antagonist, a Hamlet and a Claudius, Antigone and Creon, Othello and Iago.

Although ultimately individual men decided on the final solution and drove the Jews to their death, *it was virtually impossible for the victims in the deathcamps to perceive their situation in this way,* and thus to see themselves as heroic victims of a definable evil. The killing system itself conspired to keep murderers and victims anonymous, to each other and in their own eyes, in the sense that the death of a man or a woman in the gas chamber was not an act of memorable choice—"Thus," cries Ahab, in *his* final moment, "I give up the spear!"—any more than the annihilation of millions, as Raul Hilberg has exhaustively shown, was traceable to the decision of a single authoritative voice. When a system turns victims into "criminals" to keep themselves alive, when murder is led up to "by countless limited decisions taken by countless people as if in the void, without any emotional or even intellectual link with the objects of crime," as Wirth says (p. 46), than how is the victim to identify the hostility directed against him and to discover a mode of action that may transform him into a potential survivor? Far from striving to keep their previous system of values inviolate, most inhabitants of the deathcamps, according to

Borowski's vision, had to invent provisional rules of conduct
that might favor physical survival, but could never ensure it. As
for *moral* survival—Borowski's stories, and perhaps even his
suicide in 1951, six years after his liberation, represent a cynical
requiem to a system of belief that collapsed before the
impersonality of the gas chambers.

The title of Borowski's volume, *This Way for the Gas, Ladies and
Gentlemen* (which is also the title of the initial story), is itself an
ironic farewell to politeness, to human consideration, and an
introduction to a pitiless world of stone (as Borowski called one of
his Polish Auschwitz volumes) from which a new human identity,
a deathcamp identity, is to be chiseled. The old identities, as
Wirth observes, which attributed exceptional positive qualities to
the hero and extraordinary cruelty to the villain, were simply
insufficient to portray the actual conditions of Auschwitz. Such
efforts, Borowski felt, would sentimentalize the hero and
demonize the villain, reflecting not the authenticity of the
deathcamp experience but the commentator's habit of viewing
that experience (often instinctively) through the comforting lenses
of traditional literature. It sometimes seems, for example, as if
Frankl and Bettelheim are determined to sculpt heroic prototypes
despite the recalcitrance of their material.

Although Borowski transforms the ordeal of Auschwitz into
literature, he refuses to treat his subject as material to be
artistically manipulated. If anything, his *reader* becomes his
material, a sensibility whose premises about character and
conduct will be disorganized by the experience of reading and
reformulated after absorbing the substance of the artist's
unorthodox vision. Both the behavior and the attitude of
Borowski's characters violate our expectations of decency (and
often of monstrosity too), leaving us with the problem of
reconciling old values with a new reality. Since Borowski need not
pretend to have invented this reality—Auschwitz has already
"happened"—*his* challenge is to ensure that we do not confuse it
with familiar assumptions about the pre-Holocaust world. Wirth
makes the important distinction between a fate that is not
irrevocable, life outside the camp where significant choices are
still possible, and existence in the deathcamp where the situation
"develops according to certain fixed norms which are not 'fate' in
general but 'fate created by the system' " (pp. 47–48). By using
narrative points of view from *within* the system of extermination,

by presenting as normal, actions that we intuitively regard as perverse, Borowski moves a step beyond Levi and Lewental, who still inhabit, at least intellectually, the dual universe of free or meaningless choice. His vision of system-created fate reflects a version of survival that is inaccessible in straightforward accounts of life in the deathcamps. He simply eliminates the destroyed half of that dual universe.

One conclusion from Borowski's art is that men have put too much trust in the strength and resiliency of inner values. Gripped by the irrevocable system-created fate of Auschwitz, they found that they were daily deprived of the possibility of being human, since the idea of humanity thrives on the opportunity to assert inner values against a stern *flexible* destiny. The gas chamber, the Nazi contempt for all prisoners, including those to whom they assigned privileged positions, so eroded the sense of moral self that, as Wirth mentions, a new principle of being emerged: "once a certain limit of inhumanity is passed, the differentiation between tormentor and victim becomes fluid" (p. 52). That is, the victim was forced by circumstances not to adopt SS *values*, but to be swept along by the rule of staying alive in the deathcamps that regularly saw one man's death become another man's means of survival. Lewental and his fellow members of the Sonderkommando remained alive a little longer because there were so many dead to burn. The situation does not make them villains, but neither does it offer the chance for heroic gesture. The futile Sonderkommando revolt, as it finally manifested itself (not as it originally was planned—part of a general uprising within and outside the camp to be coordinated with the uprising in Warsaw), was not a splendid affirmation of inner value but a vain protest against approaching extermination. This does not diminish the desperate courage of the participants; but it does clarify the nature of the human options available to them. The revolt began, one notes grimly, when the prisoners thrust a hostile German Kapo and an SS man *alive* into the crematorium.

The apparent cynicism of Borowski's narrators is not merely a literary device; it represents an honest attempt to suggest how Auschwitz "denatured" human character. "It is impossible to write about Auschwitz impersonally," Borowski once said in a review of a book about the camp that praised the behavior of survivors and victims:

> The first duty of Auschwitzers is to make clear just what a
> camp is. . . . But let them not forget that the reader will
> unfailingly ask: But how did it happen that *you* survived? . . .
> Tell, then, how you bought places in the hospital, easy posts,
> how you shoved the "Moslems" into the oven, how you
> bought women, men, what you did in the barracks,
> unloading the transports, at the gypsy camp; tell about the
> daily life of the camp, about the hierarchy of fear, about the
> loneliness of every man. But write that you, you were the
> ones who did this. That a portion of the sad fame of
> Auschwitz belongs to you as well.[31]

Fear and loneliness do not breed heroes or villains in this
atmosphere. Life here breeds lice, and because of this the opening
line of the story "This Way for the Gas"—"All of us walked
around naked"—introduces us to an unrecognizable Eden, where
men and women exist not by naming the beasts but by being
confused with them, breathing (while their garments are being
deloused) not the glorious air of Paradise restored but the odor of
Cyclone B, "an efficient killer of lice in clothing and of men in gas
chambers" (p. 29). It is as if the world of organized creation were
disintegrating back into chaos through a natural process, devoid
of the signs of apocalypse, still under the control of men, while
the unprepared reader—like the confused original arrivals at
Auschwitz—must find his way around an alien terrain.

Delousing is a vital controlling image for the deathcamp
experience, not as metaphor but as literal reflection of a place
where men and women did not choose heroic death and were not
even killed like human beings, but were *exterminated*.
Extermination is part of the terminology of annihilation, and even
though the word insults our propensity for transcendence, it
accurately defines the doom that men faced in the deathcamp
universe. The first duty of commentators is no different from the
first duty of Auschwitzers: "to make clear just what a camp is."
For Borowski, Auschwitz was a place where people were
exterminated, or survived in order to avoid extermination. In
normal times, we may admire the spiritual strength of those who
can draw on a quiet faith to confront impending disaster;
Borowski allows no such luxury, not because he is an enemy of
faith, but because he knows how such an emphasis can distort

what he calls "the daily life of the camp." The following exchange reminds us of Levi's anger at Kuhn's prayer of gratitude after escaping a selection:

> Below us, naked, sweat-drenched men crowd the narrow barracks aisles or lie packed in eights and tens in the lower bunks. Their nude, withered bodies stink of sweat and excrement; their cheeks are hollow. Directly beneath me, in the bottom bunk, lies a rabbi. He has covered his head with a peace of rag torn off a blanket and reads from a Hebrew prayer book (there is no shortage of this type of literature at the camp), wailing loudly, monotonously. "Can't somebody shut him up? He's been raving as if he'd caught God himself by the feet." "I don't feel like moving. Let him rave. They'll take him to the oven that much sooner." (pp. 31–32)

Borowski's narrator—who as a non-Jew knows the privileged position he holds—is less contemptuous of the rabbi than of his misplaced traffic with transcendence, as the bodies of other men, not their souls, lie rotting around him. And their "salvation," Borowski insists with unrelenting irony, lies not in communion with spirit, but with a successful delousing operation (to protect them from typhus) and in the arrival of further transports of Jews, to provide them with additional food and clothing—since the narrator is associated with the "Canada" Kommando, whose job was to unload the incoming boxcars filled with victims for the gas chambers. When one is surrounded by the threat of extermination, proximity to suffering does not strengthen human ties, but establishes a new priority of value whose sole aim is to strengthen the chances of survival.

Just as periodic delousing is a futile struggle against a system of living that breeds typhus, so attempts to remain alive represent a futile struggle against a system that authorizes extermination—futile in the sense that success for some depends on further extermination of others. Under such circumstances, men do not react with dismay to the killing, but to the absence of transports. "We are without even our usual diversion," the narrator complains: "the wide roads leading to the crematoria are empty" (p. 30). Borowski knows how such casual diction will freeze the blood of his readers, but he also knows that no other usage can so powerfully redirect their waning attention to the exploitation implicit in the situation of survival. If the Germans "run out of people" (p. 31), as the narrator says, that situation may grow insupportable. Although the Poles receive packages from home, the Russians, Jews, and Greeks must scavenge for their food. When his French friend replies that "they can't run out of people, or we'll starve to death in this blasted camp" (p. 31), we get a devastating glimpse of the moral cannibalism that the deathcamp conditions imposed on multitudes of survivors. This cosmopolitan community has developed a culture of coping that feeds on the very human feelings that our more familiar culture is supposed to preserve.

In the culture of coping that was Auschwitz, the living did not control the dead—the dead controlled the living. The survivor depended for his life—for the time being, anyway—on the death of someone else. If the tragic figure is a man who through action or moral attitude rebels against his destiny, what are we to make of Borowski's narrator, who helps to drive victims from the cattle cars, unloads their belongings, watches them being led off to the gas chambers, feels rage at his involvement in their fate rather than pride at his triumph over his own, and finds in an attack of nausea little escape from an environment that dehumanizes everyone—murderer, victim, and survivor? Ironically, in his hierarchy of degradation the starving Greeks, those ancient bearers of the tragic spirit, occupy the lowest level now. Waiting for the transport, they devour some mildewed bread and half-rotten sardines found lying beneath the rails; after the unloading, they stuff themselves with anything they can find, including jars of marmalade. In the presence of so much casual slaughter, the narrator cannot tolerate such greedy feasting; ignoring their hunger, he denounces them as pigs and knows that many of them will die of dysentery. Life gestures are contaminated by death or become death gestures themselves. He spends his rage in impotent silence: "The air is filled with ghastly cries, the earth trembles beneath me, I can feel sticky moisture on my eyelids. My throat is completely dry" (p. 41). Earlier he had broken his silence by explaining to the Greeks in what he called "crematorium Esperanto" the challenge that lay before the Canada Kommando: "*Transport kommen, alles Krematorium, compris?*" (p. 35). In the universal idiom of extermination, words do not dignify and communication brings neither community nor communion. He is victim himself of the only permissible form of charity, the camp law that dictates that "people going to their death must be deceived to the very end" (p. 37).

Their death pollutes his life while it ensures his survival: he will get from the transport the new shoes that he needs. He is left only a choice between evils, between extermination and continued existence in Auschwitz: "Suddenly I see the camp as a haven of peace. It is true, others may be dying, but one is somehow still alive, one has enough food, enough strength to work." (p. 48). In the context of all those corpses, we are surprised by his question from another world—"Listen, Henri, are we good people?" (p. 41)—a question both irrelevant and intolerable. It is irrelevant because the idea of the "good" echoes a system of values that the Nazis have perverted, leaving a vacuum that makes such a question unanswerable; and intolerable because the narrator, powerless to denounce or attack the original agents of evil, who are unidentifiable in any case, finds himself hating their victims, a situation that he himself calls pathological.[32] And the reader, who shares with Borowski a vantage point wider than any of his characters, who still inhabits the other world that the narrator has been wrenched from, suffers most of all from what he is forced to witness: the invitation to the gas in the story's title includes us all.

Its fatal odor lingers in our memory as Borowski mercilessly confronts us with moments of dehumanization so overwhelming that they temporarily obliterate instances of compassion that might have balanced them. Compassion we expect, even in adversity; but the terror of extermination generated consequences that leave us morally speechless:

> Here is a woman—she walks quickly, but tries to appear calm. A small child with a pink cherub's face runs after her and, unable to keep up, stretches out his little arms and cries: "Mama! Mama!"
>
> "Pick up your child, woman!"
>
> "It's not mine, sir not mine!" she shouts hysterically and runs on, covering her face with her hands. She wants to hide, she wants to reach those who will not ride the trucks, those who will go on foot, those who will stay alive. She is young, healthy, good-looking, she wants to live.
>
> But the child runs after her, wailing loudly: "Mama, mama, don't leave me!"
>
> "It's not mine, not mine, no!" (p. 43)

And what is a "decent" human response to this indecent drama? A drunken Russian prisoner, a member of the Kommando, outraged by what he has seen, chokes the mother, throws her on the truck leaving for the gas chambers, hurls the child after her—"And take this with you, bitch!" (p. 43)—and is praised by the SS guard for his efficient way of dealing with "degenerate mothers" (p. 43). He growls at the guard to shut his mouth and takes another swallow of vodka, then passes the canteen to the narrator, who only feels nauseous. Misdirected scorn conceals self-contempt, forbids the kind of human growth we normally associate with extraordinary suffering, and mocks the tradition that makes of such suffering a spiritual test, for victim or witness. The columns of smoke rising into a translucent sky at the story's end effectively fuse the details of the episode into the image of stained purity, of a spreading dawn and the promise of a clear day polluted by a situation that, contrary to nature, drives the maternal instinct and the life instinct apart. Because Borowski's characters are so quick to blame the mother, his readers are moved to judge with greater moral caution. But they soon discover that in Auschwitz reality so often crippled judgment with fear that the individual was forced to shed his or her human identity and stand unadorned—"All of us walked around naked"—before his *destroyer*, not his Creator, bereft of defense and left only with the inextinguishable desire to stay alive.

Borowski is determined to follow the images of men as they evolve under the tutelage of Auschwitz, even though his pursuit may shatter all cherished humanisms of the past. The risk is great, since it raises the challenge of rebuilding new humanisms from fragments of discord that pierce the heart with potentially incurable wounds. He complicates his vision, and our task of interpreting it, by acknowledging the multiple realities of the deathcamp universe, where human reactions shift with the state of one's hunger, the relative security of one's future (depending on which Kommando one was assigned to), and the simple fact of whether or not one was Jewish. Borowski's non-Jewish narrator in "A Day at Harmenz" (Harmenz was one of the many subcamps surrounding Auschwitz) is openly contemptuous of the Jew Becker, who when he was camp senior at a Jewish camp elsewhere in Poland had had his own son hanged for stealing bread from the other prisoners. Borowski's secure narrator habitually denounces those who violate his sense of human decency with imprecations like "pig" and "swine" (favorite SS imprecations too), and Becker does not escape his scorn. But the confrontation that follows shifts our sympathies rapidly as we are drawn into a world where human decencies like the loyalty of father to son are poisoned by unprecendented conditions of being:

> Becker, the old, melancholy, silver-haired Jew, had already calmed down. He looked down at me almost with pity and asked:
>   "How long have you been in the camp?"
>   "Oh, a few months."
>   "You know something, Tadek, I think you're a nice boy," he said unexpectedly, "but you haven't really known hunger, have you?"
>   "That depends on what you mean by hunger."
>   "Real hunger is when one man regards another man as something to eat. I have been hungry like that, you see."
> (p. 54)

But just as we begin to understand the justification for Becker's version of survival, Borowski's narrator undermines our insight with a further exchange: " 'And you, you never ate anything but your own ration?' 'That was different. I was a camp senior' " (p. 55). A morality determined by diet seems a bizarre juxtaposition to readers accustomed to one founded on values less nutritive; Borowski's story records the genesis of this unfamiliar system for gauging human conduct.

Food dominates the action of "A Day at Harmenz," preserving life, indirectly causing death, alienating or binding together various characters in the story. Its opening conversation, like the introductory theme of a sonata that later will be developed through variations, sets the tone: "Working hard today, aren't you? Good morning, Tadek. How would you like something to eat?' 'Good morning, Mrs. Haneczka! No thanks' " (p. 51). Mrs. Haneczka, the patron saint of Harmenz (the Greeks ask if she is the narrator's Madonna), has access to ordinary provisions, since Harmenz has a farm and orchards; she provides food for special favorites among the prisoners, and even occasionally dispenses some potatoes among the Greeks. The narrator's refusal of food (when he is surrounded by starving men like Becker) highlights the uneven "justice" of Auschwitz; as a non-Jewish Pole, he receives frequent packages from home. But it also qualifies his later condemnation of Becker, who receives no packages and as a Jew is constantly threatened by a kind of death that the narrator need not fear. Borowski draws on his own experience here; a few weeks before his arrival in Auschwitz, the gassing of non-Jews had been suspended.

Two essential rituals of the deathcamp dominate the action of the story, framing the perimeters of the prisoners' existence: the noontime "meal," and a selection for the gas chambers. In Borowski's universe, men cannot afford the luxury of inviolate spirits or uncontaminated attitudes: the pressure of events allows no leisure for such self-indulgence. The practical law of survival motivates the narrator, who is foreman of his work detail, to snatch a large caldron of soup from the next Kommando and substitute one of his own that is half the size. A similar rule induces the Kapo to distribute second helpings of soup to the stronger and healthier workers: "The sick, the weaklings, the emaciated, have no right to an extra bowl of water with nettles. Food must not be wasted on people who are about to go to the gas chamber" (p. 70). Borowski's ironic tone cannot disguise the fact that within the inhuman limitations of Auschwitz there is a grain of reason in this sensible cruelty, similar to the principle followed by prisoner-doctors of designating hopeless cases for selection in order to save convalescing ones. The idea that men suffer in body to endure in spirit is meaningless here, as is the more traditional view of sacrifice: we suffer, that others may live. The deathcamp corrupts this to read, "Let others suffer, so that we may live," and in the wake of this perverse but inescapable system of morality given the minimal inclination toward sainthood of ordinary men, charity becomes an exclusive prerogative of the fortunate few, not a source of spiritual grace, while the reader gropes in vain to share with the victims a terror he cannot identify with.

Nor can pity for the victims lead to catharsis, since we can never be made to accept extermination as a version of man's ultimate lot on earth. Borowski's refusal to spiritualize the experience of suffering in the deathcamp creates distance rather than recognition, and the reader is left with a sense of humanity so violated (and violating) that there is nothing and no one to identify with. Perhaps this is one reason why the Holocaust as a theme for investigation continues to haunt the imagination, especially among humanists and men of devout conviction: the prolonged, unredeemable agony of victims and survivors cannot be easily adapted—though some have tried—to a tragic or religious view of existence. Even Borowski's Polish biographer was driven to conclude after reading the Auschwitz stories that in the world of stone, the living are always right, the dead are always wrong. But Jan Kott, who introduces Borowski's stories in English, corrects this misleading conclusion: "If the dead are wrong and the living are always right, everything is finally justified: but the story of Borowski's life and that which he wrote about Auschwitz show that the dead are right, and not the living."[33]

Borowski's contribution to the versions of survival we have been examining is that he refuses to gratify the reader's need to find justification in the survivor. If mutual support occasionally helped friends or relatives to hold out for a time (as Mrs. Haneczka gave food to the narrator before he began to receive packages from home), *ultimately* private support ensures one life at the expense of another, since there is not enough food to go around (as the narrator tells the Greeks who plead with him to intervene with Mrs. Haneczka, "If you're hungry, ask her for food yourself. Let her give it to you" [p. 53]). The narrator is forced, not by his own nature—and this is vital if we are to understand Wirth's theory of a tragedy beyond choice—but by the situation in Auschwitz which controls him even though he did not help to create it, to participate in a kind of deathcamp "justice" that is always allied with the death of someone else. In this sense the living are always "wrong," since they so rarely are able to perform their deeds in behalf of everyone's life. And the dead are "right" maybe only because they have not been saved by a "justice" that is not just. They do not bear the burden of lingering doubts, of unspecified guilt, of unjustified blame.

When human relationships can lead toward a stable and more fruitful future, then the virtues we commonly associate with mutual support flourish, because individuals have some control over the results. But when the purpose of relationships is to lead *away* from starvation, exhaustion, and the gas chamber—the purpose of all prisoner efforts in Auschwitz—then we cannot so easily praise or evaluate such behavior. The complex interaction of helping and hurting is illustrated by the quest for food in "A Day at Harmenz." Mrs. Haneczka gives the narrator some lard for a Russian prisoner named Ivan, who has found two bars of soap for her. She does not know that Ivan has stolen the soap that very day from the narrator, who vows revenge for the theft (forgetting his own contempt for Becker, who had executed his son for a similar deed). When the narrator accidentally discovers that Ivan is concealing a stolen goose in his effects, he leaks the information to someone who will report it to the Kapo. When the SS search for the stolen goose, they find it in the sack of an old Greek, and threaten him with execution if he does not disclose where he got it. With the narrator staring at his eyes, Ivan steps forward to certain death by announcing that he is the source: a selection has been declared for that day, and his number is written down. But he is a wretched victim, not a martyred hero.

Thus the narrator has his revenge, though the chain of events begins with the well-intentioned gesture of Mrs. Haneczka, and ends with the exchange of two bars of soap for a man's life. The narrator, who earlier in the story had taunted Becker with rumors of a selection that day, does not rejoice in his perspicacity: "I feel as if this damn selection were somehow my fault," he exclaims. "What a curious power words have. . . . Here in Auschwitz even evil words seem to materialize" (p. 80). Evil words, like evil deeds, materialize from a matrix that encompasses many motives, though the original design—the execution of men and women in the gas chamber—has no connection to the decisions of the potential victims.

The evil words are "selection" and "extermination," but the narrator and his non-Jewish friends are protected from their fatal effects. Their talisman is "food," and as the story ends, two of them go off to enjoy "a wonderful apple cake" that has just arrived "straight from home" (p. 81). The worlds of death and survival collide when Becker, who has also been chosen for the gas chamber, pleads with the narrator for a final "meal": "I've been so hungry for such a long time. Give me something to eat" (p. 80). The narrator, seated on an upper bunk, replies: "Okay, Jew, come on up and eat. And when you've had enough, take the rest with you to the cremo" (p. 80). The fundamental impulse in Auschwitz, says Borowski (who wants to tell us what a deathcamp really is), the means of remaining alive for a brief *or* a prolonged period of time, is satisfaction of the appetite. But his version goes beyond the physical, to the dreary vision of how the spiritual substance of both victim and survivor is consumed by the SS world they have been forced to inhabit. The luck of the non-Jew, who will live because of that identity, and the misery of the Jew, who will die in the gas chamber for the same reason, coexist and forbid an ordering of loyalties, a distinction between heroism and villainy, a sorting out of sympathies. We cannot celebrate survival when the living are degraded by the very fact that others have been condemned to death; the narrator uneasily senses this when he ponders his earlier joking prophecy of a selection that day: his taunt has become truth. He cannot entirely dissociate himself, any more than the reader can, from the story's final epiphany, an image of Becker reaching for his last food: "His eyes were half-closed and, like a blind man, he was vainly groping with his hand for the board to pull himself on to the bunk" (p. 81). For Borowski, the spirit cannot rise when the body has sunk so low.

Nor can the mind escape the paradox, the theme of "The People Who Walked On," that Auschwitz was a place where the ritual of soccer and the ritual of gassing were enacted simultaneously: "Between two throw-ins of a soccer game," says the narrator of this story, "right behind my back, three thousand people had been put to death" (p. 84). The endlessly flowing line of victims finally engulfs all responses, including a discussion between the narrator and a woman block elder about the relationship of justice and punishment to all this annihilation. Questions and answers within a framework of conventional morality are mere rhetoric: "And you, would you do good if you were able to?" "I seek no rewards. I build roofs and want to survive the concentration camp" (p. 90). Before Auschwitz, at least theoretically, justice had been anchored securely to the nature of the crime; but after Auschwitz, we are told, receiving a preview of a still unsolved dilemma, those who suffered unjustly will "want the guilty to suffer unjustly too" (p. 90). "Justice" in Auschwitz was a derived, not an imported principle, derived from the unequivocal fact that there was not enough life sustenance to support a general theory of ideal behavior. "You're a pretty smart fellow!" says the block elder to the narrator scornfully, while at the same time acknowledging the practical morality of Auschwitz. "But you wouldn't have the slightest idea how to divide bread justly, without giving more to your own mistress!" (pp. 90–91). How does one evaluate this implied charge of injustice when the narrator, against whom it is directed, must live as a daily witness to the slaughter of 300,000 Hungarian Jews?

The "flaming pits and the crematoria operating at full speed" (p. 95) crowd his vision, so that he seems to exist in two realms—the surface routine of staying alive, waiting for packages and letters from home, "organizing" for friends, passing time; and a deeper, more instinctive revulsion, which penetrates the veneer of ironic indifference and erupts sporadically from the darker side of Auschwitz: "I stared into the night, numb, speechless, frozen with horror. My entire body trembled and rebelled, somehow even without my participation. I no longer controlled my body, although I could feel its every tremor. My mind was completely calm, only the body seemed to revolt" (p. 85). This darker side of Auschwitz is allied, as always, with the fate of the Jews; Borowski cannot suppress the suspicion that they have paid for his narrator's survival—and perhaps for his own. Did he try to redeem this debt six years later by turning on the gas and taking his own life? We will never know. But his stories continually lead us from "sight" to insight into the tenuous bond that joins normal civilization after Auschwitz with those moments that still disrupt our efforts to believe in order after such chaos. The conclusion of "The People Who Walked On" is a summation of epiphanies, those sharply etched instants of reality that define perception and disturb tranquility:

> Your memory retains only images. Today, as I think back on that last summer in Auschwitz I can still see the endless, colourful procession of peole solemnly walking—along both roads [victims to the gas chambers, and local Poles out for a Sunday stroll]; the woman, her head bent forward, standing over the flaming pit; the big readheaded girl [the block elder] in the dark interior of the barracks, shouting impatiently:
> "Will evil be punished? I mean in human, normal terms!" And I can still see the Jew with bad teeth, standing beneath my high bunk every evening, lifting his face to me, asking insistently:
> "Any packages today? Couldn't you sell me some eggs for Mirka? I'll pay in marks. She is so fond of eggs . . ." (p. 97)

Such images not only disturb tranquility: they pollute it. All the first-person narrators of Borowski's Auschwitz stories recognize that their identities have been permanently scarred by their encounter with extermination. Even the narrative impulse is an inadequate defense against the disintegrating coherence of their lives; the profusion of images intrudes on their inner world and transforms it into a reflection of the Holocaust universe itself. One narrator, after surviving and returning home, finds—in one of Borowski's most vivid tropes—that routine living "cannot keep the world from swelling and bursting like an over-ripe pomegranate, leaving behind but a handful of grey, dry ashes" (p. 179). One senses from Borowski's vision that a thin film of ash will soil any bright hopes that may have survived from the pre-Holocaust world.

Borowski is one of the few commentators to pursue in detail the ambiguity of hope in the deathcamp universe. In a singular passage from his longest story, "Auschwitz, Our Home (A Letter)," the narrator reflects in a letter to his fiancée in the women's camp on the value of hope, and before our eyes the celebration of this traditional virtue dissolves into a bitter lament at its deceptive power:

> Do you really think that, without the hope that [a better] world is possible, that the rights of man will be restored again, we could stand the concentration camp even for one day? It is that very hope that makes people go without a murmur to the gas chambers, keeps them from risking a revolt, paralyses them into numb inactivity. It is hope that breaks down family ties, makes mothers renounce their children, or wives sell their bodies for bread, or husbands kill. It is hope that compels man to hold on to one more day of life, because that day may be the day of liberation. Ah, and not even the hope for a different, better world, but simply for life, a life of peace and rest. Never before in the history of mankind has hope been stronger than man, but never also has it done so much harm as it has in this war, in this concentration camp. We were never taught how to give up hope, and this is why today we perish in gas chambers. (pp. 121–122)

Indeed, a burning residue of psychological truth smolders in these lines, for only when they surrendered hope and embraced despair did the remnant of Jews in the Warsaw ghetto, in Sobibor and Treblinka, in the last Sonderkommando of Birkenau acknowledge that destruction was upon them and mobilize the will to action. Recognizing the urgency of deluding its victims about the future, the Nazis placed over the entrance to Auschwitz the slogan *Arbeit Macht Frei*, not Dante's dismal but accurate Abandon Hope.

The author of the abortive love letters in "Auschwitz, Our Home" wrestles with one of the crucial bequests of the Holocaust: how to reconcile his memories of love *before* the camp with anticipations of a future infected by experiences *of* the camp. Those experiences transform survival for him into a *negative* principle: "Our only strength is our great number—the gas chambers cannot accommodate all of us" (p. 113). His dialogue with his beloved is really a monologue with himself, a struggle to explain how the abnormal, through habit and familiarity, grows to seem normal—a process he records even as he disputes its logic. "If I had said to you," he writes,

> as we danced together in my room in the light of the paraffin lamp: listen, take a million people, or two million, or three, kill them in such a way that no one knows about it, not even they themselves, enslave several hundred thousand more, destroy their mutual loyalty, pit man against man, and . . . surely you would have thought me mad. (p. 112)

Confronting Auschwitz begins with assenting to what many commentators are loath to admit: there is little room for love or loyalty in a situation that pits "man against man" for very survival. With melancholy pain, not even with rage or indignation, the narrator tells how once several trucks rolled by full of naked women shouting "Save us! We are going to the gas chambers! Save us!" (p. 116) while ten thousand men, including himself, stood silently by. "Not one of us made a move, not one of us lifted a hand" (p. 116). What of mutual loyalty, to say nothing of romance, after such horror? Shall love flourish in a world subsequent to this event?

Telling the whole truth about the camp displaces expressions of affection, which are not only inappropriate in the context of Auschwitz, but absurd. "As you read this letter," writes the narrator to his fiancée, "you must be thinking that I have completely forgotten the world we left behind. I go on and on about the camp, about its various aspects, trying to unravel their deeper significance, as though there were to be no future for us except right here" (pp. 120–121). The language of love, like the language of transcendence, assumes unlimited futures, provides unlimited vocabulary for debates about the difference between physical and spiritual reality. But Auschwitz and the experience of annihilation have convinced the narrator that Plato lied: "There can be no beauty if it is paid for by inhuman injustice, nor truth that passes over injustice in silence, nor moral virtue that condones it" (p. 132). Nevertheless, ten thousand men stood by while truckloads of helpless and innocent women were driven to their deaths in the gas chambers. If this event has not canceled beauty, truth, and moral virtue forever (and Borowski does not suggest that it has), it has challenged and perhaps corrupted their meaning for the narrator and other survivors like him. The reader participates in two realities: one where love, beauty, truth, and moral virtue continue to flourish (at least in inspiration) despite the Holocaust; and another where in a perpetual present of the imagination, men reenact the ordeal of extermination. For Borowski they are separate but intersecting realms, although he reverses the connection promoted by commentators like Frankl and Bettelheim. Whereas they argue that reliance on prior values can ease the severity of the deathcamp ordeal, Borowski insists that the severity of the ordeal undermines the unity and potency of all prior values. "The fire in the crematorium has been extinguished," as one of his narrators observes, "but the smoke has not yet settled" (p. 169).

Peering through that lingering smoke from the security of survival, Borowski discovers how much his initiation in Auschwitz has altered the very fabric of his imagination. As the narrator of one of his most autobiographical stories, "The World of Stone," strolls through the city streets after the war, he encounters an apocalyptic vision that confirms the camp's influence on his present way of seeing human beings:

> Through half-open eyes I see with satisfaction that once again a gust of the cosmic gale has blown the crowd into the air, all the way up to the treetops, sucked the human bodies into a huge whirlpool, twisted their lips open in terror, mingled the children's rosy cheeks with the hairy chests of the men, entwined the clenched fists with strips of women's dresses, thrown snow-white thighs on the top, like foam, with hats and fragments of heads tangled in hair-like seaweed peeping from below. And I see that this weird snarl,

this gigantic stew concocted out of the human crowd, flows along the street, down the gutter, and seeps into space with a loud gurgle, like water into a sewer. (pp. 178–179)

The inspiration for this apparently surrealistic landscape is clear, but clearer still is how easily the recollected image of exterminated corpses can transform surrealism back into the most gruesome realism. And even more lucid to Borowski is the impossibility of following this "cosmic gale" into a realm of space where the free spirit can regain the dignity that was destroyed by Auschwitz. The prism of moral indifference through which his narrators often view their Auschwitz experience only sharpens the horror of the events. Their apparent insensitivity reflects not a perversion of their nature but, as Andrzej Wirth pointed out, a situation "created by a system which had treated man as an object, a thing, and taken away from him the possibility of being human." Deprived of separate physical identities, how could the victims take separate moral actions? "In inhuman situations," Wirth concludes, "there is no room for human actions." [34] Without physical or spiritual scope— and the deathcamp inmate had neither—the tragic gesture as we know it is stillborn, and men find themselves paralyzed by a situation they cannot transcend. Survival is then totally detached from a world of inner values.

Borowski offers abundant evidence to support his version of survival. He tells the story of a smaller camp where prisoners arrived daily. The camp had a limited quantity of supplies, and the Kommandant disliked seeing the prisoners starve. But every day the camp seemed to have a few dozen more men than it could feed. "So every evening a ballot, using cards or matches, was held in every block, and the following morning the losers did not go to work. At noon they were led out behind the barbed-wire fence and shot" (p. 119). Few examples could illustrate more effectively Wirth's notion of a situation-determined fate. The victims are offered an option that is no option, since the results of a lottery are governed by chance, not choice. And obviously anyone who refused to participate in the macabre game certified his execution the next day. The inner conflict that we identify with the tragic figure simply did not exist, though we continue to hypothesize that conflict in order to salvage some potential dignity for the survivor, if not for the victim.

Refusal to participate in the ritual of extermination was not a meaningful option for the victim because he shared no responsibility for the situation that condemned him to such an existence. He lacked the power to act physically in behalf of his own survival, and without this power (which through luck or collaboration or good connections might be *bestowed* on him) no mere control of attitude or feeling of spiritual inviolability could save him. His position was entirely different from that of an SS man who might disapprove of the process of extermination and would have to wrestle with the problem of personal responsibility and evaluate the options available to him. This *was* a matter of ethical choice, risky but possible, though few decided to exercise it. Hermann Langbein tells of a young SS doctor who returned to his quarters from his first experience with selection on the ramp in a state of collapse, virtually unable to speak. Still shaken the next morning, he donned his uniform, marched rigidly to the Kommandant, stood at attention, and officially declared that he was unable to carry out such a duty and refused to do so. He asked either to be sent to the front, or to be gassed himself.[35]

One may be disappointed to learn that instead of being reprimanded, punished, or executed, the young SS doctor was commissioned to accompany the notorious Dr. Mengele in his work for a prolonged period, while the latter tried to convince him of the necessity of exterminating the Jews. If Auschwitz did not breed many heroes among the victims, it bred fewer among the persecutors; the history of this particular SS doctor proves how adaptable all men were to the conditions of extremity in the deathcamp, and how rarely the heroic gesture surfaced under those conditions. Mengele's specious logic gives us some insight into the flexible SS mentality, if not into its moral nature; for he argued that a doctor at the front made similar "selections," insofar as he had to decide which wounded he would treat first, creating the possibility that it might then be too late to save the others. In addition, Mengele insisted that selections on the ramp only determined who would *live*, who were capable of work; it had already been decided that all Jews would eventually perish, and thus the young doctor need not feel responsible for that choice. To his discredit and our dismay, but hardly to our surprise, he let himself be persuaded by these arguments and withdrew his protests, though one of his colleagues testified later that from then on he was a broken man. Facing arrest after the war, he committed suicide.

We cannot know whether such self-destruction represented an escape from punishment or a dramatic acceptance of personal responsibility for events in Auschwitz. When Nazi sustenance for the extermination process crumbled, this SS man found himself once again facing a traditional world of justice, where categories like "guilt," "punishment," and "responsibility" resumed their former ethical force. Since his earlier behavior suggests that he had never entirely repudiated these categories, we can assume that his suicide is partly a response to the total collapse of a system that had (in his case) so tentatively supported his compromised spirit. His death may have been an acknowledgement of how badly he had used the area of inner freedom that was available to him in spite of external pressures. At least there is some logic to explaining it in this way. But we cannot use a similar logic when assessing the behavior of the victim or survivor. One could refuse to kill in the deathcamp, and accept the consequences; one could not refuse to die.

The originality of Borowski's vision is that it portrays a world where consequences are not connected to choice. Since the deathcamp universe eliminated conditions that support worth, the victim could not "choose" life and remain human. He could strive for life and, if lucky, remain *alive*; but this was a struggle between states of being, not competing values. Borowski concentrates unerringly on situations that confirm this view. In one of his stories, a Russian prisoner is trying to teach two terrified Greek Jews to march, since those who do not march properly to and from the camp become obvious candidates for the gas chamber. So the Russian's impulse is charitable. But when the SS leader of the subcamp unexpectedly appears, he summarily exclaims: "They can't march? Then kill them!" This fatal illogic is transmitted by the Kapo, who received the order, to the narrator-foreman—"Go and tell Andrei to take care of them. *Los!*" (p. 76)—who in turn tells Andrei to finish them off. Andrei is thus abruptly transformed from savior to executioner, though the long chain of command blurs the agency and dilutes responsibility. Victims become conspirators, collaborators in support of their own survival, though the original choice is not theirs and the price—as so often in Borowski's stories—is once more the lives of

Jews. Earlier the narrator had been told to prepare four "stretchers," made from branches, to carry back the dead from the work detail, and he now knows with some relief that half of the daily quota has already been filled.

Borowski challenges us to identify with the narrator, who transmitted the execution order, and Andrei who carried it out, even though the world of competing values that we inhabit comfortably as readers urges us toward revulsion at their acts. Wirth's principle of a new tragedy outside the familiar classical laws operates here; he argues that Borowski "demonstrated prototypes of situations which are tragic in themselves."[36] If we can accept the idea of human behavior resulting from situations into which men are thrust *despite* their ethical convictions, then we cannot evaluate their conduct with familiar moral imperatives, by praising survivors for clinging to inner values in adversity, or blaming victims for cooperating in their own extermination. Such attitudes, Borowski would assert, derive from a misconception of the deathcamp *situation*. Several survivors in one of his stories become spokesmen for a point of view that we might call the disenchanting truth of Auschwitz: "in this war morality, national solidarity, patriotism and the ideals of freedom, justice and human dignity had all slid off man like a rotten rag . . . there is no crime that a man will not commit in order to save himself" (p. 168). Such cynicism is part of our heritage from the Holocaust, to be measured alongside those more optimistic versions that still celebrate the individual and minimize the transfiguring—or disfiguring—power of the situation.

For those like Viktor Frankl who see life as a challenge to give meaning to being, the notion that the *situation* in Auschwitz deprived being of meaning is the highest form of impiety. He speaks of the deathcamp as a "living laboratory" or "testing ground" where he witnessed how "some of our comrades behave[d] like swine while others behaved like saints." But we have seen how misleading and inaccurate is this arbitrary division into heroes and villains, since it totally ignores the even more arbitrary environment that shaped human conduct in Auschwitz. Frankl cannot resist the temptation to incorporate the deathcamp experience into his world view, to make the events serve his theory of behavior: "Man has both potentialities within himself; which one is actualized depends on decisions but not on conditions."[37] But by now it should be plain how much evidence

Frankl was required to ignore in order to protect his image of man as a self-determining creature, no matter how humiliating his surroundings. Auschwitz was indeed a laboratory and testing ground, but if we contemplate the "experiment" without rigid moral preconceptions, we discover that men could not be divided simply into saints and swine, and that self-actualization as a concept evaporates when conditions obliterate decisions in the way that we have just examined. To speak of survival in Auschwitz as a form of self-actualization is to mock language and men, especially those who did not survive.

After having surveyed some of the agonizing dilemmas confronting prisoners in the deathcamps, we should be less persuaded by questionable half-truths like the following, from Frankl's version of survival: "Psychological observations of the prisoners have shown that only the men who allowed their inner hold on their moral and spiritual selves to subside eventually fell victim to the camp's degenerating influences."[38] The woman who was forced to drown an infant to save the mother is only one eloquent example among many of the fate of the moral and spiritual self in Auschwitz. Was she swine or saint; did she "allow" herself to make the murderous decision, or was she trapped by loathsome conditions? The journey from version to vision to revision seems endless.

But it seems endless only if we persist in trying to have the deathcamp experience conform to some comprehensive interpretation of behavior in extremity. Like Frankl, Bruno Bettelheim has a world view that makes Auschwitz an extension of a larger social issue: how, when confronted by the pressures of a mass society, "to inform the heart in the service of autonomy." But Bettelheim too is unable or unwilling to tolerate ambiguity in the matter of choice: "By destroying man's ability to act on his own or to predict the outcome of his actions, [the SS] destroyed the feeling that his actions had any purpose, so many prisoners stopped acting. But when they stopped acting they soon stopped living." We have seen, however, that when the environment supported one man's life, it was often at the cost of another's death—not because victims made wrong choices, or no choices, but because dying was the "purpose" of living in this particular environment. Hence gestures made as defense against extermination were not positive expressions of will and could hardly qualify, in Bettelheim's terms, as "minimal choices" in behalf of survival. His need to equate activity with continued existence and passivity with death reflects a desperate desire to retain some moral coherence in a chaotic universe. Perhaps aware of the profound contempt implicit in this view for the victims who "let" themselves perish, Bettelheim inconsistently tries to reclaim some credit for them on the last page of his book by announcing that "men are not ants. They embrace death rather than an antlike existence"—abruptly and unconvincingly transforming the millions who were slaughtered into heroes and heroines who "marched themselves into death, choosing to give up a life that was no longer human." [39]

But they did not march themselves, they were marched, by men who chose to kill them. For Bettelheim too, being ceases to have meaning if man does not remain to the end a self-determining creature. If the Jews are not to be censured for collaborating in their own destruction, he concludes, let them be praised! We could avoid this oversimplified option if we might only allow ourselves to believe that the Jews and other victims were not degraded by dying horribly *when the situation that consumed them permitted them no meaningful choice;* we reserve the degradation for their murderers. Bettelheim finally retreats from the complex truths of the deathcamp universe by describing it as a crisis "in which men have only the choice between such a giving up of life, and the achieving of a higher integration." He returns us to Gandhi's innocent pre-Holocaust world, heedless here[40] of a third "option" that forced men to *adapt* to a world that was no longer human, merely becuase they wanted to remain alive. His faith in choice and his vision of a better future—the central inspirations of *The Informed Heart*—would have been corrupted by Salmen Lewental's bitter description of the early years in Auschwitz, when "each man, really each one, who lived longer than two weeks, lived at the cost of other victims, at the cost of lives of other people or on what he had taken from them." [41] If we accept this even as a partial version of survival—and it comes to us from inside a mausoleum of death whose walls Bettelheim never penetrated, in person or imagination—it utterly transforms the context of his conclusion that the individual's best chance for survival was "his ability to react appropriately and to make decisions." [42] These are Levi's "free words" once again, without meaning for Auschwitz unless we temporarily abandon the innocent world that gave them birth and interpret Bettelheim's language using the dictionary of Lewental and his fellow victims. If we cannot invent a vocabulary of annihilation, we can at least redefine the terminology of transcendence.

Terrence Des Pres cannot be accused of never having penetrated imaginatively the walls of mausoleum Auschwitz. Indeed, the novice in Holocaust studies could scarcely do better than to begin his investigation with the chapter from *The Survivor* called "Excremental Assault." Nevertheless, for Des Pres too dignity means "an inward resistance to determination by external forces," and like Frankl and Bettelheim he believes that the distinction of successful survivors is that "they try to keep themselves *fundamentally* unchanged by the pressures to which they respond." But as we have seen repeatedly, the "choices" forced on prisoners by their murderous conditions—the mother who was told to "choose" one of her three children for survival, the son who "chose" not to acknowledge his father for fear of receiving a fatal phenol injection himself—literally prohibited them from remaining *"fundamentally* unchanged by the pressures to which they respond." That they *could* remain unchanged is a conviction necessary to sustain a celebratory view of human nature in the presence of atrocity; it leads to a poetics of survival, effectively expressed by Des Pres, that does not really integrate the substance of his darker vision: "There is a power at the center of our being, at the heart of all things living. But only in man does it assume a spiritual character. And only through spirit does life continue by decision." [43] "Power," "being," "spirit," and "decision"—once more, we find language seeking to transform reality with a kind of hypnotic compulsion, which is especially puzzling here, since elsewhere in *The Survivor* Des Pres is vividly aware of how the reality of Auschwitz has itself transformed both language *and* value. But to surrender the affirmative force of language is to abandon the belief that even in the deathcamp universe human nature could assert its dignity through choice. Des Pres, like Frankl and Bettelheim, is unwilling to abandon this belief, though it is difficult to determine whether this refusal is a comment on the authors themselves or on their response to the experience they are investigating. None of them is prepared to pursue the implications of the voice we met earlier: "Only to survive, to survive, everything consists in that, and the forms of survival are extreme and loathsome, they are not worth the price of life."

The problem is not one of alternatives, but of fusion. After Auschwitz, any hopeful vision, however diminished, is a *product* of despair, not a protection against it. In the unprecedented world of the deathcamps, traditional opposites like negation and affirmation cease to have separate meanings; affirmation *includes* negation, so that if at times, as Des Pres insists, survival seemed to be a collective act, at others, as we have seen, it was intensely private, even hostile and selfish. In the Warsaw ghetto—as one example—the will to survive *was* a collective act, since men were armed (though inadequately), could meet to plan resistance, hide, risk flight, could *feel* inwardly unchanged though doomed because despite the limitations of their situation they were able to behave like self-determining creatures. But in Auschwitz no prisoners were armed, resistance was surreptitious and largely ineffectual, there was no place to hide, some hundreds escaped successfully, but rarely as a collective gesture, and few men, especially Jews, because of their situation, were able to behave like self-determining creatures. The victims of the Warsaw ghetto—we cling perhaps excessively to this truth— were permitted the luxury of testimony with acknowledgement, because the ghetto was not a deathcamp. But we exaggerate when we transmit to the victims of Auschwitz a similar luxury, since their "testimony" (those who did not survive) is located in an act of annihilation unconnected to their will. To argue, as both Bettelheim and Des Pres do, that many prisoners died soon after their admission through loss of the will to live, through a kind of "moral disgust," is to perpetuate the myth that survival was somehow *primarily* determined by attitude or choice. One has only to examine the statistics in Charlotte Delbo's *Le Convoi du 24 Janvier*, which in brief biographies of the 230 members of her convoy to Auschwitz (of whom 49 survived) lists cause and approximate date of death of the victims, to learn that they died early of typhus, dysentery, malnutrition, beatings, and the inability to carry on unendurable work. The shock of initiation into an unrecognizable environment afflicted everyone's mental state and may have *accelerated* some deaths; but those who "adapted" were not better protected from the causes of death just listed than the others. To identify moral disgust as a source of vulnerability is once again to internalize the threat of exter-mination and somehow to circumvent the notion that men were destroyed by external forces they could not meaningfully respond to. It is also to imply that the reverse, a kind of moral vigor, could insulate the individual against that threat and preserve his self-respect, his sense of dignity, and thus his life. But more than thirty years after the event, we still have not established how much of this is necessary illusion, recollected in tranquility, and how much demonstrable truth.

Despite his homage—much greater than Frankl's or Bettelheim's—to the "worst" of Auschwitz, Des Pres is unambiguously explicit in his belief that the resolute victim could enhance his chances of survival by turning away from the monstrous inhumanity of Auschwitz and toward "a fabric of discernible goodness amid that evil." He says that this turning is "attended by a strong sensation of choice, a feeling of new determination, as if the decision to survive were an inner fate expressing itself through a conscious assent of the will." [44] But the monstrous inhumanity of Auschwitz has a way of asserting its presence despite the imagination's desire to transcend it: once we have turned toward it, can we ever turn away again without feeling its frigid breath chilling the warmth of our hopeful souls? As we shall see from subsequent chapters, the evolution from despair to renewed faith in the human spirit requires a revision of the very image of evolution, for organic growth ceases to be merely organic when it is accompanied by memories of disintegration. The prose of Elie Wiesel and the poems of Nelly Sachs attempt to revive a limited vision of the future that will include, as it were, the extinct species—the victims of the Holocaust. Their efforts to reclaim a life for the surviving world (and for themselves), the very language they use, are dominated by the voices and the presence of the dead. They are less concerned with what survival meant for the survivors than with what the fact of extermination means for all of us and for our era. And they wrestle with the agonizing question of how *any* insights gained from this exacting heritage are to be reconciled with the price we have paid. The perpetual dialogue—between voice and voice in Wiesel, between word and word in Sachs—reflects our own continuing struggle to find a way of *expressing* (to say nothing of understanding) the incompatible universes of gas chamber and human dignity, extermination and human choice.

THREE

"What are you after, Zeide?"
"The truth."
"There are many truths. Each one denies the others."
"I want the one that contains them all."
"Even if it's inhuman?"
"Even if it's inhuman."

The Gates of the Forest

Elie Wiesel:
DIVIDED VOICE IN A DIVIDED UNIVERSE

When the Chosen People became the people chosen, when "selection" replaced "election" as the key term to describe the future of a human being, we might have been forewarned of the fragility of a vocabulary of decent assurance when confronted by the murderous ambitions of indecent men. But the appeal of affirmation remains enormous, and we still struggle in the twentieth century to find a comfortable balance to sustain its overwhelming weight. Inspired by scriptural injunction to choose life, and by existential authority to choose oneself at every moment of one's life, a writer like Elie Wiesel—disciple of Jewish religious thought and postwar Paris's feverish intellectual activity[1]—wrestles to reconcile this twin heritage of stern hope with the disproportionate influence of that single despairing year of his youth in Auschwitz and Buchenwald. If one source of inspiration (to borrow some lines from one of his novels) perceives man as dust turned to hope, another, with equal force, imagines him as hope turned to dust. It would be convenient and orderly to view Wiesel's growth as a writer (and some have done so)[2] as an arc ascending slowly from dust to hope, as the Holocaust recedes in time and his vision restores a sense of promise to what was once a landscape of brooding gloom. But as we have already seen (and his works will furnish further evidence), the passage of chronological time does not diminish memory of that event. Dust mingles with hope, soiling its shining face, staining the future. If we search for an image appropriate to this turmoil, we turn not to an ascending arc but to a circular labyrinth, sending out ominous echoes from its central darkness even as the wanderer approaches the outermost corridor, with daylight beckoning at its exit. That echo resounds long after we have escaped the maze, reminding us that what we have found in release cannot be separated from what we have lost during the days and years of confinement.

Except for his autobiographical memoir *Night*,[3] Wiesel has not devoted much literary energy to events inside that labyrinth. He is less concerned with how one survives *in* the camp—the central issue for most of the works we have examined so far—than with how one survives afterward, having left part of oneself behind. The problem does not end with liberation—it only begins. His version of survival stresses keeping alive the *dead*, not the living, to find a way of enabling the victims to enter and remain in the consciousness of those who shared with them the Holocaust ordeal, but managed to escape its fatal snare. This is the first step in a sequence that continues when both kinds of "survivors," the living and the dead, combine with the memory and intelligence of the reader, who slowly discerns how *their* merged existence can alter the substance of his. Gradually the scope of the challenge widens, until we find ourselves facing one of the great unsettled dilemmas of our time: how to cope with the wasted lives of millions in a culture already witnessing a waning reverence for the individual human life.

The kingdom of night, spreading out from Wiesel's own first volume, casts its shadow over everything else he has written. It causes the foundations of our civilization to totter, but provides only scattered light to illuminate the path toward a rehabilitated future. Tragedy as a literary form offered catharsis to men contemplating with pity and terror the image of their own fragile mortality; but we have not yet discovered a form to fuse six million unnecessary deaths into a coherent reflection of our destiny in the modern era. In his own quest for insight (so urgent as cause, so elusive as effect), Wiesel himself is capable of the following dubious analysis of survival behavior: "To die struggling would have meant a betrayal of those who had gone to their death submissive and silent. The only way was to follow in their footsteps, die their kind of death—only then could the living make their peace with those who had already gone." The sentiment—which I do not find convincing—is less important than the need that inspired it, a desperate desire to discover some alliance between the living and the dead that permits a feeling of continuity from one to the other. We cannot accustom ourselves to the fact that during the Holocaust, in the absence of a tragic atmosphere dignifying choice (and hence the possibility of moral and physical heroism), men were forced to meet their death "submissive and silent," through no fault of their own. We cannot imagine a reality so freighted with terror and confusion that victims could be made to feel, in Wiesel's own words, "that they were neither worthy nor capable of an act of honor." [4] Among his most striking achievements is his ability to crystallize the dilemma, still unresolved, of what to do with the meaningless deaths of so many. The fate of the Jews is a persistent irritant to those who still echo Enlightenment rhetoric about progress and culture.

Almost from his first volume to his last, Wiesel's writing has been an act of homage, a ritual of remembrance in response to a dreadful challenge: "to unite the language of man with the silence of the dead." [5] The dialogue at the heart of his work between language and history forestalls the advent of what Camus called the "crippled judgment," crippled by a transposition peculiar to our times whereby "crime dons the apparel of innocence" and "it is innocence that is called upon to justify itself." [6] What an inversion of values: that the survivor should be burdened with guilt for being alive, and that we should still have to proclaim the innocence of the dead by reminding ourselves almost daily of their existence! Somehow, Wiesel suggests, our diminished humanity is related to those victims, its survival contingent on our finding a way to acknowledge their meaningless deaths. As time passes and memories fade, the imagination may be the only link between silence and the extermination of an entire people.

In confronting so complex an issue, we need to be prepared for contradictions and unusually wary of generalizations about survival behavior that lead us in a single (and usually upward) direction. There is no doubt, as one commentator has claimed, that some Holocaust literature "posits a future tense" and attempts "to retrieve some ongoing life" from the dismal details of the event. And this emphasis can be found in Wiesel. But it is equally true that much Holocaust literature posits a *past* tense and strives to retrieve some ongoing memory of the *dead*. This emphasis too is central in Wiesel, and reasserts itself throughout his work, reminding him and us of the special responsibility imposed on the writer's talent by the sheer mass of anonymous dead. That burden is one feature of the altered consciousness that our age requires of us, and it is not eased by celebrations of scattered examples of human dignity in the deathcamps. Indeed, a danger exists that such celebrations may deflect our attention— and our respect—from those who did not survive. The spirit of tragedy is unable to absorb them; neither time nor history has silenced their wail in the ears of those, like Wiesel, who cannot cease listening. The heritage they bestow brings us to what has properly been called "the threshold of new and more difficult beginnings." [7]

This is a strenuous challenge for readers nurtured on life, hope, and the future. To argue that the most vital survivors are those who did not survive—vital in the sense of their continuing influence on our perception of moral reality—is to plunge us into a world inhabited by creatures who do not inspire us with prospects of human possibility. They remind us how much of Holocaust literature has to do with nonbeing. "We play at dying," begins a memorable poem by Nelly Sachs. "Those who had no papers entitling them to live lined up to die," begins "Soul of Wood," Jakov Lind's most famous short story. "Dead though they be, the dead do not immediately become ageless," begins Pierre Gascar's "Season of the Dead." And the well-known final lines of Wiesel's *Night* only sum up a recurrent concern with this particular truth of the Holocaust universe: "From the depths of the mirror, a corpse gazed back at me. The look in his eyes, as they stared back into mine, has never left me." If we multiply that corpse a hundred, a thousand, a millionfold, we may begin to understand more clearly what is implied when we are told that because of the Holocaust, "the imagination has come to one of its periodic endings and stands at the threshold of new and more difficult beginnings."

It is scarcely accidental that in his first novel, *Dawn* (and his first work after *Night*), Wiesel imposes on his protagonist, one of the many Holocaust survivors who will populate his fiction, the awful role of becoming an executioner. When exploring the Holocaust experience, we are not confounded by the question of why evil men kill, or how guilty criminals die, but of why otherwise decent men agree to kill, and how innocent and helpless victims die. If for some the survivor is one who has affirmed and chosen life, to Wiesel he is even more one who has been confirmed and chosen by death—even though still alive. In Buchenwald, says the narrator of *Dawn*, "the living were transformed into dead and their future into darkness." By accepting the assignment to execute an innocent British hostage in retaliation for the execution of a member of the Jewish underground in Palestine, the narrator becomes an agent of atrocity himself, and although this may seem to be a way of purging residual unresolved hostility from the deathcamp, Wiesel knows that such equations simplify an insoluble dilemma. When the militant Gad in *Dawn*, the leader of the narrator's group, argues that "We [the Jews] shall kill in order that once more we may be men," he introduces a principle of being representing an unexplored (and unflattering) heritage from Auschwitz. Much of the source of modern terrorism (and also a desperate lesson implicit in the Holocaust) is concealed in Gad's belief that "we must become more unjust and inhuman than those who have been unjust and inhuman to us." [8] Without necessarily endorsing them, Wiesel tries not to flinch at the brutal contradictions to the generous tendencies in human nature exposed by the Holocaust. It may seem that the living are contaminated by the omnipresence of the dead, but perhaps what we really mean to say is that the humanistic impulse, as evolved through the centuries, can no longer contain the old polarity between being and nonbeing. It requires, like the experience that transformed our conception of it, fresh definitions and images, a notion of survival fusing, as in Auschwitz itself, vitality with decay, the resurrected phoenix with the crematory flames that forever warm its wings.

The act of execution in *Dawn*, which is part of a struggle for liberation and hence (at least in Gad's terms) a necessary and justified form of violence, cannot be separated, in Wiesel's terms, from the lingering presence of the Holocaust dead. At least for the Jew in the post-Holocaust era, every act of affirmation includes a gesture toward that unsettling and continually unsettled past. The will to survive is never merely a triumph of value over nihilistic or self-destructive impulse, of spiritual strength over moral

weakness or decay. The will to survive contains an acknowledgement of what has destroyed others and thus destroyed
a part of oneself. One version of survival concludes that
after Auschwitz, the soul is doomed to limp forever. "There lies
the problem," says the narrator in this novel: "in the influence of
the backdrop of the play upon the actor. War had made me an
executioner, and an executioner I would remain even after the
backdrop had changed, when I was acting in another play upon a
different stage" (p. 90).

The analogy with the deathcamps requires little commentary.
That kind of survivor also remains, in part, what he had become in
the camp even though survival transforms the setting of his life.
Neither "progress" nor "regression" adequately captures the
movement of one's life before, during, or after the experience. We
need, as I suggested earlier, an image of fusion, of two worlds
blended, of the presence in one's life of ghosts *and* living beings,
inseparable in their appeal—like Hamlet facing in his mother's
bedchamber her anguish *and* his father's troubled spirit, and being
driven by the demands of both, even though no one else perceives
the tension that is splitting his consciousness. The claims of the
murdered father on the son are like the claims of the deathcamp
victims on the survivor: not only not to forget, but also so to live
as to commemorate in some adequate fashion the violence done
to them. Gertrude, an outsider (and later the king) who cannot
participate in this tension, thinks Hamlet mad, the "sane" world's
explanation for such eccentric behavior. No wonder that the
theme of madness dominates Wiesel's vision, as if the survivor
knew that he were poised on its brink throughout his existence,
while wrestling with the need to incorporate his ghosts into a
world that denies them or shrinks in terror from their reality.

The vision of a moment frozen in time and space—the year in
Auschwitz and Buchenwald, with its associated memories—is a
recurrent leitmotif in Wiesel's works. It stands as a ponderous
barrier between an innocent past and a burdensome future.
Among the ghosts who haunt the narrator in *Dawn* is "a boy who
looked strangely like myself as I had been before the
concentration camps, before the war, before everything" (p. 76).
The Holocaust radically severs life "before everything" from life
"after everything," leaving only nostalgia in place of the normal
inclination to seek connections between one's youth and one's
maturity. Wiesel ridicules, by implication if not intention, the

thesis set forth by Frankl, Bettelheim, and others that it was possible to live in the camps and afterward by values inherited from one's precamp existence. According to Wiesel, the rupture between "then" and "now" is so complete that the ghosts of victims hovering in an intermediate realm between the two are themselves doomed to wander in search of a means of rejoining the fragments of their splintered reality. This quest, saturated like Hamlet's story with questions of vengeance and justice, reflects the pursuit of an elusive and perhaps an impossible goal. No Grail lures the searcher with hopes of final reconciliation; the execution of additional innocent men, as in *Dawn*, cannot bring redemption or peace to the spirits of the dead.

Hamlet is charged with the execution of a "guilty" man; his path is clear, though his mind finds obstacles to advancing along it. In addition, he has the choice of a "proper" way of dying, commensurate with his heroic spirit. The Holocaust victim had no such choice; the survivor, no way of identifying the source of that victim's destruction. "We are what you do," say the narrator's ghosts in *Dawn*; but they urge no action, no revenge, no way to pacify their troubled spirits. Their wasted lives simply hover in the memories of survivors. Unlike the ghost of Hamlet's father, they do not murmur "Remember us" and remind the narrator of his all too blunted purpose. He has no purpose, other than to hear their silences and the words they imply, and to seek words of his own to penetrate the meaning of their silence. To survive—and this may be the core of Wiesel's vision—means not to live, but to *tell*, to say, to find language rather than acts or gestures. Hamlet's monologues forestall his tragic destiny. Wiesel's tales and legends unconsciously differentiate between the tragic demands that burden a Hamlet and the painful—and more paralyzing—load that oppresses the soul of the survivor, who must speak without the assurance that he will be heard, or that his words are adequate to his intention.

"Occasionally you may see us," proclaim the survivor-ghosts in *Dawn*, "but most of the time we are invisible to you. When you see us you imagine that we are sitting in judgment upon you. You are wrong. Your silence is your judge" (p. 97). Few passages could more clearly distinguish between the traditional existential appeal, which makes man an agent of a difficult action and tests his resourcefulness and his moral stature by measuring his ability to act, and the doom of the Holocaust survivor, who in the absence of a definable antagonist must use language as his weapon against a surging sense of impotence. Hamlet's uncle is a barrier between what Hamlet's father has suffered and a proper ritual of mourning. Wiesel knows that the execution of John Dawson in *Dawn*, or any other violent act of vengeance, cannot restore the imbalance between atrocity and remembrance, not because an adequate act is too elusive, but because of the nature of the atrocity—which is unredeemable. We are back in the disfigured universe of Tadeusz Borowski, where a situation of unparalleled brutality ensures the futility of conventional moral gesture to control it. In Wiesel's world, the ghosts of the victims persist, while the spirit of silence hovers in the wings, reminding the survivor-spokesman, like a mocking director of a failed tragedy, of the poverty of his words.

When a messenger arrives in Sophocles' *Oedipus* who ultimately informs the king of his real identity, Oedipus knows what he must do to restore his integrity as a man. Despite Jocasta's pleas to ignore the truth, he embraces the altered sense of his fate and accepts the suffering that, in conjunction with chance and destiny, he has brought upon himself. He knows the path he must follow to redeem his anguished past. As a messenger of another kind, Wiesel bears not one message, but many. His quest presumes no journey's end, only arduous ascents up steep crags and along rock-strewn paths. He sheds light on the ways we may go; as for The Way, it is still lost in the night with which his journey began. Time and dedication to his theme have pierced the obscurities of that night, but its darkness is a perpetual presence in his universe, which is so densely populated with ghosts that they threaten to crowd out the living souls. When he says that he entered literature through silence, does he not mean that his task as a writer is to give a voice to those ghosts, whose anguished past would otherwise be buried beneath the nontragic rubble of unfulfillment?

A chorus of ghostly voices haunts Wiesel's pages from *Night* (1958) to *A Jew Today* (1978), and the recitative is always a variation on the same theme. "In their frozen world the dead have nothing to do but judge," says the narrator in *Dawn* (though "judgment" here assumes an unfamiliar form), "and because they have no sense of past or future they judge without pity. They condemn not with words or gestures but with their very existence." [9] "Our dead take with them to the hereafter not only clothes and food," says the narrator in *The Accident*, "but also the future of their descendants. Nothing remains below." [10] "Each of us has a ghost that follows him everywhere in this life," says Michael in *The Town beyond the Wall*, adding later: "It's heavy work carrying the dead on your back." [11] "To live is to betray the dead," thinks Gregor in *The Gates of the Forest*, expressing one of Wiesel's favorite motifs. "We hasten to bury and forget them because we are ashamed, we feel guilty towards them." [12] All those "who entered, by night, the crucible of death," says Wiesel in his own voice in *Legends of Our Time*, after meeting an apparent reincarnation of Moshe the Madman, "emerged from it by day more healthy and more pure than the others who had not followed them." [13] Again in his own voice, in *One Generation After*: we need to face the dead to appease them, "perhaps even to seek among them, beyond all contradiction and absurdity, a symbol, a beginning of promise." [14] And in *A Begger in Jerusalem* Katriel brings the narrator to a sudden moment of insight:

> "I" had remained over there, in the kingdom of night, a prisoner of the dead. The living person I was, the one I thought myself to be, had been living a lie; I was nothing more than an echo of voices long since extinguished. . . . I thought I was living my own life, I was only inventing it. I thought I had escaped the ghosts, I was only extending their power." [15]

This fictional confession of a decade ago persists in its application to the present day. Although Wiesel has announced many times in recent years that he is finished with the Holocaust as a subject for public discourse, it is clear from his latest work that the Holocaust is not yet finished with him. His problem reenacts and anticipates our own. In *A Jew Today* he maintains a fragile balance between two worlds: pride in the future (for which Jewish destiny in the twentieth century is a paradigm), and despair at the past (for which Jewish destiny in the Holocaust is also a model). He dramatizes the dilemma of fashioning a possible future out of an impossible past—is not this the survivor dilemma par excellence?—in a story told to him by one of his students: "My father is sad and silent; his wife and their children perished *there*. My mother is sad and silent; her husband and their children perished *there*. After the Liberation my mother and father met and were married. I am their son—but every time they look at me, I know it is not me they're seeing." [16] Two realities coexist, a new and an old, and there seems no way to separate them: a past without a future strews its ashes over a present desperately trying to shape one, and the imagination is left with the sad task of living with a stained vision of dignity and love.

The student's story has personal overtones too. In three brief, melancholy dialogues from *A Jew Today* called "A Father and His Son," "A Mother and Her Daugher," and "A Man and His Little Sister," Wiesel's private worlds of "there" and "here" collide, and we get a glimpse of the painful truth that survival may not be the supreme blessing after all. Those who were left "behind" still possess the power to summon the survivor back into the realm of night. The dialogues, in which Wiesel resurrects the voices of his family lost in the Holocaust, typify language's attempt to solace memory, arrest extinction, preserve in a frozen moment of literary time images of a ruined past. We are silent partners at this verbal ritual to rescue from oblivion the uncompleted lives of a mother, a father, and a sister who did not survive but left a heritage of unforgettable anguish for the son and brother who did.

No one will ever write the biographies of these dead, because biography inevitably elicits patterns of meaning from the lives of its subjects. In the dialogue "A Man and His Little Sister," we find the following exchange:

> When you speak of your little sister leaving you like that, without a hug, without a goodbye, without wishing you a good journey, will you say that it was her fault?
> *It was not your fault.*
>
> Then whose fault was it?
> *I shall find out. And I shall tell. I swear it to you, little sister. I shall.*[17]

But who can keep such a promise, whose successful fulfillment might indeed add pattern or meaning to the life of the victim? Beyond the hope of knowing lies a deeper conviction. Wiesel hurls at his readers some unpalatable truths, which a world raised on a more optimistic diet has difficulty digesting:

> Auschwitz signifies not only the failure of two thousand years of Christian civilization, but also the defeat of the

intellect that wants to find a Meaning—with a capital M—in history. What Auschwitz embodied has none. The executioner killed for nothing, the victim died for nothing. No God ordered the one to prepare the stake, nor the other to mount it. During the Middle Ages, the Jews, when they chose death, were convinced that by their sacrifice they were glorifying and sanctifying God's name. At Auschwitz the sacrifices were without point, without divine inspiration. If the suffering of one human being has any meaning, that of six million has none.[18]

If this is literally true, if it was all for nothing, if the effect had no morally distinguishable cause, if the episode is merely an excrescence on the flesh of history—then what is there to discuss?

We discuss the experience of atrocity itself, the reality that divides men into victims and executioners, and the qualities in them that make each capable of being both. To clarify the relationship, Wiesel invents a third category, the spectator, but his analysis of the triumvirate warns us to regard even so reliable a witness as himself with caution, since he suddenly drifts into a sentimentality that one can only regard as the momentary lapse of a stubbornly clear-sighted intelligence. "At the risk of offending," he begins, as if to forestall criticism,

> it must be emphasized that the victims suffered more, and more profoundly, from the indifference of the onlookers than from the brutality of the executioner. The cruelty of the enemy would have been incapable of breaking the prisoner; it was the silence of those he believed to be his friends— cruelty more cowardly, more subtle—which broke his heart.

More subtle than selection for the gas chamber? Such a comment seems to fall under Wiesel's own charge, in another context, that to "find one answer or another, nothing is easier; language can mend anything." [19] For who among us, after Auschwitz, fears a broken heart more than a mutilated body? What victim of physical torture suffered more from the indifference of his torturers than from the pain inflicted by their cunnng devices? *Restrospectively* the survivor may suffer more from the indifference of the world (which he only came to understand fully after his return) than from his remembered pain; but who will ever be

convinced that the immediate threat of physical extermination
and cremation was not the greatest source of terror to the
potential victim?

Obviously, Wiesel needs to include the rest of the world
beneath the mantle of guilt that, by his own confession, still
weighs heavily on the shoulders of so many survivors. Whether
that guilt is justified, in survivor or spectator, is a question that
still requires investigation, since a category like "guilt," together
with all those human values celebrated by Frankl, Bettelheim, and
Des Pres, depends on choice for its continuing appeal. If the idea
of choiceless choice in the deathcamps has any validity, then
post-Holocaust guilt may have less substance than we often
assume. The Nazis were so determined to exterminate the Jews
that one wonders whether any protest, short of direct invasion
and liberation, could have inhibited the machinery of death *once
the victims were at the mercy of the executioners.* The illusion that moral
opposition might move such executioners, like the illusion that
one could keep one's moral nature intact in the deathcamps, dies
hard, because the cynicism implicit in the alternative is so
contrary to the coherence of the humanistic vision.[20] Wiesel
himself clings to that vision even as he multiplies evidence to
contradict it. His charge that the cruel indifference of the onlooker
broke the heart of the victim more than the physical brutality of
the executioner reflects the ambiguity of his own position, which
seeks some basis for cause and effect in his fate—and hence some
minimal meaning—while simultaneously conceding that
Auschwitz embodied no meaning at all. But any interpretation of
the Holocaust that requires us to shift the ordeal of atrocity from
the locus of the body to the palpitating regions of the heart
projects our own (understandable) needs more than the ferocious
nature of the event.

Perhaps Wiesel's exaggeration about the victim's heart broken
by the onlooker's indifference originates from his own private
impulse to lay sufficient blame on the world of the living, as a
kind of penance for the dead, a world that now struggles to find a
way of identifying its part of the responsibility for the
catastrophe. The more we examine the issue, the more we
encounter *disbelief* rather than *refusal to act* as a source of
indifference, and this adds an important gloss to Wiesel's charge
against the spectator: "the further I go," he writes, "the more I
learn of the scope of the betrayal by the world of the living

against the world of the dead. I take my head in my hands and I think: it is insanity, that is the explanation, the only conceivable one." Concepts like "blame" and "guilt" reduce the Holocaust to moral and psychological order, and though Wiesel occasionally is tempted by the intellectual "neatness" of such explanations—as in the passage on the cruelty of the world's silence about the deathcamps—his ceaseless dialogue on the Holocaust introduces opposing voices that complicate our vision of the event. The world's indifference may reflect cowardice or insensitivity, but it also may be a commentary on the survivor's instinct to melodramatize his ordeal. The Wandering Jew from *Legends of Our Time* disturbs Wiesel because he seems so untouched by the Holocaust: "If, for him, the past is nothing, the future is nothing, then is death nothing either and the death of a million Jewish children?" But the Wandering Jew is not indifferent; he is simply sensitive to the limitations of words, which "die away in the night without enriching it." He knows that a "beautiful answer" is nothing more than an illusion, that present attitude is now more important than remorse for the failure of past action, that man "defines himself by what disturbs him and not by what reassures him." [21] The search for reassurance exists within the context of an ancient humanism that proclaims the fundamental dignity of man; its vocabulary of affirmation, so alien to the modern inhumanism of the Holocaust, is more closely linked with "beautiful answers" than we are perhaps prepared to admit.

"Answers" about the behavior of survivors, as we have seen, can be selectively manipulated to support numerous conclusions. "Answers" about the behavior of the victims range from impertinence to impiety. "Not to understand the dead," observes Wiesel in one of his subtlest comments on the subject, "is . . . the only way to ask their pardon" (p. 234). For where does it lead us to ask how many victims "permitted" themselves to be murdered, as if they had any real choice once their deaths had been determined and they had been deprived of means of physical defense? That unfortunate and inappropriate expression, "like sheep to the slaughter," distorts the truth of extermination in innumerable ways. It deflects our attention from the slaughterers and the "slaughter," too terrible for most readers to confront, to the "sheep," as if the impotence of human fear were in any way comparable to the mindless confusion of innocent beasts. "The lesson of the Holocaust," says Wiesel, "—if there is any—is that our strength is only illusory, and that in each of us is a victim who is afraid, who is cold, who is hungry. Who is also ashamed" (p. 237). This is a crucial counterpoint to Frankl and Bettelheim, who argue the opposite principle that in each of us is a survivor whose inner strength, pride, and dignity are potent enough to combat and defeat the assaults of fear and humiliation, starvation and cold. Ultimately, Wiesel dramatizes both positions in his literary universe, forcing us constantly to reconsider which illusions are truths and which truths, illusions.

In the heat of agrument he occasionally is victimized by his own illusions, though one says this not to criticize the authenticity of his vision, but to illustrate how the delicate subject of survival can sometimes lead astray even the most wary emotions. Understandably, like the rest of the world, Wiesel is frustrated by the failure of the Hungarian Jews to act concretely on their own behalf before, during, or after their deportation to Auschwitz. Unwilling to concede that in Auschwitz significant resistance by unarmed men, women, and children was futile, heedless (at this moment) of his own traumatizing account in *Night* of the terrifying journey to the camp and its paralyzing effect on the victims, he insists in an essay called "The Guilt We Share" that a Hungarian Jewry forewarned by international denunciation of what they might expect in Auschwitz would have been forearmed upon arrival and prepared to act in support of their own survival:

> Had they known, they could have made a dash for it, been saved. Not all, maybe, but the great majority. Mountains surrounded the area, and the Jews might have fled into these mountains and hidden out for a while. The Red Army had advanced to within eighteen to twenty miles from Auschwitz, and at night the rumbling of their guns could be distinctly heard. It was only a matter of a few days before the liberators would appear. But these pious Jews of Transylvania were told that they had nothing to fear, that they were only being transferred further inland—were told and believed, for there was no one to tell them anything else.[22]

Future generations will be baffled or misled by this passage, depending on how determined have been their efforts to recreate the concrete situation in the deathcamps. All investigations of survival must begin with such efforts. To expect starving and frightened men, women, and children, however forewarned, to flee through the barbed wire surrounding Birkenau (to say nothing of SS bullets), to run miles to distant mountains, to survive there without food, clothing, or shelter, not knowing Polish, subject to the hostility of a suspicious native population—is bizarre and absurd. Moreover, in the spring of 1944 (the period of which Wiesel is speaking), the Red Army was not a few days away but more than six months, since the Soviets did not arrive in Auschwitz until the end of January 1945. But even more basically, there is little evidence that the informed mind, any more than the informed heart, found survival easier in the situation I have described as choiceless choice. The Jews in occupied areas of the Soviet Union who were forced to dig their own graves prior to execution knew their impending fate but rarely fled. Among the many temptations that beckon from the pit of the Holocaust, one of the most engaging is the instinct to invent myths of more favorable outcome, as if the parched imagination might somehow transform irrevocable extinction back into potential survival. If Wiesel himself is not immune to such temptations, how careful must we be in assessing the interpretations of other commentators, survivors and nonsurvivors, who like him are struggling with the question of human behavior during and after the deathcamp ordeal.

We will probably never be able to establish whether the burden of guilt that Wiesel imposes on survivor and nonsurvivor is the creation of the retrospective imagination or accurately reflects the feelings of those involved. Insofar as "guilt" is a useful category for incorporating the contradictory responses of the individual into a conventional view of human behavior during and after the Holocaust, it forestalls further analysis of how these responses may have disturbed the conventional view. One wishes Wiesel had pursued the implications of his final line in "The Guilt We Share": "Guilt was not invented at Auschwitz, it was disfigured there" (p. 212). We have already seen how "dignity" and "suffering" were so disfigured in the deathcamps that they required some other designation to liberate the mind from traditional associations. Is not Wiesel imprisoned by the limitations of his own vocabulary here? When guilt is dissociated from choice—as it was when the victim was spared selection for the gas chamber—what happens to Wiesel's formula, which transforms instinctive relief into feelings of guilt? That formula he expresses in the following: "*I am happy to have escaped death* becomes equivalent to admitting: *I am glad that someone else went in my place*" (p. 212). But since the "selection" was made by the Nazis, why should the survivor feel responsible? "I am alive, therefore I am guilty" (p. 210) may be a spurious piece of psychological logic within an intellectual tradition that cannot surrender its universe of cause and effect to the moral chaos of choiceless choice.

And Wiesel is not unaware of these paradoxes. He knows that survival can be destructive rather than triumphant: "If to live means to accept or to engender injustice, to die quickly becomes a promise and a deliverance" (p. 210). But he also knows that such "deliverance," deprived of the martyr's halo of heroism, was not frequent in Auschwitz. He knows too that a ghetto inhabitant permitted (temporarily) to "save" one family member while watching the others deported to their deaths cannot celebrate the freedom of his "choice" or rejoice that he can still be an agent of destiny. Such a man, he says, "thereafter lives in a suffocating circle of hell; and whenever his thoughts turn to himself, it is in anger and in disgust" (p. 211). How can a sense of guilt define such a man? Such choiceless choices are perversions of power and will; they proclaim the impotence of the victim, who contaminates his future by the very compulsion to survive in which his oppressors seek to drown his moral nature.

That compulsion to survive may be viewed through the lens of existential guilt, as Wiesel so often does in his search for some minimal connection between the fate of the Jews and the attitude of victim, survivor, and spectator toward that fate. But it may also be seen as a unique form of existential innocence, or "innocent guilt," unjudgeable by any known ethical system, since no human gesture could alter the Nazi policy of annihilation once the potential victims were deprived of effective physical defense. Moral protest only has meaning when the oppressors maintain *some* respect for the moral intention of the protestor. Gandhi's hunger strikes were effective; but when prisoners in the Soviet Gulags, as Solzhenitsyn reports, tried a hunger strike to improve their conditions, the guards charged into their cells and beat them without mercy.[23] Hunger strikes quickly ceased. In an analysis of deathcamp behavior, existential guilt may be little more than a convenient formula for clarifying an otherwise morally incomprehensible situation. "I am alive, therefore I am guilty" is as much a rationalization of an unpalatable consequence as the position we encountered in an earlier chapter: "I have retained an inner commitment to human dignity; therefore I am alive."

Without the overriding sense of guilt, chiefly for deeds undone (his failure to react when an SS guard beat his father, the world's failure to respond to the persecution of the Jews in Europe), that is so central to Wiesel's version of survival, the individual would be condemned to emotional and intellectual chaos. It is as if a vast desert separates a destroyed ancient civilization from a flourishing modern one, while a few men wander its trackless wastes searching for some sign of connection, a buried path, a vestige of vegetation, a broken monument, to prove that the desert is not an anomaly, that beneath its arid, faceless mystery lie human roots. With a part of his being, Wiesel seems unwilling to concede the total inhumanity of the Holocaust. Perhaps this helps to explain his recurrent return, in fact and fiction, to the ruins of his own youth. His compulsive need to keep alive a part of himself that will always be a stranger to the world he inhabits now is merely a microcosm of the larger responsibility we all share—so he believes—to keep alive an image of the Holocaust desert, so alien to the world *we* inhabit now. The man he did not become besieges his imagination and compels him to confirm his appointments with a past that holds him prisoner. Although he knows that only failure and madness lie at the end of the journey back to Sighet, he offers versions of that return in his essays and novels again and again. What it does for him is an enigma; what it does for us is to verify, lest we forget, that once there was a Jewish past that is no more, and that there are moments when futile gestures to recapture it are as necessary as sensible efforts to create a meaningful future.

But the gestures *are* futile. Wiesel does not celebrate the rediscovery of his vital roots; he mourns their withered remnants. Is it any wonder that the only place he feels at home on his first return (which, ironically, he calls "The Last Return" in *Legends of Our Time*) is the town cemetery? The dead of pre-Holocaust Sighet have a local habitation and a name. Nothing can erase their link with tradition. But the Holocaust dead have only a monument "to the memory of a generation that had died elsewhere" (p, 162). Instead of finding a longed-for orientation, the visitor encounters once more an image of disruption: "A tomb with no corpses. A gravestone with no graves instead of innumerable graves"

(p. 162). Rather than locating an old source of coherence, he uncovers the reason why ghosts still haunt him: the Holocaust victim continues to survive because tradition provides him with no place of burial. Nothing can irrigate the total aridity of the desert intervening between the past of memory and the future of possibility. Wiesel carries away with him from his visit to Sighet "nothing but the feeling of emptiness" (p. 164). Roots, in this instance, do not restore dignity or continuity: "My journey to the source of all events had been merely a journey to nothingness" (p. 164). Wiesel's inability to identify with his origins confirms the Holocaust's power to wrench both time and place from their familiar frames of reference, to invalidate ancient values and leave the survivor frustrated in his quest for a human gesture to rejoin the pre- and post-Holocaust worlds.

This does not mean that the search is useless; but the results thus far, in Wiesel's universe, are ambiguous. He inhabits two worlds of truth, but has not yet found a means of repairing the broken circuit that keeps them apart. Commentators like Frankl and Bettelheim try to repair that radical rupture with familiar abstractions, the vocabulary of transcendence, drawing our attention to pre-Auschwitz associations with moral and spiritual conduct that enable us to leap over the event itself with the help of phrases like "the value of suffering" and "the dignity of choice." One of the many paradoxes in Wiesel is that he longs to make that leap himself, wants to celebrate the intact humanity of victim and survivor, includes passages in essays and novels where he does precisely that, but simultaneously confesses to himself how deceptive is such a strategy, and how impoverished the vocabulary that describes it. He does not really believe in the intact humanity of victim or survivor. The Holocaust has destroyed for him the modern notion of the integrated self. His characters are descendants of Ivan Karamazov, whose vision of injustice and needless suffering (however intellectualized, de-Christianized, disapproved of by Dostoevsky himself) splits his consciousness, divides his being, frustrates his desire for harmony, and finally afflicts his brain with seeds of madness. Just as Ivan cannot reconcile human aspiration with human fate, so Wiesel cannot resolve the violent discord in the Holocaust universe between a man's life and a man's death.

A lucid example of the problem appears in the essay on "The Death of My Father," an important supplement to the dramatic account in *Night*. Wiesel here confirms a vital principle for students of the Holocaust: the version of survival we endorse cannot be separated from the vision of dying we can tolerate. Without curtailing the private impact of his father's death, he manages to make of it a parable of a crucial dilemma in the deathcamp, one that confounds us still: the victim who was deprived of his life was also deprived of his death. "No link between it and the life he had led," says Wiesel of his father. "His death, lost among all the rest, had nothing to do with the person he had been. It could just as easily have brushed him in passing and spared him. It took him inadvertently, absent-mindedly. By mistake. Without knowing that it was he; he was robbed of his death" (p. 15). The very basis of character, in fiction and psychology, is that we become what we have been and done. Despoiled of "doing" and doomed for "being" (a Jew), the deathcamp inhabitant, in the manner of his dying, violates every idea of human continuity that we have inherited from literature and history. At least we must concede this for those millions of victims—and they were the majority—who were crowded into the gas chambers lacking strength or opportunity to offer a gesture reasserting this continuity. The Nazi imagination, which believed it was snuffing out vermin, not men, created a situation that made such gestures virtually impossible.

How much of our celebration of survivors, and the gestures they allegedly made to ensure survival, represents a compensation for our failure to find a proper way of mourning the dead? Wiesel cannot discover an appropriate ritual to acknowledge the anniversary of his father's death because he cannot establish a connection between human response and the manner of that dying. Memory, as so often with survivors, becomes an instrument not for recalling truth, but for recovering possibilities. There is no precedent, verbal or intellectual, for such a confrontation between dying father and surviving son. "I am ignorant of the essentials," writes Wiesel: "what he felt, what he believed, in that final moment of his hopeless struggle, when his very being was already fading" (pp. 17–18). The reason is not his father's chosen silence, but the place of his dying (Buchenwald, after a murderous journey from Auschwitz), and the cause—the Nazi program to exterminate the Jews. Unceremonious extinction does not inspire customary forms of ceremony. The annual sense of desolation and futility that overcomes the son because of his failure to find a way to commemorate the father's death has no outlet other than the word: "the act of writing is for me often nothing more than the secret or conscious desire to carve words on a tombstone" (p. 26). Writing itself is a ritual, perhaps the only form of continuity left for Wiesel between a vanished world and a future that cannot absorb it.

One reason why Wiesel returns in his works to similar or identical versions of the Holocaust period and the years preceding it may be that only through this process of multiple layering can history gradually be transformed into legend. Do we lose the immediate meanings of the Holocaust by pursuing such a strategy, or do we gain access to possible interpretations otherwise not available? Certainly the turbulent details of his own survival in *Night*, at the beginning of his long chronicle of the Holocaust and its aftermath, paralyze the imagination without luring it on to further inquiry. Only when his private woe becomes part of the legend of our time, only when we realize that for the post-Holocaust consciousness confronting Auschwitz, choosing life always *includes* remembering death, will atrocity be raised to a public level and the individual reader be given a means of encountering its ambiguities. Then we return to the difficult distinction between truth and interpretation, literal history and the encompassing vision of what it implies.

Wiesel's imagination moves in two directions at once— backward toward death and forward toward life. There is no question of alternatives. His characters are condemned by a past they cannot escape; absorption, not liberation is their goal. They are thus never wholly free to even imagine that they can throw off the shrouds of the past and go forth, like Stephen Dedalus, to forge anew the uncreated conscience of their race. That conscience has been damaged beyond renewal; the Holocaust survivor, and those who reconstruct the implications of his ordeal, move forward, as it were, while standing with their backs toward the future. The process of reconstruction illustrates what I have called "versions of survival," but by now it should be clear that it cannot be dissociated from versions of annihilation. Wiesel offers a brief but critical example of the process near the end of *A Beggar in Jerusalem*, where his narrator alludes to the famous photograph, retained as a souvenir by a German officer, of a "father and his son, in the middle of a human herd, moving toward the ditch where, a moment later, they will be shot. The father, his left hand on the boy's shoulder, speaks to him gently while his right hand points to the sky." [24] How *do* we interpret this visual image of atrocity, a faded and melancholy moment of frozen silence that cries out for words to rescue its victims from oblivion? What *does* a father say to his son in the vestibule of eternity—or on the edge of chaos? Is there a reasonable explanation for such a fate, that will console a young boy about to surrender a life he has not yet lived—and under such harrowing circumstances? Fathers protect their sons, they do not invite them to accept annihilation with equanimity. Do we violate the sanctity of that moment by trying to endow it with verbal life? Do we violate it if we refuse to do so? This photograph is emblematic of the difficulty facing readers *and* writers of the Holocaust: many of its essential truths we will never understand, but it challenges the imagination to penetrate a history that greets us with silence, a past of committed and irreversible atrocities like the murder of this father and son.

Wiesel transforms history into legend by imposing words on the silence, as his narrator in the novel accepts the responsibility of interpretation. Speaking of the father, he says:

> He is explaining the battle between love and hatred: "You see, my child, we are right now losing that battle." And since the boy does not answer, his father continues: "Know, my son, if gratuitous suffering exists, it is ordained by divine will. Whoever kills, becomes God. Whoever kills, kills God. Each murder is a suicide, with the Eternal eternally the victim." [25]

These enigmatic words, carved on a tombstone of memory that might otherwise stand vacant, represent one voice echoing from the wilderness of the Holocaust. Truth or legend? Is the son baffled, consoled, or terrified? Explanations resurrect spiritual possibility without guaranteeing authenticity, because there is no way to establish a connection between the death of this "human herd" and the lives its individual members have led. Like Wiesel's father, they are robbed of their deaths as they are robbed of their lives. The retrospective imagination here invents a theodicy that makes God the victim of man; it offers the reader a way of

thinking about the human and divine in the Holocaust universe
that satisfies the yearning for connection. But neither man nor
God emerges triumphant from this interpretation.

And there are moments when Wiesel cannot bring himself to
move beyond history to legend, when mired in the diabolism of
atrocity he knows that "progression into the inhuman transcends
the exploration of the human." At such moments, mesmerized by
the misery of the victims, he admits that "evil, more than good,
suggests infinity." Leafing through a volume of Holocaust
photographs, he cannot escape from the concrete realities of the
inhuman. In an essay called "Snapshots" from *One Generation
After*, he encounters the faces of innumerable victims, "fathers
and sons who spoke or remained silent before tumbling into the
trench," and suddenly it seems impious to reconstruct legends
from such fear and hunger and shame. Now history poisons the
future:

> Deep down I know that every eye staring into mine cuts off
> the new branch of a tree and adds yet another stain to the
> sun. I know that every image robs me of another reason for
> hope. And still my fingers turn the pages, and the shriveled
> bodies, the gaping twisted mouths, their screams lost in
> space, continue to follow one another. Then the anguish
> clutching me, choking me, grows darker and darker; it
> crushes me: with all these corpses before my eyes, I am
> afraid to stumble over my own.

The survivor pores over these vivid images of atrocity to know
more about the event that mutilated his identity; the reader peers
over his shoulder to discover, belatedly, a truth that eludes them
both: "how—and why—they were spared." [26] Both are in search
of an image of the human they thought extinct.

When he transforms history into legend, Wiesel reinvents that
image of the human, even among the victims on the edge of
annihilation. He knows that such writing represents "a passion to
testify for the future, against death and oblivion." But with
another voice he admits that such testimonies are fragmentary,
that all questions about Auschwitz lead to anguish, that "every
witness expresses only his own truth, in his own name," not a
representative Truth, and that "it is not enough to have listened to
the survivors, one must find a way to add the silence left behind

by millions of unknowns." [27] Perhaps ultimately all writers
depend on language to animate the past and to kindle their
readers' imaginations with visions of distant events. But when,
prior to the Holocaust, did they have to account for the stifled
voices of so many innocent victims in this drama of
extermination? Tolstoy's panoramic description of the French and
Russian armies at Borodino evokes the futility and human waste
of all such battles, from Marathon to the Marne. But neither
panoramic sweep nor the deflation of military glory suffices to
convey the human waste and anguish of Auschwitz. Words are a
threat, not a treasure hoard, and Wiesel records his memory of
the "Selishter Rebbe's" warning about their danger: "Be wary of
them. They beget either demons or angels. It's up to you to give
life to one or the other." [28]

The paradox of the Holocaust, as we have seen, is that it gives
birth to both, to angels with demonic faces, to demons with
angelic wings. Death is surcease and unmanageable terror;
survival is relief and a guilt-burdened curse. If, according to the
Zohar, when Israel is in exile so is the word, what are we to say
when Israel is literally reduced to ashes? Must the tongue remain
entirely mute? Of what other historical episode has it been said so
earnestly: "Survivors and witnesses have done their best to
describe their experiences, yet their writings have perhaps no
substantial relationship with what they have seen and lived
through"? [29] Once again, we ascribe such "failure" not only to an
inadequate mind approaching an elusive event, but to the limits of
a language too orderly in its structure, too coherent in its content,
to chronicle the disorder and incoherence of the deathcamps. Just
as Adam would have hesitated if asked to name the items of chaos
that preceded creation, since his available vocabulary had been
designed for the idyllic atmosphere of Eden, so the survivor and
witness stumble, Wiesel alleges, when they use what Primo Levi
called "free words" to describe the dead world they lived through.
"It was by seeking, by probing silence," he says, "that I began to
discover the perils and power of the word." [30]

We cannot dismiss this as mere mystification. As we shall see,
it lies at the heart of Nelly Sachs's poetic vision too, whereas
Gertrud Kolmar's confidence in the word, and the durability of
the values it could express, only increased her vulnerability.
Indeed, such confidence increased the vulnerability of all those
who believed that naming a value endowed it with meaning and

power. The distrust of language that followed World War I moved, after Auschwitz, beyond disenchantment to an overwhelming sense of the discrepancy between the ordeal and verbal images potent enough to communicate it. The question was not the betrayal of words, but their impotence. In a searching analysis of the problem, Wiesel discredits the "language of day," pre-Holocaust vocabulary, as a source for presenting or interpreting the survivor experience:

> The word has deserted the meaning it was intended to convey—impossible to make them coincide. The displacement, the shift, is irrevocable. This was never more true than right after the upheaval. We all knew that we could never, never say what had to be said, that we could never express in words, coherent, intelligible words, our experience of madness on an absolute scale. The walk through flaming night, the silence before and after the selection, the monotonous praying of the condemned, the Kaddish of the dying, the fear and hunger of the sick, the shame and suffering, the haunted eyes, the demented stares. I thought that I would never be able to speak of them. All words seemed inadequate, worn, foolish, lifeless, whereas I wanted them to be searing. Where was I to discover a fresh vocabulary, a primeval language? The language of night was not human; it was primitive, almost animal—hoarse shouting, screams, muffled moaning, savage howling, the sound of beating. . . . A brute striking wildly, a body falling; an officer raises his arm and a whole community walks toward a common grave; a soldier shrugs his shoulders, and a thousand families are torn apart, to be reunited only by death. This is the concentration camp language. It negated all other language and took its place. Rather than link, it became wall.[31]

Once words joined; now they separate. In order to surmount this barrier, one must first perceive it; and to perceive it, one must recognize that it is built not of bricks, but of a pile of corpses rising to the sky.

Can the reader be brought to the other side? Wiesel's divided voice is nowhere more evident than in his response to this question: "I knew the answer to be negative, and yet I also knew that 'no' had to become 'yes.' It was the wish, the last will of the dead. One had to break the shell enclosing the dark truth, and give it a name. One had to force man to look." In the role of an unblessed Adam, the survivor-witness names the creatures of night, not to celebrate the splendor of God's creation but to fix for future generations the desecration of man. Here, seeing precedes knowing; and after having seen, the mind questions the basis of all prior knowledge. Beyond the wall of corpses one finds not fair fields of living folk, but only endless acres of the dead. That some survived does not alter the dominating image of the deathcamp as the morgue of the Jewish people. For Wiesel, the loyalty of the survivor is not to those values that enabled him to survive, but to the victims who perished despite all values. Survivors, he insists, "owe nothing to anyone, but everthing to the dead." [32]

Every statement about the Holocaust that Wiesel makes, every fiction he invents, is saturated by the presence of perished victims. A shadow of *Night* falls over all his subsequent volumes, by design, a permanent reminder to himself to resist the temptation of lapsing into the "language of day." Bettelheim, we recall, begins his analysis of human behavior in extreme situations—by which he means the German concentration camps—with a significant disclaimer: "I have no intention of recounting once more the horror story of the concentration camps, since it is now common knowledge that prisoners suffered extreme deprivation and were deliberately tortured." [33] But by journey's end, when Bettelheim celebrates the will's determination to affirm its dignity, the reader has long since forgotten the world of "seeing" in favor of the safer universe of "knowing." Similarly, Frankl begins his account of "Experiences in a Concentration Camp" with the caution that his tale "is not concerned with the great horrors, which have already been described often enough (though less often believed), but with the multitude of small torments," [34] thus evading the challenge of using a "language of night" that "was not human." As a result, his interpretation of the experience, like Bettelheim's, is a link between past and present, rather than a wall. Neither would care to understand the insight of Wiesel's narrator in *The Accident*, who offers a crucial revision of the existentialist view of man: "The problem is not: to be or not to be. But rather: to be and not to be. What it comes down to is that man lives while dying, that he represents death to the living, and that's where tragedy begins." [35]

Choosing life in the camps—Borowski makes this clear—often meant allying oneself with the forces of atrocity. Impure decisions sully "pure" ideas like "choice" and "tragedy," though we continue to use them because we lack verbal alternatives. For the survivor, who embodies Wiesel's question whether one can die in Auschwitz *after* Auschwitz, familiar options lack meaning; and this is also true for all those who struggle to approach the survivor by moving through seeing to knowing. If the survivor who measures himself against the reality of good—of dignity, compassion, sharing, self-respect—emerges triumphant, as he does in Frankl, Bettelheim, and ultimately Des Pres, the one who "measures himself against the reality of evil," Wiesel contends, "always emerges beaten and humiliated." [36] Both measures are essential in the post-Holocaust world, though the gain of "being" cannot negate the loss represented by those who did not survive. The very imbalance of numbers between the living and the dead prohibits the usual celebration of survival. It prohibits too the usual *definition* of survival, since men and women continued to exist—we often overlook this—only because their turn to die had not yet arrived, not because they had *permanently* outwitted the enemy. The image of the deathcamp as a morgue for certain populations persists, as we consider what would have happened had the Nazis *won*. Perhaps this is why so many continue to die in Auschwitz after Auschwitz, in imagination if not in fact, in deference to the destiny so few managed so narrowly to avoid.

More than any other writer on the Holocaust, Wiesel has explored the ambiguity of this dilemma. In "A Plea for the Dead" he urges the reader to leave the dead in peace, not to analyze their motives before they perished, not to judge their behavior now that they are no longer present to defend or explain. But simultaneously, in book after book, he insists that the dead will not leave *us* in peace, that their tombless ghosts are and will remain part of our present and future reality. They infiltrate the memories of his characters, who respond to this legacy by allowing it to shape the design of their lives. How are we to respond to this dual adjuration—not to trouble the dead, yet to be constantly troubled by them ourselves? From one point of view, Wiesel's work is a sustained dramatization of counterpositions, a long monologue disguised as a series of dialogues, revealing his own divided self. His inconsistency is both real and imagined, the reflection of a writer who feels trapped by two necessities—to speak and to hold his tongue—and who incorporates this very tension into the substance of his vision. Even in one of his most recent works, the text of *Ani Maamin*, the complaints of the Patriarchs are opposed by God's silence—for in Wiesel (as in Chekhov and Beckett) silence too is a feature of dialogue. Patriarchs and God—the two are tenuously joined by a few divine tears and an intermediate Voice, which consoles but does not—cannot—establish a final reconciliation to banish the tension in the dialogue between man and transcendence, hope and despair, speech and silence, soliciting and burying the dead. That dialogue is a heritage from Auschwitz, and Wiesel offers no reassurance that a new Voice from the Whirlwind will emerge to satisfy the spiritual needs of Job's descendants. In the balance between the human and the divine—indeed, in the balance between the human and the inhuman—the dead still weigh too heavily on one side of the scale.

As a messenger from those dead, Wiesel's task has been to explore how men respond when the line "between humanity and inhumanity becomes blurred." If on the one hand he affirms that a literature of the Holocaust is a contradiction in terms, on the other hand he is dedicated to helping men discover "the link between words and the ashes they cover." [37] The image is central to our theme, and illuminates some of the objections to it. To uncover ashes is to unbury the past, to expose the dead; most human beings would prefer to celebrate the phoenix that rises from them. The literature of the Holocaust is not a literature of hope, though Wiesel's personal mood has veered away from the opposite pole of despair often enough so that he cannot be identified with either party. His strategy has been to pour hope and despair into the crucible of experience, without losing sight of the event that inspires and modifies them both, and to permit his characters to work out the implications on the stages of their lives. If the results are not harmonious, they are nonetheless faithful to his vision of the night: his shifting positions are themselves an imaginative statement on the futility of seeking to escape its eternal shadows.

From the victims' son in *Dawn*, who (as we have seen) reluctantly becomes an executioner, to the futile sacrifice of that ancestor and contemporary of victims, Moshe the Madman in *The Oath*, men seek a gesture to affirm the human in the midst of threatened chaos—but who among them has succeeded? They only confirm the contradictions implicit in the attempt. The quest is Wiesel's theme, not the arrival, and a quest is literally the beginning of a question. His work is one entry into the labyrinth of the Holocaust, and though he guides us through its inner corridors with an acute sense of sudden turns, he has not yet discovered an Ariadne who possesses the secret of the way out. One of the darker twists in this labyrinth is illuminated by the narrator of *Dawn*, who wrestles with the paradox that he must be an agent of the very violence that destroyed his own past, and seeks a principle to bolster his waning courage:

> Why do I try to hate you, John Dawson? Because my people
> have never known how to hate. Their tragedy, throughout
> the centuries, has stemmed from their inability to hate those
> who have humiliated and from time to time exterminated
> them. Now our only chance lies in hating you, in learning the
> necessity and the art of hate.[38]

Scarcely a humanist position, this attitude solves nothing, as Wiesel understands, since the victim is an innocent hostage, not an enemy executioner. Yet a morality of hatred is allied with the possibility of survival, and qualifies if it does not obliterate the dignity that others avow as a main source of strength for those who would survive.

The voice defending this position in *Dawn* is a vigorous one. In most tragic art, evil finally exhausts itself and society regains equilibrium as justice restores order among men. But justice cannot restore order to communities that have been annihilated; for this reason, the Holocaust dead who troop through the pages of Wiesel's work do not clamor for revenge. Wiesel perceives that atrocity of such magnitude disclaims the spirit of tragedy, and the redeeming moral dignity of which it was the supreme expression. Nor are the traditional consolations of religion any more effective. When the executioner arrives before the Messiah, as he elsewhere suggests, we are left facing the impossibility of finding a position commensurate with both Jewish destiny and a reality mutilated by atrocity. Hence we should not be surprised to find Wiesel, in another of his voices, in his letter "To a Young German on the New Left," contradicting the earlier attitude: "No, I shall never hate you. Not for yesterday and not even for today. It is something else: for yesterday you have my pity; for today, my contempt." [39] Which position ensures survival: the shocking one of turning executioner in self-defense or the conventional one of meeting hostility with pity or contempt, but not the aggressive posture of hatred? Or is there a middle ground? We begin to understand what Wiesel means when he says that to be a Jew is to ask a thousand questions—about surviving in a hostile universe, about reason and unreason in history, about meaningless suffering, about God's silence, in and after Auschwitz.

The problem then, for Wiesel at any rate, is not the nature of the Holocaust itself, which may indeed be indescribable in its essence (though not in its consequence), but how to respond to it. In his use of dialogue, in the diversity of his voices, he confirms a principle we need to remember: "One's spiritual legacy provides no screen, ethical concepts offer no protection" [40] against the metamorphoses of character in victim and executioner when mass extermination becomes the rule of existence. The insights his characters acquire in their journey through his tales divide the personality as often as they unite it; they are descendants of Ivan Karamazov, though their "devil" is far more real than his, rooted in history rather than intellectual (and spiritual) despair. The stories they collect of suffering innocence are not from books and legends, but from their own lives; and Dostoevsky's ideal of active love is powerless to heal their wounds. For them, drowned in the misery of remembrance, returning their "ticket" to heaven would be a luxurious privilege, a superfluous gesture, a vain effort to affirm a mutilated identity.

In the universe of Wiesel's imagination, the ordeal of survival is an extension of the ordeal of atrocity, not a triumph over it. "To a victim of the 'concentrationary' system," he writes,

> it no longer mattered that he had been intellectual, laborer, angry student or devoted husband. A few beatings, a few screams turned him into a blank, his loss of identity complete. He no longer thought as before, nor did he look men straight in the eyes; his own eyes were no longer the same. Camp law and camp truth transcended all laws and all truth, and the prisoner could not help but submit. When he was hungry, he thought of soup and not of immortality. After a long night's march, he yearned for rest and not for mercy. Was this all there was to man? [41]

With the primacy of body over mind and spirit, the growth of character as we traditionally understand it is disrupted, suspended; and when that growth resumes after the event, a

certain malformation is evident in the result. To some extent, the
principle of choiceless choice continues to exert its control
beyond Auschwitz, since the survivor is not "free" simply to
forget. "Dead souls have more to say than living ones," [42] says the
narrator of Wiesel's second novel, *The Accident*, acknowledging a
possibility that Gogol's Chichikov discovered to his comic
dismay. Their voices inhibit the reintegration of identity that
Wiesel's characters struggle toward, as they strive to negate the
implications of his question: "Was this all there was to man?"

And in the beginning there were *many voices*, not only *one word*:
this is a major clue to Wiesel's literary tactics. He is determined to
complicate the reality of the Holocaust past by multiplying the
tongues that speak of it. It is an art of chorus, of dialogue, of
language in quest of conscience. Words are more fluid than
characters, who become fixed in time and place. Perhaps this is
why his characters are less memorable than what they say: a voice
must flow into the present, not echo with regular vibrations from
the past. Oddly enough, in his tales based on legend and history,
where his art is less visible, his figures are more vivid than the
words they speak: Rebbe Nahman of Bratzlav, Menahem-Mendl
of Kotsk, Abraham and Moses, are more fully realized than
Michael and Pedro in *The Town beyond the Wall* and Gavriel and
Gregor in *The Gates of the Forest*. The latter are more disembodied
voices than men, perhaps because they are wrestling with
post-Holocaust problems that the rebbes and patriarchs did not
have to confront. In those days the world was not yet a
slaughterhouse, so that men still had time to be themselves and
affirm the human in the face of injustice. For Wiesel, as for other
authors in the tradition, the Holocaust has ruptured human reality
and shattered the durability of time: man can't afford to wait for
God's decision to send the Messiah, concludes one of the voices
from *The Gates of the Forest*, because his life hangs in the balance.

The narrator of *The Accident* is a survivor whose life illustrates
"how man can become a grave for the unburied dead." He does
not cherish such a burden. First humorously, then angrily, he
repudiates the role of sainthood thrust upon him by "false
prophets" among his friends. Their conception of suffering, based
on the familiar language of transcendence, consoles and protects
them, but it does not define his ordeal or its injury to his soul. He
offers them a description more consonant with the Holocaust
experience:

"Suffering brings out the lowest, the most cowardly in man. There is a phase of suffering you reach beyond which you become a brute: beyond it you sell your soul—and worse, the souls of your friends—for a piece of bread, for some warmth, for a moment of oblivion, of sleep. Saints are those who die before the end of the story. The others, those who live out their destiny, no longer dare look at themselves in the mirror, afraid they may see their inner image. . . ." [43]

But there is no place for this definition in the lives of his auditors, who do not share the images, like his grandmother ascending to heaven through a smokestack, that jostle his memory as he tries unsuccessfully to adapt to the routines of daily living in the post-Holocaust world. His mind conceals not an archetypal past, uniting him to the secret fears and longings of all men, but a private terror, creating barriers between him and those he exists among. The woman who loves him, the doctor who heals him, the artist friend who paints his portrait and tries futilely to imprison in the eyes on the canvas the demons that haunt this survivor's imagination—all choose life, whereas the dead have chosen the narrator before he can make a choice of his own. He does not rejoice in his fate, but cannot escape it. And the more he seeks to communicate his dilemma, the more he discovers that he cannot share it with anyone.

Some have seen "the abstract, somewhat disembodied quality of experience" in much of Wiesel's fiction, "its frequent disconnections, and its heavy reliance on a world made up of words alone" as significant weaknesses.[44] And they are, for those devoted to the kind of novel where character evolves within a certain texture of experience. But as the palpable terrors of the deathcamp recede, the phenomenal world that gave them birth grows more unreal, and that distant Holocaust universe, alive in memory but fading as a realm of concrete detail, merely numbs the mind by casting a glow of unreality over the present. The intense life of the senses is attenuated for characters who spend much of the time carrying on disputes with their dead. Those dead exert a hold over the survivor-narrator of *The Accident* that no one around him understands. Unspoken (as well as spoken) words occupy so much of his existence, dialogues and interior monologues so crowd out normal responses to the phenomenal world, that he appears withdrawn even when engaged in the most explicit enounters, like making love. The "disembodied quality" in Wiesel's fiction reflects the divided universe that he and his characters inhabit. This early in Wiesel's career (the date of *The Accident* is 1961), attempts to find an accommodation between the two halves of that universe—like the narrator's reluctant agreement to see a Hollywood version of *The Brothers Karamazov* with the woman he so hesitantly loves—may prove fatal. He is struck by a taxi as they cross the street to reach the theater.

The narrator disturbs, offends, exasperates the doctor who tries to save him, because he seems indifferent to life, refuses to "choose" it. The doctor represents a point of view that he unwittingly shares with Holocaust commentators like Frankl, Bettelheim, and Des Pres: "What fascinates me in man is his capacity for living." [45] What attracts Wiesel in other men—his survivors—is the necessary compulsion they feel for responding to a certain kind of dying—in the deathcamps of the Holocaust. For Wiesel, Auschwitz threatens the laws of equilibrium that traditionally drive all men to favor life over death, no matter what their circumstances. Living abstractly in the present, his narrator does not view Death, as Camus might, as an irrational force that by definition humiliates Man; his memory is more concrete than his immersion in the present. The images of past "seeing" obscure the clarity of future sight. The thought of his grandmother's death in the camp, like a flame, "chased away the sun and took its place. And this new sun," he thinks, "which blinds instead of giving light forces me to walk with my head down. It weighs upon the future of man. It casts a gloom over the hearts and vision of generations to come" (p. 79). But the special source of this image, a new sun that blinds instead of illuminating, changes our view of cosmic order—Nelly Sachs will explore similar images—and of human existence within its orbit.

One version of survival stresses the disintegration rather than the reintegration of the survivor. Wiesel's narrator in *The Accident* shares this view. "Anyone who has seen what they have seen cannot be like the others, cannot laugh, love, pray, bargain, suffer, have fun, or forget" (p. 79). Whatever we name their ordeal—suffering, martyrdom, extermination—or their response to it—dignity, compromise, surrender—for Wiesel, in his initial imaginative visions of the consequences of that ordeal, the survivor is different, maimed, imprisoned by what he has survived. "These people have been amputated," thinks his narrator, as he tries to sort out in his own mind what the doctor could never understand; "they haven't lost their legs or eyes but their will and their taste for life. The things they have seen will come to the surface again sooner or later. And then the world will be frightened and won't dare look these spiritual cripples in the eye" (p. 79). Later Wiesel will have to contend not with the fear but the embarrassment of the world, as his amputees blend into a reality that has no way of and little interest in acknowledging their unique inheritance. Other men will know how to celebrate the heroic forms of survival, because these rise from a shared source of values; they are, the narrator believes, texts men know by heart. But who will chant the unfamiliar texts that tell of the crippled spirits; and who, other than the handful of survivors like the narrator, will know how to mourn the victims who through their ghostly presence continue to mutilate him?

The Accident, through dialogue and reflection rather than dramatic action, suggests the impossibility of crossing the gulf between remorse and consolation where the narrator has been cast adrift. In one of his essays Wiesel alludes to Sartre's phrase that in love, one and one are one. "For us, contemporary Jews," he adds, "one and one are six million." [46] In *The Accident*, the memory of atrocity corrupts the anticipation of love, infecting the sentiment that once overcame all obstacles to human intimacy. "You claim you love me," complains Kathleen to the narrator, "but you keep suffering. You say you love me in the present but you're still living in the past. You tell me you love me but you refuse to forget" (p. 110). The form of the disputation, the reduction of complex inner anguish to apparently simple verbal formulas, should not deflect our attention from the gravity of the argument. "Anyone who has been there," replies the narrator, echoing a charge that reverberates beyond the specific locus of the Holocaust, "has brought back some of humanity's madness. One day or another, it will come to the surface" (p. 111). The narrator's inner world is saturated by such suffocating gloom that Kathleen would find it intolerable were he to express it. He knows that survivors must not give other men and women "the sour taste, the smoke-cloud taste, that we have in our mouth" (p. 113). But this leaves the narrator shrouded in a gloom that not even the act of love can pierce.

For him at this moment in his life, love and happiness are a mirage. The entire vocabulary of transcendence has migrated to the heaven of cemeteries, along with the victims. "You say 'love,' " he admonishes Kathleen:

> And you don't know that love too has taken the train which went straight to heaven. Now everything has been transferred there. Love, happiness, truth, purity, children with happy smiles, women with mysterious eyes, old people who walk slowly, and little orphans whose prayers are filled with anguish. That's the true exodus. The exodus from one world to the other. (p. 113)

The earlier exodus led men out of bondage to a promised land, a new covenant with God, a future mingling sorrow with glory. This one cancels the future, mingling present sorrow only with remembered pain, as if the forty years of desert wandering were stretched to an inner eternity. In the privacy of his mind, the narrator confronts his new identity, as survivor-witness, precisely but with apprehension; his words never spill over into speech: "He is the incarnation of time that negates present and future, only recognizing the harsh law of memory. He suffers and his contagious suffering calls forth echoes around him" (p. 122). But they are reluctant, resentful echoes, ultimately provoking contrary voices that listen to but do not hear the pleas of his "contagious suffering." As his battered body slowly heals, we get a deeper glimpse of the trauma that afflicts his spirit. The drained planet he inhabits dries up the verbal springs of hope: "And you speak of love, Kathleen?" he concludes sadly. "And you speak of happiness? Others speak of justice, universal or not, of freedom, of brotherhood, of progress" (p. 114). The dialogues in the novel resemble concurrent monologues because each participant's terms of discourse derive from totally alienated universes of words.

The final exchange in the novel—the narrator calls it a "silent dialogue" (p. 123)—takes place between himself and an artist friend who is painting his portrait, to assign a place to the dead, he says, in the eyes of his subject. Perhaps art can transfix a poisoning reality and give the victim a chance to exorcise it. The painter mouths truths that emerge as platitudes, not because he is insensitive but because, for the narrator, the Holocaust experience has anesthetized the words used to describe it. "Suffering is given to the living, not to the dead," exclaims the painter. "It is man's duty to make it cease, not to increase it. One hour of suffering less is already a victory over fate" (p. 124). But this is both the method and the language of reason, assuming a connection between action and consequence; whereas the narrator's dead populate a realm where life was extinguished for nothing. To whip the dead from memory, as his friend admonishes him, is to desanctify their ordeal, since memory is the only form of commemoration that may honor them. The narrator-survivor cannot invent himself anew, as his artist friend asks, because he has already been invented by a past whose rigid limits imprison his character. The flexibility of character we have learned to expect from art, whereby man opens himself to fresh experience and is renewed by it, is inaccessible to one who stubbornly refuses to interpret his existence as a choice between the living or the dead. He alone defines growth as a permanent encounter with both, but has not resolved the dilemma of how one chosen by death is to choose life too. If he embraces love, it will be with self-deceit, deceiving others, with an ironic acceptance of the discovery that "lies can give birth to true happiness" (p. 126). Recognizing the failure of his portrait-sermon, the painter burns his canvas. The narrator, who like Wiesel reveres art for what it reflects, not for what it cures, weeps at its destruction; he mourns the loss, but instantly acknowledges the remnants—a small pile of ashes—as one more image to cherish in his private gallery of the dead.

Relationships are left in suspension at the end of *The Accident*, a novel in which confirmation (of the past) precedes and thus prohibits affirmation (of the future). Wiesel's subsequent fiction moves in both directions, as his spokesmen seek ways of absorbing their burden without paralyzing the possibilities for human growth. Although the titles of Wiesel's first three works, *Night*, *Dawn*, and *Day* (the original French title of *The Accident* is *Le Jour*) suggest a clear progression toward vision and insight, the contents of the works do not support this simple assumption. Melancholy accompanies hope throughout his fictional journey, from his first work to his last. Indeed, a decade after *The Accident*, in *The Oath*, Wiesel still questions the potency of art as testimony, the role of the witness, the meaning of past atrocity for those who did not feel its immediate force. Unlike Bunyan's Christian pilgrim, Wiesel's Jewish survivor cannot be liberated from the burden of memory as he slowly enters the realm of grace. This survivor may improve the condition of his soul through reverence for the victims—who, we must remember, were not "fallen" but fallen *upon*—through human gesture if not through holy deed. But the discontinuity of their deaths, which did not "belong" to them as Wiesel's father's did not belong to him, dooms them to a spiritual limbo. Among the revelations derived from the various voices in Wiesel's later novels is one asserting the limited power of words and acts to redeem the dead from their innocent suffering and unchosen fate.

Thus the rebirth of the protagonist, Michael, in *The Town beyond the Wall* is simultaneously a "redeath": he returns, first in mind, then in fact, to the locale of his birth, but instead of establishing a continuity in his identity, he confirms the radical rupture that has divided his childhood from his youth. His teachers, like Wiesel's, include a Moishe the Madman, who counsels madness as the only source of human wholeness; a Kalman the Kabbalist, an ascetic and religious fanatic who preaches the offense of the body; and his own father, whose support of the humanist position creates one more dialogue between opposites that contain their own contradiction: "If the soul is the link between you and God, the body is the same between you and your fellows. Why destroy it?" To live for man is the proper worship of God. Only later does Michael realize and try to confront the crisis in religious and humanistic belief introduced by the Holocaust, which destroyed Moishe, Kalman, and his father:

> "In those years, nineteen forty-three, nineteen forty-four, you had to be crazy to believe that man has any control over his fate. You had to be crazy to hope for a victory of the spirit over the forces of evil, to imagine any possibility of redemption, of consolation; you had to have lost your reason, or sacrificed it, to believe in God, to believe in man, to believe in a reconciliation between them." [47]

Before he can move into the future, Michael must sort out these voices from his childhood, not yet ghosts or victims, but spokesmen for vital principles of being that perished indiscriminately in the nightmare of atrocity.

Michael recalls himself as a little boy sneaking into the forbidden garden of an ancient neighbor named Varaday (a kind of pre-Holocaust Lord of a humanistic Eden). Here he had been enchanted by Varaday's titanic vision of human capacity: "I love men only when they shatter their mold, when they assault the immutable barriers of the past, present, and future; when they possess the strength and courage to impose their will on the universe, on death" (p. 28). In the post-Holocaust universe, this tribute to Enlightenment energy and romantic optimism sounds like an elegy to a vanished world, what Michael himself remembers as a "blasted Paradise where all had once seemed so simple" (p. 78). The little boy who visited there has been driven from its gates not by a committed or transmitted sin, but by the intrinsic failure of the values that had given the place vitality. Figuratively, he was annihilated along with the other victims of the deathcamps. "He didn't survive," says Michael about himself, though his memories contradict his denial. "He's dead. . . . I have nothing in common with him" (p. 80). But later he confesses: "I know he's dead, but I also know that he won't leave me. He follows my trail; he walks in my footsteps; I can hear his own" (p. 80). Two selves survive, not one evolving into another, and the tension between them becomes the meaning of being for a survivor like Michael. He follows the footsteps of his dead self back to their source, since he cannot run fast enough to escape them.

If the return to the city of his childhood seems artificial in *The Town beyond the Wall*, one reason may be that both reader and author know in advance that they are about to plunge into an impalpable reality. Nothing is the same: the Jewish community is gone, no one recognizes Michael, he is betrayed and arrested again, this time by the local secret police—and he can find no way to revive an identity from the past. Quickly he learns the folly of his earlier hope: "Soon he would see himself, know himself, compare himself" (p. 126). The return is a gesture both futile and necessary, a quest for links and the discovery that they have melted in a caldron of forgetfulness and indifference. His quest for self dissolves into a more agonizing question: how to understand *"those who watched us depart for the unknown; those who observed us, without emotion, while we became objects"* (p. 148). The real mystery for Wiesel is not what happened to the moral identity of victim or survivor, but how what he calls the "Other" or spectator permitted the human bond to be violated without protest.

This rankling enigma exacerbates the belief in community, in shared suffering, in all those values that for generations and centuries supported the idea of a humanistic civilization. Any coherent image of the survivor to emerge from the Holocaust experience depends on a prior need to understand "those who watched us depart for the unknown; those who observed us, without emotion, while we became objects." Wiesel is as baffled as was Dante, trying to find a place in the world of moral order for this spectator of atrocity, who "says neither yes nor no, and not even maybe" (p. 151). Disciples of the neuter gender, they countenanced the Holocaust by pretending to ignore it. One of the protagonist Michael's alter egos in the novel, a friend named Pedro, with whom Michael engages in mental dialogues while in captivity, offers sensible advice: *"The only valuable protest, or attitude, is one rooted in the uncertain soil of humanity. Remaining human—in spite of all temptations and humiliations—is the only way to hold your own against the Other, whatever it may be"* (p. 172). The message comes straight from Camus, but it sounds as if Pedro has been reading Frankl and Bettelheim too: the language of reason, the vocabulary of transcendence, resounds loudly from his lines. Indifference to suffering is the ultimate inhumanity, the final betrayal. It is wise counsel: but only one voice among many.

Thus Wiesel adds the "Other," the spectator, to his cast of characters who haunt the survivor in the present; like the dead, they exasperate memory and intensify anguish without offering an opportunity to reconcile persisting tensions. If the dialogue between Michael and the man from his town who now occupies his childhood home lacks an authentic ring, perhaps it is because the exchange reflects too obviously the need for catharsis. Here and elsewhere in his fiction, Wiesel introduces episodes that are less dramatic than purgative, as if a private compulsion to reenact lost possibilities might somehow make them more tolerable to memory. Art momentarily seems therapeutic, as the victim charges the spectator with cowardice for refusing to help, while the spectator in turn condemns the victim for failing to resist. Each has his explanation, neither satisfactory, though Wiesel is careful to distinguish victim from spectator by the ordeal of atrocity that the former has survived. Nonetheless, the reader is left with an overwhelming sense of the futility of such retrospective attempts to give a meaningless history a context of meaning: no insight can mitigate the compulsive despair inspired by the event itself.

Michael's return to the city from which he and his family and the rest of the Jewish population were deported (most to their deaths), his arrest, torture, imprisonment, his behavior in prison and his effort to formulate an attitude to facilitate survival, all suggest that on one level of being it is possible to exorcise the past. After his confrontation with the spectator, Michael himself concludes: "The task is accomplished. No more concealed wrath, no more disguises. No more double life, lived on two levels. Now I am whole" (p. 162). But what appears to be climax is really only beginning, since shortly after this decision he is arrested and the cycle of his return to the past will start again. His "wholeness" is challenged by a cellmate, mute and withdrawn, resembling the self-abandoned Muslims of the deathcamps, and Michael realizes that he will never achieve release for himself until he can pierce the identity of his miserable companion, locked in the silence of an uncommunicated past. Those who celebrate the affirmative tone of the closing pages of *The Town beyond the Wall* forget that Michael's hopeful words represent only a planting, with a possibility but no assurance of a good harvest. These pages may be seen as another example of monologue disguised as dialogue, Wiesel in communion with two strains of his own nature, the silent cellmate whose future is blocked by an unarticulated anguish, and Michael, who pays verbal homage to "the art and necessity of clinging to humanity" (p. 177) and who thus acknowledges that his destiny is bound to, determined by the young boy who cannot or will not speak. Meanwhile, both remain in prison, and neither executioner nor spectator shares the benefit of Michael's sanguine words. The test of remaining human in spite of all remembered humiliations has just begun, a bulwark against the legacy of death, one that permits Wiesel to shift the direction of his vision upward without abandoning the opaque realm of the deathcamps that still menaces from below.

That upward turn is neither solution nor resolution, only a further complication of the principle of divided voice that governs Wiesel's fiction and sense of character. The growth of that character is like the life-and-death struggle, described at the beginning of his next novel, *The Gates of the Forest*, between the angel of love and the angel of wrath: "Imagine the laugh that would rise above their corpses as if to say, your death has given me birth; I am the soul of your conflict, its fulfillment as well." [48] The death of promise (for the victim) marks the triumph of evil; the death of evil (for the survivor) marks the triumph of promise. Although temporal sequence and the logic of history require the survivor to outlive the victim, the Holocaust's violation of these axioms enables the victim to outlive his death and coexist with the survivor. In this way, victim and survivor are victorious; but because the bond between them is both memorial *and* burden, victim and survivor are defeated too. Neither can attain his proper rest from the experience of atrocity.

The survivor is one who lives with the knowledge that the angel of wrath and evil has won an irrevocable victory during the Holocaust. The battlefield is strewn with six million corpses. Subsequent affirmations of the spirit, human or divine, exist in the shadow of that fact. In *The Gates of the Forest*, Gregor passes through four stages in the growth of his identity as a survivor, though his anguish is inward, not physical, as he searches for reasons to resist despair and not to surrender to death. His encounter in the cave with the first of his alter egos, the mysterious Gavriel, leads to a series of dialogues about the Messiah that have their counterpart in the fourth and final stage of the novel when Gregor after the war enters into dialogue with the Rebbe and other Hasidim about man's relationship to the divine. The middle two stages represent man in action as well as verbal contest, achieving identities rather than a single identity as the exigencies of being a Jew during the Holocaust prevent the development of an integrated self. For Gregor, those exigencies exert their force after the event too, dividing his life, frustrating his love, leading him finally to a clarifying if not purifying vision of how the Holocaust has caused a permanent rupture between the "self and its image, between being and acting" (p. 219). That divorce, as Gregor will learn, does not paralyze action, but complicates the task of the survivor who still searches for what seems righteous and just. For Gregor, a son who has lost his family in the deathcamps, a pretended deaf-mute Christian boy among hostile anti-Semites, a Jew among Jewish partisans who suspect his devotion, and a Jew among Hasidim disturbed by his gloom, the challenge of unifying his roles appears insuperable, once the history of the Holocaust is behind him.

Perhaps the first security undermined by the Holocaust was a transcendent faith in the coming of the Messiah. In the dialogue within dialogue that is part of the narrative form of the novel's first section, Gavriel tells Gregor how he tried to convince the Messiah, in the person of Moshe the Mute, to save the Jewish people at the risk of upsetting the order of creation. The formation of character in the presence of the Holocaust, for Wiesel, requires an encounter with this principle of redemption, which is not only an article of belief but an image of coherence, purpose, and universal order. Without it, the direction of human growth is threatened by incoherence and chaos. Gregor never forgets Gavriel's conclusion that "the Messiah came, and nothing changed," that despite his "presence" (in imagination or fact) "the executioner goes right on executing . . . and the world is a vast slaughterhouse" (p. 56). Behind the theological dispute lies the more practical question of how the Holocaust has corrupted hope for those who would cling to pre-Holocaust spiritual traditions. The story of the Holocaust, for the Jew, is a story of separations, not reunions; hence Gavriel's final words to Gregor, as he leaves the cave to sacrifice himself so that Gregor may escape, furnish a clue to the tension that will govern Gregor's life throughout and after the war: "separation contains as much of a mystery as meeting. In both cases a door opens: in meeting it opens on the future, in separation on the past. It's the same door" (p. 59). The ambiguity of identity that Gavriel bequeathes to Gregor—which, in a more subtle sense, Gregor-Gavriel bequeathes to himself— gives him the strength to endure his subsequent ordeals.

His brief sojourn among Christians, pretending to be a deaf-mute, teaches him the limited value of silence, which conceals rather than reveals identity. War enriches character, he thinks, imposing on men a double life; he distinguishes between "actual being," what one literally does, and "the image it casts over both past and future" (p. 94). Although he is not alluding to the deathcamp experience, his words illuminate that event, since henceforth the survivor can no longer think of "identity" or "self" as a progress from there to here, then to now. The same door, as Gavriel had suggested, opens on both. When Gregor agrees reluctantly to play Judas in the Christian community's Easter pageant, he initiates a momentum that will ensure his return from silence to speech, from Christian waif to Jewish refugee. He discovers that over the centuries anti-Semite and Jew have remained the same, "and yet in the farthest corner of their being, and of mine too, something has been transfigured" (p. 110). The context of the novel makes clear that the Holocaust itself, the Nazi program of genocide, which has infiltrated this tiny village, has wrought changes in the self-concept of Jew and non-Jew that range far beyond the ancient rivalry born of orthodox Christian doctrine. What had previously been a ritual of hatred swept out of

control by "the memory of old wounds" suddenly becomes a
different kind of hostility when Gregor confesses, "I am a Jew and
my name is a Jewish name, Gavriel" (p. 118). Drama fuses with
reality and the prospective fate of the single victim merges with
the annihilation of anonymous throngs as the bloodthirsty crowd
advances on the defiant Gregor:

> The executioners are moving close to the stage, about to
> invade it and avenge their honor in blood. Gregor did not
> flinch. At this same moment, in the crimson fields of Galicia,
> smartly turned-out officers were shouting the order: "Fire!
> Fire!" A hundred Jews, ten thousand Jews were tumbling into
> the ditches. He would not die alone. (p. 119)

At the last minute he is rescued, but he will not live alone either.
Their death shapes his life, at this crucial instant and into the
future. When he reaches the Jewish partisans, he will bring the
tale of extermination to their incredulous ears, reshaping the
destiny of them all.

Gregor has inherited Gavriel's role as a messenger from the
dead to the living; he transmits to the innocent partisans the story
of the destruction of the Jews. Their task then becomes to liberate
Gavriel, to confirm the tale but even more to restore the identity
of this prophetic figure and thus somehow assure their own
identity as men. Rescuing Gavriel—an illusion they subscribe
to—may reverse his prophecy that "the Messiah is not coming,"
as Gregor repeats to the partisan leader Leib: "he got lost along
the way, and from now on the clouds will obscure his sight. There
are no more men" (p. 124). Or there are no more men, with rare
exceptions, in the old sense of commitment to a human goal.
Gregor is uncomfortable in the role of "a messenger incapable of
deciphering his message" (p. 134), since the news of
extermination he brings is useless unless he can translate it into
meaning or value. And this he cannot do. His story has raised the
possibility of a new and terrible kind of community, the idea
"that men were there to kill rather than to help one another, that
they were there to massacre the Jews, letting them go hand in
hand to death, defying solitude" (p. 134). The image reverses the
sad but human future of Christian man and woman departing
from Milton's Eden—"hand in hand with wandering steps and
slow"—toward the promise of salvation and the restoration of

spiritual communion with God. The effort to rescue Gavriel is futile, symbolically and literally; it costs the life of Leib instead. The Holocaust has added to love a new burden, has made the heart of man a cemetery as well as a reservoir of affection: *"the more open it becomes, the greater is the cold,"* thinks Gregor, who cannot escape the painful realization of how Jewish fate has altered his sense of Jewish origin: *"In the beginning God created man in order to kill him; he created him because he has no pity"* (p. 137).

This is another plateau of his perception; he does not leave it behind but bears it with him, as it were, as he struggles to higher peaks of insight. Like Wiesel, Gregor does not wish to dismiss Scripture, but to expand it by adding the Holocaust to the canon. Secular atrocity is enacted on the stage of Jewish faith, but the new script includes a cynical voice that unites survivor and audience in a fearful if not final role: "He who is not among the victims is with the executioners" (p. 168). The challenge to the survivor is to find a way, in memory or imagination, to be among the victims though having survived them. This is the only legitimate form of rebirth; and if, as suggested earlier, it requires a "redeath" to make it possible, Wiesel does not flinch at the challenge. The danger, as Gregor discovers when he falls in love with Clara, who had been betrothed to the dead partisan leader Leib, is that homage to the victim can imprison as well as liberate. Clara's heart has grown cold from the memory of her loss.

The failure of the plan to free Gavriel and the consequent capture of Leib, together with Gregor's inability to do anything to reverse the defeat, convinces him that the real problem is not hate (of the murderer), but shame (at his own impotence to dethrone him). Perhaps this is what he means when he admits to himself that to "live is to betray the dead" (p. 174). The source of shame and guilt is not the failure to act but the recognition that the system of values on which he had depended to help him in an extremity like the Holocaust had left him powerless. His bitterness, his initial refusal to acknowledge his love for Clara, is an expression of fidelity to that other world of no values that consumed so many millions. Typically, Wiesel introduces a countervoice to Gregor's stubborn reticence, a voice proclaiming that in "an inhuman world like this one love is the great reward and the greatest of victories" (p. 180), but as so often in his fiction, this argument has the force of formula, of lecture or sermon rather than dramatized truth:

It's inhuman to wall yourself up in pain and memories as if
in a prison. Suffering must open us to others. It must not
cause us to reject them. The Talmud tells us that God suffers
with man. Why? In order to strengthen the bonds between
creation and the creator; God chooses to suffer in order to
better understand man and be better understood by him. But
you, you insist upon suffering alone. Such suffering shrinks
you, diminishes you. (p. 180)

The speaker, a partisan appropriately named Yehuda, offers
familiar verbal security by espousing the value of suffering and
the redeeming power of love. They are words both appealing and
weary, considering Yehuda's own fate: he is murdered by a
peasant during a partisan raid for food. The counterpoint between
yearning for unity and the law of retaliation that drives Gregor
and his companions to kill the peasant in return, only highlights
the rupture between memory and aspiration, dissolution and
hope. Gregor's declared love for Clara is nourished by ghosts: of
Leib, Clara's former lover, tortured and deported by the Nazis; of
Yehuda, brutally murdered, though himself a gentle philosopher
of love and suffering; and of the peasant, killer of Yehuda, whose
wife—though she betrayed him to the partisans—prefigures
Gregor's own future with Clara by lamenting, "You've killed my
man, the man who loved me. Nobody will ever love me again"
(p. 185).

After the war, in the fourth and final section of the novel,
Gregor must learn to live with a future mortgaged to the cries that
echo behind him, in a present where "too many roads are open,
too many voices call and your own is so easily lost. The self
crumbles" (p. 219). His encounter with the Hasidim and their
Rebbe, whose transport transcends memory, remorse, pain,
accusation, and regret, offers the fervor of song as a way of
uniting the dissonances of past and future in the ecstasy of the
present moment. Gregor is both drawn and hesitant; his disputes
with the Rebbe remind us of the struggle between the angel of
love and the angel of wrath that opened the novel. The Rebbe
speaks of their dialogue as a reflection of Jacob wrestling with the
angel, though neither is sure of which role is his. For the Rebbe,
Auschwitz merely confirms the primeval war between love and
hate; for Gregor, if the death of the victims has no meaning, "then
it's an insult, and if it does have a meaning, it's even more so"

(p. 195). The Rebbe shares with Yehuda the belief that "suffering contains the secret of creation and its dimension of eternity" (p. 199), and as long as we translate gas chamber and crematorium into the generalized concept of suffering, and speak of Auschwitz, as the Rebbe does, as a "trial," we have the verbal terms and the psychological coherence to understand his reasons for "giving triple thanks to the Almighty" (p. 199) for such trials. Gregor's aspirations are more modest, the ghosts that haunt him (his father, like Wiesel's, died in Buchenwald) more concrete: his only purpose is "not to cause others to suffer" (p. 194). Whereas the Rebbe celebrates the mysterious ways of the Creator, Gregor mourns the all too lucid deaths of the victims. One is tempted to call their contest a stalemate, but when Gregor decides that it is "better to sleep on the trodden ground, if the ground is real, than to chase mirages" (pp. 222–223), one senses that his choice, respectful but firm, has been for man *despite*, not because of the allure of divinity.

The conclusion that man is saved by his own love, not God's, does not prevent Gregor from praying in the final gesture of the novel for his father's soul—and for God's. But as at the end of *The Town beyond the Wall*, we have no assurance that the struggle to survive, which Gregor interprets as a struggle against the ghosts that continue to haunt him (and Clara), will vitalize their love or retard the progress of the crumbling self. As he recites the Kaddish for his father, the prayer for the dead, he has a trembling sense of a renewed relationship "between death and eternity, between eternity and the word" (p. 223), and this is precisely the source of continuity that the survivor searches for. But it is nothing more than a sense, since the novel ends before the reader has a chance to witness in the lives (not the minds or attitudes) of the afflicted the arduous journey from atrocity back to language. The need for the journey has been established, the determination to undertake it has been expressed: but whether Gregor and Clara have the emotional resources to indemnify their mortgaged future remains, as so often in Wiesel, a tenuous question, shrouded in uncertainty. The will is still child to the deed, and the deed—thus far in Wiesel's fiction—conceals hidden terrors.

It takes a mighty deed to liberate the will from so much remembered pain, and for a time, in *A Beggar in Jerusalem*, Wiesel's next work of fiction, it seems as if history has finally furnished one. The episodes in this novel alternate between memories of extermination and the triumphant reunification of the Holy City, as Wiesel's characters waver between nocturnal vision and daily truth in their effort to define the significance of the Six Day War in the context of Jewish tradition and experience, especially the experience of the Holocaust. One says "characters" from habit, since here too his figures are less living and substantial men than *spokesmen*, who whisper legends from the past or hopes for the future, then withdraw or vanish like shadows in the night. Their "being" retreats behind their "saying," as if their selves were absorbed by the words they uttered, equally ambiguous, equally impermanent. "Kill a Jew," declares the narrator in one of the many aphorisms scattered through the novel's pages, "and you make him immortal; his memory, independently, survives him." [49] This "immortality," though, contrary to normal experience, cannot lead to a celebration of continuity in living, since what is remembered is always associated with the "killing," polluting the joy that is commonly identified with immortality.

Wiesel is shrewd enough in this novel to see, despite the heady triumph of the Six Day War, that though the victors survive, survivors are not always allowed a victory. Like so many of his other works, *A Beggar in Jerusalem* retraces his steps back to his town, to deportation, to the deathcamps, but does not succeed in erasing their imprint; while simultaneously he follows a path forward in time, to the consolidation of Israel and to the agonizing paradox that is the Jew's heritage from the Holocaust: "Victory does not prevent suffering from having existed, nor death from having taken its toll." Against one character's conclusion that the dead have no right in Jerusalem, city of victory, the narrator balances the irrepressible question that still haunts Wiesel's vision and complicates the existence of the survivor: "How can one work for the living without by that very act betraying those who are absent?" (p. 210). Answers are as impossible as amnesia; they congeal in the process of formulation. But the sharing of questions is part of the creative act, certainly of Wiesel's, and as the voices in this novel contend with their questions, we explore with them, in the context of the Holocaust, the implications of Samuel Beckett's observation that speech can be a desecration of silence.

The tensions between the need to remember and the compulsion to remain silent are dramatized in a dialogue between

the narrator, a survivor called David, and an enigmatic alter ego
named Katriel. Katriel mistrusts words because they "destroy
what they aim to describe, they alter what they try to emphasize.
By enveloping the truth, they end up taking its place" (p. 135).
There may be no "pure" description of any event, but the
particular atrocity that rumbles beneath the narrative surface of *A
Beggar in Jerusalem* (and Wiesel's other works) eludes even
"impure" ones—hence Katriel's skepticism. Earlier Katriel had
distinguished between two kinds of silence, the sterile one before
creation that contains chaos, and the one accompanying the
revelation on Mount Sinai, which suggests plenitude. David, the
survivor, whose past includes a vision unknown to Katriel,
defends words, though his argument is less aggressive: "You
prefer to feed truth with silence? Good. But you risk distorting it
with contempt" (p. 135). In the absence of a trustworthy style for
speaking of atrocity, the dispute over whether one exists becomes
part of the drama; and the question for the artist becomes not *what*
words convey, but whether they can. The impotence of words
burdened by a theme beyond their capacity shares center stage in
the novel with the fragility of a future rebuilt on the blasted
foundations of a Holocaust past.

Now history in the form of the Six Day War has given Wiesel
an opportunity to cement the two with more durable mortar. Can
triumph in Jerusalem finally appease the specter of Auschwitz?
Can this affirmation of heritage restore the interrupted rhythm of
time and unite the fragments of the divided self? For a moment it
seems so, as the narrator, in a kind of mystical awakening,
enthusiastically insists: "Haunted by the holocaust, the people of
Israel and the State of Israel again had but a single memory, a
single heart, and that heart vibrated with pride" (p. 116). The war
is thus a crucial episode in the destiny of the Jewish people (for
whom no *single* act can offer redemption); the Holocaust is now
seen as the penultimate experience in the crisis of Jewish faith.
Defeat will mean total annihilation, a holocaust of the spirit
completing the work begun by the earlier genocide. Victory will at
least tempt one to believe in the reprieve of sorrow, the
restoration of dignity to the dead, the assurance of a Jewish future,
the vindication of hope.

The urgency of the crisis is reflected on a personal as well as a
historical level, for on the eve of the conflict the narrator David
suffers a migraine attack, during which, in a phantasmagoric

dream-vision, he is confronted by "all the people who once occupied a place in [his] life." This pantheon of victims, including his mother and Kalman the Kabbalist, all murmur "Too late!" to his frenzied appeal for a parable or story to integrate his fragmented heritage. He finally dredges up the destiny—a familiar one in Wiesel's imaginative universe— of "the man who, having fled from himself, was condemned to mark time forever" (p. 130). In so doing he offers us a situation that Wiesel has tested in each of his previous novels and reexamines here, perhaps hoping to find in the Six Day War a talisman to release himself and his survivor-narrator from their schizophrenic doom, to uncover in Israel's victory a means of resuming a unified destiny once more harmonious with the passage of time. The excitement of triumph on the heights of Jerusalem parallels the gloom of "the secret subterranean kingdom where the beginning has a voice, throbbing and melancholy" (p. 130). The search for a link is at the heart of Wiesel's Holocaust vision.

Can literature create a consciousness that real life has thus far anesthetized? This seems to be a major purpose of *A Beggar in Jerusalem.* David associates the night before the beginning of battle with the night before his deportation to the camp: he recalls first his father's returning to a courtyard and reporting helplessly, "It's for tomorrow, it's for tomorrow," then turns his own imagination resolutely toward the next day, and himself murmurs, "it's for tomorrow, it's for tomorrow" (p. 167). The Six Day War thus potentially restores to Jewish consciousness those qualities of possibility of which the Holocaust mercilessly deprived it: a sense of connection between human action and human fate (the expectation of victory), of a future opening out instead of clanging shut like the ominous sealed doors of the gas chambers. But this is a promise for public consciousness; private memory cannot succumb so easily to such illusions, and the division between the two sustains its tension to the closing pages of the novel, as Wiesel's fictional voices continue the dialogue between the liberator of tomorrow and the hostage of yesterday, between hope and despair.

As Israeli shells hurtle through the predawn darkness after the attack has begun, David whispers to Katriel an ambiguous discovery: "Do you know what war is? A journey to the end of silence" (p. 174). Katriel later replies that the children of Israel cannot escape the past of Israel, that the wish to be "healthy, normal, cured of obsessions and complexes, relieved of mystery and burden" (p. 188) is a delusion proved by the war itself, which only creates more victims and the foundations for future conflict. But for a time, the momentum of the narrative silences Katriel's reservations, as another voice rapturously exclaims: "Israel defeated its enemies—do you know why? I'll tell you, Israel won because its army, its people, could deploy six million more names in battle" (p. 202). The liberation of the ancient Temple Wall briefly introduces the germ of a new legend that may balance the old horror of the Holocaust, as the spirits of its victims infiltrate the ranks of the living troops and march with them in sacred communion toward the source and goal, the beginning and end of Jewish destiny—the Wall. For a thrilling instant one is tempted to believe that Wiesel has achieved what no one before him has been able to accomplish—the writing of a worthy epitaph for all those unnumbered dead.

But to accept this without qualification is to ignore the principle of divided voice that characterizes his art—even here. Collective victory leads to common celebration, but the private split in the narrator's self before the battle does not change afterward. "I was nothing more than an echo of voices long since extinguished . . . ," he had realized. "I thought I was living my own life, I was only inventing it. I thought I had escaped the ghosts, I was only extending their power" (p. 133). His pact with Katriel, to help Katriel conquer fear in exchange for remembrance, confirms the burden that makes David's identity hostage to others, since Katriel disappears during the fighting and David inherits only one more ghost to mourn. When he tells Katriel's desolate wife Malka that the "worst thing is to have dead eyes and still be alive" (p. 146), he reaffirms the dilemma that liberation has not solved for him. And though Malka offers him her love in an attempt to establish a link with the missing Katriel, David cannot accept it because it seems to him a betrayal of the dead—and of the living who cannot share it. But repudiating it is also a betrayal, since it opens the possibility of a fulfillment that was denied the victims, who can be affirmed if not reborn through its consummation in their behalf. "There lies the trap," concludes David, the survivor-narrator: "the yes and the no carry the same weight, open or shut the same gates to the same redemption" (p. 142).

But if, as he continues, love is not a solution to the atrocities of the past, whereas "outside of love there is no solution" (p. 143), how are we to escape from the paradox?

We are not; we are left only with shifting attitudes, voices expressing points of view that cannot cohere into a unified vision. Wiesel undermines his own efforts at imaginative integration, almost as if he were convinced that integration might prove irreverent. It is worth repeating some of the closing words from *A Beggar in Jerusalem*, echoing the sober and even weary tone of Camus at the end of *The Plague*: "Victory does not prevent suffering from having existed, nor death from having taken its toll" (p. 210). The cheering crowds in that novel, celebrating the lifting of the quarantine, resemble the rejoicing soldiers in this one, standing reverently by the Wall, whose stones are souls, says the narrator, rebuilding an invisible temple. But he also recalls that the soul of his mother (like Wiesel's) "found shelter in fire and not in stone" (p. 197). No matter how much he may dream in her place beside the Wall she never saw, he knows that any request he may slip between its cracks cannot be addressed to the future but must acknowledge the power of the other victims and herself to punish or forgive, "to take pity on a world which has betrayed and rejected them" (p. 208). In the end, victory in Jerusalem cannot undo defeat in Auschwitz, whose legacy is still "ambiguity and the quest arising from it" (p. 210). Long after the Six Day War, history has ceased to beckon with illusions of final victory and redemption; and the survivor continues to search for gestures—including an appropriate gesture of silence—to tranquilize the memories that goad his existence.

Wiesel continues that search too; it is his destiny, which the passage of time does not change. The successor of the Six Day War, the Yom Kippur War, confirms his belief that "a Jew lives in more than one place, in more than one era, on more than one level." Oppression unites the defenders and reminds them that to be Jewish "is to be possessed of a historical consciousness that transcends individual consciousness." But this is Wiesel in his affirmative mood, inspired by the need to unify a nation and a people, dispersed throughout the world. We know from his other writing that to be Jewish is also to be a survivor possessed of an individual consciousness so victimized by memory and remorse that historical consciousness seems a timid palliative. Historical consciousness here is a brave but impotent diversion from the ungraspable fact that at its worst the Holocaust does not speak with the voice of history, but with a private, unprecedented vocabulary awakening no resonances in previous or future events. Its voice cannot be transcended; it must be deciphered before it can be heard. Like the Jew in history, the Holocaust survivor "lives in more than one place, in more than one era, on more than one level." What better illustrates Wiesel's divided perspective than these words, which celebrate Jewish resistance in an essay called "Against Despair," but are equally appropriate to describe the insulated fate of the survivor, who is not—who never will be—"possessed of a historical consciousness that transcends individual consciousness" because the kind of death he has experienced blocks all transcendence. "Every survivor will tell you," Wiesel announces elsewhere in a clear countervoice, "that he could easily have stayed *there*, and in a way that is where he still is." 50

Wiesel's most recent novel, *The Oath*, suggests—perhaps unintentionally—the impossibility of fusing historical consciousness of Jewish destiny with individual consciousness of Holocaust fate. By choosing an anachronistic theme—a twentieth-century, pre-Holocaust pogrom that desroys all members but one of the Jewish community of Kolvillàg—he plunges us into a violent but familiar world of traditional anti-Semitism that has little connection with the technological genocide of gas chambers and crematoriums. The carnage that concludes the novel represents not a dispassionate, systematic program of extermination but a temporary outburst of animosity, an expression of ancient superstitious rage against supposed Jewish ritual murder of Christian children. If the cause is artistically unconvincing, however, the effects are not, since we know how easily mass slaughter can coexist in our time with the modern "civilized" state. The more dramatic theme of the novel is not what happened, but how and whether to tell about it. The sole survivor, Azriel, has taken a vow of silence (for reasons that we shall examine); then, in order to convince a suicidal youth that his despair is based on ignorance, not lucidity (echoing a conviction of Camus), he breaks his vow. The destruction of Kolvillàg has taught him an unappealing truth, whose connection with the Holocaust is obvious: "Whether life has meaning or not, what matters is not to make a gift of it to death. All you will get in return is a corpse. And corpses stink—I know something about that." [51] The idea that silence must be integrated into this vision of reality—a silence expressed *through* speech—achieves its fullest paradoxical statement by Wiesel in this novel, and indeed is the major source of its originality and power.

Azriel announces his dilemma clearly:

> "The story that is mine, I have been forbidden to tell.
> And so, what am I expected to do? I should like to be able to speak without betraying myself, without lying.
> I should like to be able to live without self-reproach.
> I should like to remain silent without turning my very silence into a lie or a betrayal." (p. 41)

The Oath is a crucial novel because it contains a coherent rationale for this position, far more sustained than anything that has previously appeared—the sermon of Moshe the Madman. It offers the most cogent argument to date for the counterposition to Wiesel's own earlier conviction that to "be a Jew today . . . means: to testify." [52] Moshe's action—his willingness to sacrifice himself in order to save the town, by "confessing" to the ritual murder—is a gesture of martyrdom in an age that no longer supports such heroism. His deed prevents nothing because the morality of atrocity—or its amorality—recognizes none of the conduct that once lent credence and meaning to martyrdom. The pogrom—this is perhaps one of its inconsistencies—proceeds beneath the shadows of certain Holocaust truths. Moshe's act begets nothing, but his words survive through the medium of narrative art.

Moshe's sermon illustrates the dialogue within the monologue that is characteristic of Wiesel's literary manner. He speaks eloquently for both sides, and if he finally chooses one, its opposite lingers in our imagination, absorbed but not supplanted by the "victorious" position. From Job to the present, the impulse to bear witness to suffering has been a major impetus to survival: "And I only am escaped alone to tell thee." Many Holocaust survivors, having lost all else, cite this as a main reason for clinging to life in an otherwise hopeless situation. Moshe sums up that view before repudiating it: "Since the executioner seemed to be immortal, the survivor-storyteller would be immortal too. Jews felt that to forget constituted a crime against memory as well as against justice: whoever forgets becomes the executioner's accomplice" (p. 237). But when a holy responsibility is transformed by events, by the empirical consequences of the act of testifying, into a platitude that leaves auditors indifferent (or justifies further atrocities), then it is time to reexamine the adequacy of that responsibility. "Words have been our weapon, our shield," says Moshe; "the tale, our lifeboat. . . . Since, in the end, someone would be left to describe our death, then death would be defeated; such was our deep, unshakable conviction" (p. 238). But he himself pierces the facade of this rhetoric and leaves a gaping wound in its logic: men have been merely distressed or annoyed by the survivors' tales of woe. History, as one more extermination threatens his people, has finally convinced him that dependence on the value and importance of testimony represents an exhausted faith, adherence to a belief that an age of atrocity no longer supports. Several of Wiesel's literary themes coalesce at this moment, as a voice proclaims death's triumph, not defeat—and then suggests silence as the only remaining strategy to arrest its further aggression.

To propose the abdication of the word, the *refusal* to testify, as a sacred alternative to the legendary obligation of bearing witness is indeed a unique approach to the ordeal of extermination. Moshe's argument forces the imagination to cross new frontiers of possibility. Wiesel himself has contended that the publicity accorded the Holocaust after the event made later atrocities easier to commit and easier to absorb into the capacious sponge of history. From this point of view, Moshe's logic, though unconventional, is irreproachable: "If suffering and the history of suffering were intrinsically linked, then the one could be abolished by attacking the other; by ceasing to refer to the events of the present, we would forestall ordeals in the future" (p. 239). Is he correct? Such a question is itself incorrect. At this moment, fiction has little to do with literal truth. Moshe's position represents imagined reality, a voice from the depths of art, adding a new proposal for facing (not mastering) the riddle of meaningless death, the burden of dying for nothing. If obsession with the history of suffering, says Moshe, surveying the past of his people, ironically sanctions its proliferation and repetition, then muting that obsession seems a viable option. For the first time in Wiesel's work, the cry for silence is more than a spontaneous impulse, nurtured by his sense of language's inability to capture the unspeakable. The fact that the rationale falls from the lips of a fanatic, a man called Moshe the Madman,

only intensifies its ambiguous appeal. And Wiesel's epitaph to
him—"last prophet and first messiah of a mankind that is no
more" (p. 281)—further complicates the strength of his entreaty.
The reader is left with a twin legacy: the voice of Moshe and a
village reduced to ashes; a vow of silence and the concrete images
of charred dwellings, charred corpses, charred dreams and
prayers and songs.

The Oath is itself a response to the other oath that Moshe
imposes on his fellow townspeople—never to reveal "how I
survived . . . . Nor how the dead perished" (p. 242). Since Azriel
is the lone survivor, he inherits the full responsibility of keeping
the pact. If he ultimately breaks it, he does so through
compromise rather than repudiation, establishing a precedent for
Wiesel's own confrontation with the world of Auschwitz and its
tale of agony. Ever since *Night*, that confrontation has been elusive
and indirect, carried on in the eerie half-light of a consciousness
that protects itself from intrusions while admitting visitors to
scattered glimpses of a haunted realm. "I shall not allow a
stranger to desecrate your sanctuary," Azriel assures his dead
when deciding to speak, then carefully defines the limits of his
revelation: "The event shall remain whole. I shall tell neither
cause nor effect. I shall not reveal the enormity of the secret, I
shall only indicate its existence. I shall show only the spark"
(p. 13). But by the end of the novel, when the spark erupts into a
conflagration and the idea of "cause and effect" disintegrates into
a *Totentanz* of frenzied massacre, the "secret" is not so obscure: we
witness the orgiastic mayhem that results when irrational
prejudice goes berserk.

But this is precisely what we do not witness in the systematic
annihilations of the Holocaust; hence some readers may find
dubious Azriel's observation on the final page of the novel: "On
that night man's work yielded to the power and judgment of the
fire. And suddenly I understood with every fiber of my being why
I was shuddering at this vision of horror: I had just glimpsed the
future" (p. 281). The ultimate effect of *The Oath* is just the
opposite: the unprecedented future of the Holocaust finds no
precedent in the flames of this pogrom. It is a consummation of
past hatreds, not a prediction of the one to come. *The Oath* finally
persuades us of *difference*, not similarity. "When death reigns,"
Azriel discovers, "no one is spared"—and the principle still
governs our understanding of the Holocaust, and of human

behavior beneath its shadow. But the subsequent insight is less relevant: "When the avenging gods are human wolves, there can be no hope for man" (p. 279). When the avenging *men*, the murderers in the deathcamps, were human *beings*, not ravenous beasts or demons, there was also no hope for man: and *this* is a secret that Holocaust victims, misled perhaps by the very theory of "human wolves" explaining pogroms like the one in *The Oath*, failed to comprehend. Denied outside aid, paralyzed by fear of a mob threat that was all too vivid in memory and history, the Jews of Kolvillàg await their fate with a clear foreknowledge of its contours. Moshe the Madman's vain attempt to "confess" the crime of killing a Christian child has proven the futility of individual gestures of martyrdom. How much more clearly can we now understand the situation of the Holocaust victim, who was not even faced with the allegation of crime, who confronted a danger that could not be allied with a motivated hatred or a reason for annihilation. One might say that the "version of victimization" dramatized in *The Oath* is no more satisfactory for understanding the behavior of victims in the deathcamps than are the versions of survival woven from traditional vocabulary about human dignity for comprehending the conduct of survivors.

But each one, each version, encourages us to discriminate, to refuse to lapse into comfortable and comforting simplifications of a catastrophe that will not be contained. Even a rationale for silence, tempting as it may sound, does not clarify the other dilemmas generated by the Holocaust. Not talking about it is one thing; not knowing about it is another. In one sense, all writing about the Holocaust represents a retrospective effort to give meaningless history a context of meaning, to furnish the mind with a framework for insight without diminishing the sorrow of the event itself. *Knowledge* of this past cannot be exorcised: Wiesel discovered this melancholy truth when he tried to visit Germany after the war, and during his brief returns to his native town of Sighet. These journeys were in vain—what should he have expected to accomplish? Perhaps the failure to exorcise the past in life compels him to recreate crucial moments from it in his art—though aesthetically he achieves no more resolution than he did in life. The theme of "return" does not lead to rebirth, but only to a greater sense of frustration and a fresh encounter with grief. The ruthlessness of the executioners, the impotence of the victims, the indifference of the spectators float in bewildering suspension; the need to understand meets stubborn resistance from recalcitrant facts that defy the mind's urge to interpret. The events run in advance of critical attitudes that may one day unlock their mysteries.

In 1968, Elie Wiesel ended *Legends of Our Time* with an essay called "A Plea for the Dead." A decade later, in 1978, he ended *A Jew Today* with an essay called "A Plea for the Survivors." There is both logic and justice in the evolution, since the two concerns have been interwoven in his work from the beginning. His version of survival is explicit and unambiguous on one point: "If you have not grasped it until now, it is time you did: Auschwitz signifies death—total, absolute death—of man and of mankind, of reason and of the heart, of language and of the senses. Auschwitz is the death of time, the end of creation; its mystery is doomed to stay whole, inviolate." Before we can understand what the survivor has survived *to*, we must comprehend what he has survived *from*; and once we have achieved that, we can no longer view the survival experience—as Bettelheim, Frankl, and Des Pres do, each in his own fashion—as a resolute turning from annihilation to life, from humiliation to dignity, from death to affirmation. Our burden would be eased, our task simplified, if Wiesel's insistence that survivor testimonies "seem to have been written by one man, always the same," [53] were *true*; but as we have seen, this is far from the case. Survivors' voices are as divided as his, though his vision is far more comprehensive because it *includes* the contradictions that separate one survivor account from another.

His occasional lapses into melodrama or exaggeration are inconsequential when compared to the ruthless honesty of his portrait of survivors on Liberation Day 1945, lifting the experience out of the secure moral frame of choice (and consequence) and suspending it in the disconcerting moral void of chance:

> They did not know how they had eluded the enemy and cheated death. They knew they had nothing to do with it. The choice had not been theirs. Intelligence, education, intuition, experience, courage—nothing had counted. Everything had been arranged by chance, only chance. A step toward the right or the left, a movement begun too early or too late, a change in mood of a particular overseer, and their fate would have been different. In the ghettos the question had been whether it was wiser to hold on to the

yellow certificates or, rather, to the red attestations? Whether
to hide in the attics or in the cellars? In the camps, would it
have been better to take initiatives and call in sick? To stand
up straight, or to make oneself so small as to disappear in the
amorphous mass? Invented and perfected by the killers, the
pattern of concentration-camp rules eluded their victims,
who, submissive and stunned, were in no condition to
discern the traps, the warning signals of death.

Our blessing is that such a world was temporary; our curse is that
it was at all. The deathcamps prove, if we need such evidence, that
for their moment in time, the universe was not governed—by
human power or divine—for man's benefit. No theory of suffering
or redemptive behavior, whether religious or secular, embraces
the random, impenetrable threat to existence as Wiesel describes
it here. Both ancient and modern images of human dignity crumble
when the combined values of western civilization—intelligence,
education, intuition, experience, courage—prove futile against the
contrived cunning of the murderers. Perhaps we crave reassurance
about the dignity available to victims and survivors in the
deathcamps to shore up our own waning sense, in this undignified
century, of the dignity still available to ourselves. Wiesel calls the
Holocaust a world where "the living and the dead are no longer
separate." [54] It is a line that defines our century, if not yet our
consciousness of it, our legacy from Auschwitz and all its
successors, where mass slaughter and mounds of corpses fracture
the horizon of hope that once tempted us with the promise of an
unimpaired future.

For Wiesel, that future will never be the same, though he is the
first to admit the futility of trying to explain why. When he says
that a Holocaust literature is a contradiction in terms, he does not
imply that it is impossible to write about the Holocaust; he
signifies, and he says so, that Auschwitz "negates all theories and
doctrines; to lock it into a philosophy means to restrict it." Words
inevitably distort the event, which is why any version of survival
can be only that—a version, limited by memory, insight, and
vocabulary. Wiesel would go further, and add imagination,though
all would not share his belief. He tells his audience in "A Plea for
the Survivors" that it was easier for a survivor "to imagine himself
free in Auschwitz than it would be for you to imagine yourself a
prisoner there," though some commentators, as we have seen,

attempt to close the gap by relying on traditional language to describe what Wiesel calls "being painfully, excruciatingly alive" in the deathcamp. That excruciating sense of death in life, which resulted in real death for most, survival for too few, forms the incommunicable core of memory for the latter, whose experiences still seize us with their essential paradox: "It is as impossible to speak of them as not to speak of them." Wiesel's conviction that one "would have to invent a new vocabulary, a new language to say what no human being has ever said" [55] is both admonition and challenge, and returns us to a central issue of this book: that access to the event (as well as distortion of it) is intimately allied to the language, the terminology, the very nuances of words that we use to give it substance.

If anyone ever *were* to write a definitive unholy scripture recording man's extermination and God's absence in Auschwitz, it would resemble no Bible or other holy text we know of. Satan, that restless spirit, would finally get *his* turn to be an author. As if to confirm this, one Auschwitz survivor called his memoir of the experience *Was Dante Nicht Sah (What Dante Did Not See)*.[56] "And who says the truth is made to be revealed," asks the irascible Menahem-Mendl of Kotzk, in Wiesel's *Souls on Fire*: "It must be sought. That's all." [57] But this "all" does not follow the path of normal discourse, ordinary inquiry, familiar imaginative endeavor. More than truth is concerned: we meddle with the integrity of the dead. This explains much of Wiesel's aversion to "making literature"of the Holocaust, since one runs the risk of transforming the human beings who suffered it—as victims or survivors—into "characters" defined by epithets: "abject," "pitiful," "dignified," "heroic." As we shall see, Nelly Sachs virtually discards the adjective from her poetic vocabulary as a usable grammatical form, whereas Gertrud Kolmar employs it as a literary bulwark against an encroaching terror she was unable or unwilling to define. The pre-Holocaust voice of Kolmar still celebrates the marriage between art and vision, vision and value. The post-Holocaust poems of Nelly Sachs proclaim the sundering of all such consoling alliances. They introduce us to an unmoored reality; they seem to be written, like the survivor memoirs that Wiesel praises, "not with words but against them." Wiesel provides us with a frame, if not with a formula, for the kind of writing appropriate to an unspeakable event: "Every word contains a hundred, and the silence between the words strikes us

as hard as the words themselves." [58] Language must learn to
include that thundering silence, from a darkened cosmos as well
as from man's whispering lips, when it confronts the Holocaust—
just as versions of survival, to be faithful to the event, must
acknowledge the ashes that cling to the garments of the survivor
long after he is restored to the community of the living.

FOUR

You! When the bitter hour ripens, I
will rise up here and now,
I will be your arch of triumph,
through which agonies proceed.
Gertrud Kolmar, "We Jews"

O such a death!
Where all helping angels
with bleeding wings
hung mangled
in the barbed wire of time!
Nelly Sachs, "Why the black
answer of hate?"

Gertrud Kolmar and Nelly Sachs:
BRIGHT VISIONS AND
SONGS OF LAMENTATION

"It is an old dream of the poets," says Heinz Politzer, speaking of
the German Jewish poetess Elsa Lasker-Schüler, who died in
Jerusalem in 1944, "to find a language in which feeling and vision
can express themselves without subservience to the rules of
linguistic logic." [1] Poets like Gertrud Kolmar and Nelly Sachs,
wrestling respectively with the impending or completed doom of
the Holocaust, faced a similar if not an identical challenge: to find
a language in which feeling and vision might express themselves
without subservience to the rules of linguistic habit. Their concern
with "feeling and vision" rather than literal truth returns us to the
distinction in Charlotte Delbo between *"vrai"* and *"véridique,"*
what actually happened and how one attempts to express that
event. We have seen how the choice of words can control
response and manipulate interpretation, making of the Holocaust
a *verbally rendered* event, a *recaptured* reality offering the
contemporary reader (and future generations) accounts of the
deathcamp experience covering a wide spectrum of implication.
With the exception of the few narratives buried in the vicinity of
the gas chambers, all accounts are filtered through memory and
imagination, to say nothing of the unconscious tensions that afflict

any author working with such unmalleable material. The survival narrative can thus serve personal needs as well as objective truths. The encounter with Holocaust disorder paradoxically encourages the discovery of refuges from its chaos and even, as we have seen, of some vessels of meaning scattered beneath its unruly terrain.

Writing from the safe sanctuary of Palestine, Elsa Lasker-Schüler could nevertheless distill in a single stanza the dilemma facing the poet in search of the *mot juste* at a time when neither language nor precision could be trusted:

> *Ich habe zu Hause ein blaues Klavier*
> *Und kenne doch keine Note.*
> *Es steht im Dunkel der Kellertür,*
> *Seitdem die Welt verrohte.*

> I have in my home a blue piano
> And yet don't know one note.
> It stands in darkness near the cellar door
> Since the world turned brutal.[2]

The brutality of the Holocaust universe, against which Gertrud Kolmar built psychological defenses, resolutely playing her own "blue piano" while hoping to retune the times to its resonance as those times threatened to stifle her spirit; upon which Nelly Sachs cast vagrant flashes of illumination, as word and spirit clashed in her poems over a landscape of corpses—this brutality continues to perplex a vocabulary determined to join a combat for which it was never properly armed. Between the indomitable towers that recur in Gertrud Kolmar's verse and the melancholy chimneys of Nelly Sachs hovers the mournful history of extermination, which consumed the one poet while the other narrowly escaped—only to make what she called the tragedy of the Jewish people her perpetual theme. Together they offer us a vivid commentary on the potential metamorphoses tugging at the idea of human dignity, and the language affirming it, before and after the Holocaust era.

If, as I have been suggesting, that idea would be radically altered by the deathcamp experience, Gertrud Kolmar had little premonition of the fact. Her letters and poems offer eloquent testimony, almost a summation, of how powerfully a vocabulary and imagery of reassurance could operate to sustain the human spirit against vague threats of annihilation. How much of Jewish (and world) refusal to accept the tangible reality of Auschwitz resulted from a failure or inability to verbalize and imagine what it really meant, and from the easy availability of a language of transcendence to express what Camus would call the nostalgia of hope? Dante's disciplined punishments in the *Inferno* were no precedent for the unthinkable, which had not been assaulting the human imagination for centuries and millenia, as had the promised blessings of his *Paradiso* and similar ethical, philosophical, and religious systems. The values of those systems supported Kolmar during her dismal years in Berlin prior to her deportation. Indeed, that pre-Holocaust period in her life seems to enact the drama of survival that commenators like Frankl and Bettelheim attribute to inmates who endured the oppressions of the camps—a circumstance that does not validate their views, but that testifies to the undiminished force of those values in the post-Auschwitz era. Kolmar's life before Auschwitz may have depended on them; but once her extermination had been decided on, they could do nothing to prevent it.

Gertrud Kolmar did not live to hear the acclaim her work would one day receive: it was the final irony in a career that resembled a tragedy of unfulfillment, the story of one representative victim among millions whose deaths, like Elie Wiesel's father's, were irrelevant to the lives that preceded them. She never enjoyed a steady reciprocity to the love she felt so capable of giving, never bore the child she longed for, never even suspected the reputation her art would one day earn her in her native land. Yet she never surrendered hope and clung to the solace that she could still control her attitude toward her destiny, if not the events that shaped it. Her imagination quickened as the difficulties of her daily existence grew, and we are left with the paradox of her determination to perceive life more intensely even as the prospects for expressing her exuberance diminished. Her tragedy of unfulfillment is thus mitigated—up to a point—by the ripening of her inner vision.

Our access to this vision is aided by a unique volume, her *Briefe an die Schwester Hilde*, letters written to her sister in Switzerland from September 1938 to February 1943, when together with other Jewish forced-laborers she was rounded up in a "factory action" in Berlin and deported to Auschwitz. She was never heard from again. Thus she does not write as a survivor, but as one who was convinced that she could bear any persecution imposed on her with dignity and inner strength. She still believes in the moral authority of language, a legacy that Nelly Sachs will question in virtually every line of her verse. In a limited sense, Kolmar's letters comprise her spiritual autobiography, but from a wider perspective they give us a glimpse of the reasons why so many potential victims misread the nihilistic truths of the deathcamp universe: not because they refused to believe the worst, but because their own system of values, and particularly the language that articulated it, was not flexible enough to admit the possibility of that "worst's" eventual success. The failure was not one of belief, but of *vision*: and who can be censured for not envisioning, for not possessing the verbal or imaginative capacity *to* envision such a totally unprecedented catastrophe?

If in 1943, in Berlin, after *Kristallnacht*, after the mobile killing units had nearly completed their work in the Soviet Union, after Belzec and Chelmno had been in operation for almost a year, after numerous friends and neighbors had "disappeared" and her own father had been transported to Theresienstadt (though it is not certain that she knew of his destination or what kind of place it was), after three-and-a-half years of military victories for Germany, Kolmar could *still* write about mastering her destiny—then surely she was not merely a naïve victim of propaganda or self-deception. She had no illusions about avoiding a harsh fate (though she could not have known its exact nature); but she genuinely believed—she will be perfectly explicit about this—in the power of the will to transfigure physical suffering into moral strength and to accept even death (not extermination, but simply cessation of living in some "manageable" and potentially heroic form) with equanimity. Under duress, action seemed less important to her than attitude: and whether this confirms a truth of religious or secular humanism, individual human psychology, Jewish mentality or heritage, or—as is more probable—a combination of all three, we gain from her letters an under-standing of how the sense of dislocation induced by Nazi strategy against the Jews could paralyze the will to action and lull the victim—but only before deportation—with illusions of inner security. We should not be surprised that so many survival narratives, notwithstanding the radically different environment of the deathcamps, transfer this belief in the power of attitude to the inmates themselves, and use it to explain or justify their survival.

Kolmar's letters to her sister between 1939 and 1943, some of the darkest years in modern Jewish and European history, are all the more dramatic because she had no way of knowing for certain how very black these years would turn out to have been after all the postwar evidence was assembled. Because her letters were subject to censorship, she could not mention significant daily events (like her father's deportation) except in the most allusive way; thus they cannot contain an explicit history of Jewish anguish during this fatal period. But they do contain equally important revelations, about a kind of preliminary version of survival that is relevant to the theme of this study. They record the struggle of the poet to retain her spiritual independence while history sought to quench its flame. Because of the censorship and her own sister's need for psychological support in a strange land, she virtually banished despair from her letters and even apologized for inadvertently making her sister believe that she was suffering excessively. Whatever pain she feels she turns inward, and it emerges in a series of searching analyses of the creative process and the dilemma of the artist at a time when external reality was hostile to her imaginative endeavors.

Heinz Politzer, describing the dilemma of Elsa Lasker-Schüler in "exile" in Palestine, a "Hebrew poetess in the German tongue," conjures up the image of the Jew—"homeless but at home in his homelessness"—as a new source for the myth of modern man.[3] We recognize his features in Kafka's Joseph K. and Bellow's Herzog, men confused and distracted by external reality though unlike Lasker-Schüler they are not alien to their environments. And so for Gertrud Kolmar, who seeks for a "home" amid her feeling of homelessness as a way of ensuring continuity in an otherwise disrupted existence. For fifteen years she had lived with her family in Finkenkrug, a Berlin suburb, with its spacious gardens and appealing natural surroundings. She never recovered from the forced sale of this home near the end of 1938, when harsh Nazi laws against Jewish ownership of real estate were enacted. Together with her father (her mother died in 1930) she moved to an urban neighborhood in Berlin, where they were forced to take in lodgers, and the quality of *Fremdheit* or strangeness that infuses so many of her later poems owes part of its inspiration to this unhappy experience. She reported to her sister with some dismay her failure to accustom herself to her new surroundings:

The day before yesterday I was walking along
Martin-Luther-Strasse and Neue Winterfeldstrasse, which I
don't know very well. I suddenly realized with some
bewilderment that contrary to my usual custom I hadn't
really noticed at all the houses, the shops, or the people I
encountered. "Be observant and pay attention," I
commanded myself. Good. But five minutes later I stopped
"seeing" again, and my gaze once more turned inward, as it
were, like a day-dreaming and inattentive pupil in school.
Soon we'll have been here for six months, and I simply can't
establish a relationship—bearable or unbearable—with this
neighborhood. I'm as alien here as I was on the first day.[4]

How many Jews across Europe, some still in their own homes,
some shifted to new areas or to ghettos, struggled with a similar
sense of dislocation, so overwhelmed by the need to continue
feeling at home in their homelessness that like Kolmar they
turned their gaze inward and ceased to "see" the reality around
them? This was neither cowardice nor denial, unconscious
collaboration with forces intent on one's own destruction or even
a naïve failure to recognize crisis. Although it is impossible to
reconstruct exactly the atmosphere of persecution preceding
actual deportation to the deathcamps, "turning inward" appears
to have been a common psychological phenomenon, not as an
escape but as a *positive* (though ultimately ineffectual) response to
oppression. Unlike Gandhi, who *was* naïve in this respect, Kolmar
had no illusions about changing the views of her enemies; her
version of survival at this moment in her life (May 1939) was
perfectly legitimate, since she faced only physical inconvenience,
not physical annihilation.

Ironically, in the same letter she informs her sister that she has
turned her face "toward the East," acknowledging an impulse that
has been in her since she was a child. "I am really a kind of
'restrained Asiatic,' " she confesses, "and would be happy if the
restraint could be removed" (p. 24). Lurking behind this
fascination with the East—which of course would be the locale of
her doom and not of her salvation—is a partial explanation of her
refusal to flee westward like other members of her family: a
brother went as far as Australia. "My duty," she writes, "has
always lain, as it were, within me; it still does, and I only seek the
appropriate place to devote myself to it. And I don't know . . . I've

always thought that in America I wouldn't find the appropriate place" (pp. 24–25). We have no way of knowing what fate her inner commitment to duty might have suffered in an "inappropriate" place like Auschwitz; had she survived, she might well have joined the chorus of voices who insist that just such a commitment enabled them to come back alive. But we must consider the possibility that such views represent a necessary confirmation of pre-Holocaust values more than a revelation of successful survivor strategies in a moral jungle. Kolmar clung to them as her raison d'être: four months after the outbreak of war she still was prepared, like Boris Pasternak after her, to accept harassment even unto death rather than exile from the atmosphere that nourished her creative vision. The inhospitable welcome Switzerland accorded her sister, who was having great difficulty establishing a life for herself and her little daughter, must have strengthened Kolmar's resolution to remain in her native land. And she could not abandon her aged father, who said he was too old to leave.

The intensification of anti-Jewish legislation and finally the war itself suffused her with a sense of the rapid transformation of external reality. She retreated inward in a desperate attempt to find a stable point of reference, a refuge from the uncertainties threatening her identity as human being and Jew (though she was forbidden to mention the latter):

> It seems to me that things are changing their face and shape today with a furious swiftness; everything is altered, whirls about, nothing remains still, and what once took years or decades to change now needs only a few days. And meanwhile I've withdrawn deeper and deeper into what endures, into what *is*, into eternal process (which does not have to be only "religion," it can also be "nature" or "love"). (pp. 29–30)

She writes as if on the edge of chaos, but without words or images to describe it, offering us insight into a troubled imagination that nevertheless lacked an idiom to define precisely the source of its uneasiness. Even if rumors or actual reports of atrocity were to combine with the less extreme features of Nazi reality that she daily endured, she would have been unable to fuse them into a coherent vision of the unthinkable, because like most victims she needed an *inner* verbal irritant to crystallize how altered "things" really were. She speaks of the kaleidoscopic shifting of temporal experience and confesses the impossibility, not to say pointlessness, of organizing it into meaningful patterns. "In the street," she writes, "I often have a feeling of numbness and stupefaction, and yearn to awaken from it—but to no avail" (p. 30). The rupture between inner value and outward fact that proved to be one of the most devastating afflictions of the deathcamp here induces an incipient paralysis of the kind of vitality that permits the individual to interact effectively with her environment. That vitality was one of the first victims in the deathcamp, as the more fortunate inmate drifted into a "program" for survival. Gertrud Kolmar in Berlin had no idea how prophetic her description of her own dilemma would become.

Eventually her sense of disorientation must have affected her poetic impulse, since she appears to have written very few poems during the final five years of her life—in any event, none has survived. In 1940 she began studying Hebrew, almost as if she wished to liberate or revive that impulse by turning to a fresh idiom in a different language, though one also close to her heritage—becoming, as it were, a "German poetess in the Hebrew tongue." She did indeed compose some verses in Hebrew that her teacher thought worthy of publication—but these too seem to have disappeared. Nevertheless she devoted considerable space in her letters to the *idea* of art, and this helped to sustain her during these last years. It was not a flight from an unpleasant reality, but a journey into a more significant one, a deep source of affirmative vision that could not, however, arm her, that in fact *disarmed* her for the negative vision that loomed ahead. Her imagery, as she wrote to her sister about form, about the need to germinate the seed and nurture in the imagination the full flower of a poem or story (her last writing during this time was short fiction) before committing it to paper, was intuitively organic, celebrating growth rather than decay. Her every view of the creative act—and one wonders how many nonpoets among her fellow victims shared this instinct—assumed an infinitely expanding future, interrupted, to be sure, by pauses and setbacks (to be Jewish was to know disappointment) but ultimately responsive to persistence and determination. One would have to understand that the Germans had simply eliminated words like "germinate" and "nurture" from active Jewish vocabulary to realize how vulnerable Kolmar and the others made themselves by insisting on their current validity. But the poet drew on her image of herself as a positive sustaining force, and pitted it against the humiliating image that history imposed on her. If this made her more vulnerable—and it did—the reason is not a self-deluding hope that "things would be all right" (from Berlin to the ghettos "things" were already so bad that few could still entertain this illusion) or an ancient Jewish tradition of accepting suffering and oppression as one's destiny, but a mind so accustomed to *thinking* (whatever the brutal actuality) in words and images of reassurance that they left no space in the imagination for cultivating a darker idiom.

Kolmar saw her alienation as a private matter. She deplored the practice of her father's writer acquaintance, who was busy working on the end of a biography when the opening chapters were already in print. *Fabrikbetrieb*, "factory labor," she scornfully called such assembly-line procedure, which offended her sense of artistic integrity; her own work habits required a manuscript to lie for weeks or months before she took it up for revision. "She creates for the times," she distinguishes herself from her father's friend, "and I, probably with insufficient energy, try to create for eternity. In any event, she has success, and I—well, it's not important enough to me" (p. 107). This is the very vocabulary of martyrdom, as all those over the centuries discovered who, determined to "live" for eternity, were forced to "die" for the times. The nobility of language takes on a moral force—as it did in Gandhi's advice to the Jews—but the heroic overtones were silenced by the manner of their collective dying and the anonymity of their individual deaths.

What *was* important to Gertrud Kolmar was her unviolated sense of herself, though as we have seen, this notion of psychological and spiritual integrity could be virtually annihilated by the conditions of deathcamp existence. She was exasperated by the talk of her tenants about relatives who had emigrated; one wonders whether her displeasure betrays a secret misgiving about her own decision to stay behind. Her analogy, when writing to her sister on the subject, is illuminating:

> for me it's a little like what I observed during the last war [World War I] in soldiers returning from battle: without really noticing it, they and those who had remained behind didn't understand each other any more, and spoke different

languages. And a mutual good intention to draw closer
together changed nothing. Perhaps a similar situation exists
between the emigrés and those who remained here. (p. 110)

Talk of emigration in the autumn of 1941 was indeed an exercise
in illusion, and Kolmar was too honest to waste any of her
previous intellectual energy on it. She was on the verge of
discovering that different languages also separated those in the
deathcamps from those outside, though she never had time to
translate *that* insight into words. The harshness of her external
situation crystallized her isolation, and in an odd way helped to
"justify" it in her own mind. Her goal was a kind of autism of the
imagination, that would allow undistracted free reign to the
vigorous power of her inner vision. At work one day she noticed a
young Gypsy woman whose tired face betrayed an enviable
aloofness:

> an impenetrable seclusion, a tranquility, a distance that was
> now unreachable by any word or glance from the outside
> world . . . and I knew: this was what I always wanted to have,
> but still couldn't possess completely; because if I had it,
> nothing and no one from outside could touch me. But I'm
> well on the way to getting there, and that makes me happy.
> (p. 114)

No wonder the geography of space did not tempt her; the inward
geography of the mind and imagination was the crucial locus of
her existence.

The aspiration to nurture an imaginative—and imagined—life
until it became an impenetrable fortress may sound futile and
perhaps even irresponsible to our retrospective ears; but by the
autumn of 1941, when Kolmar envisioned a state in which
"nothing and no one from outside could touch me," gestures of
defiance or resistance must have seemed even more futile to her.
Although Berlin was not a ghetto or deathcamp, her persecutors
still determined where she could live and work and controlled the
other limits of her physical freedom. She rapidly realized that the
only area accessible to her own power of choice was that inner
empire of attitudes, over which she continued to rule. Before
deportation, that made a significant difference in her existence; it
still plays a vital role, as we have seen, in numerous versions of

survival, as a cultural inheritance from the difficult pre-Holocaust years. As a source of security and of confidence in the durability of the human spirit Kolmar's increasing dependence on her inner strength is admirable; but she had no illusions about using it as the basis for a shared communal regeneration. Nor did she ever dream of testing its force against the unimaginable travail of a place like Auschwitz.

Perhaps the most revealing admission about the secret of her ability to endure her destiny as a Jew in wartime Berlin with a kind of heroic resignation occurs in a letter of July 1942. Perverse as it may sound, the hardships she faced under Nazi persecution challenged the resourcefulness of her spirit as the comforts of peacetime Germany could not. She was determined to resist Nazi efforts to erase her dignity and humanity; in fact, she seemed to grow inwardly stronger as the external situation began to deteriorate. But she was not facing slow starvation, beatings, exhausting work, and the omnipresent threat of the gas chamber. Her struggle did not unite her with the other oppressed. There is even some evidence that she enjoyed her martyrdom, though one speaks here only of the "martyrdom" of forced labor in Berlin, not of the horrors of Auschwitz. "Unfortunately," she laments to her sister,

> what depresses me so is that my view or attitude, wherever I express it, almost never finds an echo. So I express it seldom enough. I can't transfer to my fellow-sufferers any of the spiritual strength that I possess. If I enter into a deeper relationship with any of them, they can only diminish it in me, without having any benefit from it themselves. They don't understand me, perhaps consider me supercilious. (p. 160)

As a child, she writes, she wanted to be a Spartan woman, and later, a heroine. The circumstances of Nazi oppression in Berlin provided her with an opportunity to become what she needed to become in order to express her inner resources, and she modestly acknowledged that such simple logic deserved no special admiration. She simply required an antagonist commensurate with her capacity for spiritual strength and self-assertion; her resolution to meet the oppressor with a posture of firmness, betraying no vestige of the craven or submissive, confirms the heroic quality of her inner life. But how serviceable was the myth of the Spartan woman—or man—in Auschwitz? Only today do we savor the bitter irony of Kolmar's celebration of Goethe's aphorism about a human destiny that did not foresee the deathcamps: "What we wish for in youth achieves fullness in age."

Gertrud Kolmar's letters represent not so much a growth of the poet's mind as a gradual disclosure and assertion of qualities within her that had long sought expression. Her loneliness is not new, but it has been brought into sharper focus by National Socialist policies against the Jews. Similarly, her impulse to embrace her destiny, whatever it may be, is not new, though external conditions have clarified its importance in her life; but before we discover analogies between the possibilities of dignity in Berlin and those same possibilities in Auschwitz, we need to remember that Kolmar's "external conditions" did not include deportation in a sealed boxcar, gassing, and cremation. As she so often does, she conjures up a metaphor to define her situation, one characteristically ripe with organic form. Unlike Napoleon's soldiers who, she says, returned home after his fall from power proclaiming that they had forgotten nothing and learned nothing, Kolmar declares that she has forgotten nothing but learned much from her ordeals: "Above all, this: *amor fati*—love of fate. To be sure, the germ has always been within me, perhaps even as a green stalk; but only now have blossoms developed and burst forth from their buds" (p. 196). The vitality of the image contradicts the resignation implicit in the idea of *amor fati*, but such a tension is at the heart of Kolmar's personality, and much of her art. Her statement about love of fate appears in a letter written little more than a month before her deportation, and reveals the struggle of a vital spirit to survive in an atmosphere polluted by hatred and oppression. But much of the struggle is *verbal*, a saying rather than a doing; her letters (like her poems) replaced deeds, *became* deeds—they were her lifeline to reality.

We can illustrate this process through the content of a letter she wrote to Hilde on Christmas Eve of 1941—the longest letter in the collection. Although she obviously had more time just before a holiday, the subject was clearly of crucial importance to her. It is impossible to tell today how much of her story is real, how much fantasy, but she presents the account of her unconsummated love affair with a twenty-one-year-old fellow factory worker (she herself was past forty-seven) with such patient detail and attention to gestures and nuances that one is encouraged to accept it as true in the reading of it. At moments like these one penetrates the essential loneliness of Gertrud Kolmar's life and realizes that her poems were a celebration of *and* a shield against the reality that she longed for and feared. Evidently Hilde was disturbed by this exaggerated love story, because in her reply, as we discern from Gertrud's own response, she warned her sister against disappointment and confusing illusion with reality. Gertrud was defensive and even truculent as she sought to justify the authenticity of her relationship with the young man, as if deep down she herself suspected the fragility of her expectations. Through her argument shines the essentially tragic nature of her world view—a view that prepares one for the worst, but not for the unthinkable. She did not fear disappointment because she recognized in advance the high price a human being had to pay for the brief radiance of love. Perhaps this explains her ability to accept her situation in Berlin with such equanimity—she had no illusions about her ultimate fate, because her tragedy of unfulfillment was not unprecedented: the Spartan woman was only one of many prototypical heroines who had already enacted the unhappy destiny that (she thought) lay before her. But there is also a touch of pathos in her confession to her sister some months later: "what I experience, slight as it may be, somehow affects me more forcibly than it used to" (p. 152). If the uneventful life is not worth living, the invented one must take its place. Experience not only becomes the stuff of her art; in regard to her factory romance, it becomes an expression of art itself, where words assume the reality that life denied.

Probably no one who has not experienced the constant uneasiness of this period—especially for a Jew still living in Berlin in 1943—can fully imagine the anguish Gertrud Kolmar must have suffered during the final weeks of her life, with the fate of her deported father unknown and her own future so uncertain. But anyone with the patience to trace her spiritual history through her correspondence during the crucial years 1938 to 1943 cannot fail to admire her resolution to retain her equilibrium as her burdens increased. Near the end of 1942 she recorded a conversation with a certain Dr. H., a Spinoza scholar, about the freedom of the human will in the midst of bondage. "I felt," she says, that I understood this very well from my own experience. Since I had not had the option to accept or reject this factory work, which I had been ordered to do, I had to acquiesce and was compelled to do it. But I was free to consent to it or refuse it *inwardly*, to approach it reluctantly or willingly. In that moment when I *consented* to it in my heart, it ceased to oppress me; I was determined to regard it as "education" and to learn as much as possible. In this way I've remained free in the midst of my bondage. (p. 187)

But freedom in the midst of bondage in a Berlin factory while living under what one could call comparatively comfortable conditions is radically different from forced labor in a concentration camp. What consolation could Sonderkommando member Salmen Lewental have gained *inwardly* by consenting to (or refusing) his grisly task, agreeing to (or rejecting) it in his heart while resolved to regard the transportation of dead Jews to the crematorium as part of his "education"? The analogy is both irreverent and impossible.

We err grievously by trying to translate Gertrud Kolmar's personal formula for spiritual survival in Berlin into a universal principle of resistance against more unimaginable forms of oppression. From today's vantage point her determination is both admirable and naïve, overestimating as it does the power of the will to control human response to external reality. She did not and of course could not yet recognize the severer restraints to her physical freedom, to say nothing of the will's capacity to resist them, that lay before her eight weeks hence. Her philosophical exertions to master present hardships and prepare for future pain echo for us with a mournful irony, since nothing in her prior experience, or in Jewish experience, or in human experience, could possibly have prepared her for the cynical brutality of the Nazi final solution. Her increasing reliance on ancient stoic formulas of conduct evoked familiar images of heroic resistance to private pain; they did not and could not include images of anonymous extermination in a deathcamp. Camus has taught us to face the death implicit in a hostile or indifferent universe with a Sisyphean courage beyond despair; but Sisyphus had only his rock to face, not the gas chambers and ovens of Auschwitz. When that fabled variation on the rock of ages crumbled into dust, to be replaced by Des Pres's succinct and graphic image of "excremental assault," then both imagination and will were challenged to redefine the meaning of "struggle" and "resistance," of "spirit" and "dignity," of "stoic endurance" and "humanity" itself.

So if we are ever tempted to praise Gertrud Kolmar—or any victim—for heroically embracing in advance the destiny that awaited her at the end of her journey, we must tread carefully, distinguishing between the victim's blind hope and our own manufactured sentimental expectation. There is no evidence that she had the slightest conception of where the sudden factory roundup of Berlin Jews in February 1943 would end—nor would she have embraced such a destiny if she had. The strength she derived from acknowledging and accepting the possibility of a tragic denouement to her life was a natural fruition of her previous spiritual development, as woman, as poet, and as German Jew; but it must be understood within the context of her relatively secure Berlin years between 1938 and 1943, and not of her postdeportation experience, about which we know absolutely nothing. To speculate, as her American translator does, that she would have accepted her "ultimate destruction" (for which we read gassing and cremation) "with perfect equanimity because she had developed an almost superhuman capacity to accept the inevitable" [5] is to pervert her idea of inner freedom and fall prey to rhetoric, since her annihilation was anything but inevitable—not fate, but murder. Her idea of dignity was based on a tension between freedom and fate, and since both terms disappeared from speech and reality beyond the gates of Auschwitz, her notion of dignity would have disintegrated too. Like Camus, whose austere sense of human tragedy resembles her own, she would have rebelled passionately against the ruthless, impersonal disregard for individual dignity that characterized the extermination of millions of her fellow Jews—though her passion could not rescue her from anonymity, or save her life.

Indeed, her conviction that *"seelische Kraft"* or spiritual strength was sufficient to combat the physical humiliation of the Jews was one of the last illusions to be shattered by the grim details of the Holocaust: will such faith ever be on firm ground again? She speaks near the end of 1942 of meeting her fate with a fierce, almost scriptural intensity, though unlike Job or Camus she is not prepared to charge her God or the universe with injustice:

> I want to walk beneath my fate, be it tall as a tower or dark and oppressive as a cloud. Even though I'm not aware of it

yet: I've consented and adjusted to it in advance, so that I
know it will not crush me or find me inadequate. . . . I will
bear it without complaint and somehow find that it is fitting,
and that with the essence of my being I was created and have
grown up to endure and somehow surmount it.
(pp. 187–188)

Her brave and noble resolution to accept and transcend suffering
without cringing or lamentation is in the tradition of Jewish moral
dignity, and hers must be one of the last pre-Holocaust voices in
that tradition. But Kolmar's language only reminds us how
deliberately the Nazi method of genocide was designed to show
contempt for that tradition and its proponents. Whether courage
or wariness of the censor prompted her to ignore her persecutors
in this passage (she of course knew nothing of deathcamp
conditions) and place the full burden of survival on herself, she
unconsciously established a precedent for future commentators,
who like her would find it more important to affirm the self than
to examine an unspecified (or specific) disaster that might erode
the foundations of that sacred image. Her sturdy eloquence, for
example, is repeated almost verbatim by Viktor Frankl, who can
still argue that in Auschwitz "man's inner strength may raise him
above his outward fate," [6] and by Terrence Des Pres, who
suggests that stripped of everything "prisoners maintained moral
identity by holding some inward space of self untouchable." [7] If
we can use the same language about dignity and the self before
and after Auschwitz, then what difference has Auschwitz really
made—to language or our idea of the self? That is why the work
of Primo Levi and Nelly Sachs, both of whom explore in depth
Auschwitz's assault on the individual *and* the word, adds such a
crucial dimension to our understanding of the Holocaust and the
meaning of survival.

Gertrud Kolmar found less reason to question her ordering
legacies from the past. The allusive style she invented to
circumvent the censor's wary eyes cannot completely disguise her
devotion to her religious heritage. "For me a part of what has been
has grown so deeply into what is," she wrote a month before the
end, "that I can't tear it out without gravely injuring myself"
(pp. 198–199). The context makes clear that she was speaking of
her Jewish destiny, but if there is any doubt that her imagination
was moving in this direction during the closing days of her life,

one need but turn to her last letter of all, written a week before
her deportation. Its opening words ironically anticipate her own
doom and the fate of her people, but more important, and
perhaps not so unconsciously, they celebrate an ancient Jewish
tradition and link it with a modern equivalent. The final letter to
her sister begins, "The sun has just set," and continues, "and I
intend to read several of Martin Buber's 'Chassidic Tales' for
Oneg Shabbat" (p. 201). But she lays Buber aside to write this
letter—and presumably it is the last literary act of her existence.
Was it foreboding, or some other hidden force, that led her to
compose instead a description of her creative process, a lucid
assertion of the artist's self against the force that was about to
crush her?

> I never create from a feeling of exultation or strength, but
> always from a feeling of impotence. Should I allow myself to
> be lured to my desk following a sudden inspiration or
> creative impulse, I usually don't carry through to the end: the
> fire burns down, the well dries up, and the poem remains a
> fragment. When on the contrary I begin a new work in a
> state of impotence or despair, I'm like someone who
> prepares in the lowlands to climb a mountain; first the goal is
> still far away, the view is obstructed, but as I advance the
> prospect becomes broader and more beautiful. By such
> gradual climbing I don't grow weary, as happens to me when
> I give way to a swift upsurge of the imagination. . . . Only
> after I say "I can do nothing more. My strength is exhausted.
> I won't accomplish anything more," is the proper hour there.
> (p. 206)

Given this philosophy of composition, what might she not have
written had she survived Auschwitz, where "I can do nothing
more. My strength is exhausted" was translated from imagination
into the body's daily refrain, and feelings of impotence and
despair ruled most victims' existence during every waking
moment of their ordeal? Her vision of broader and more beautiful
prospects, as her remaining "proper hours" diminished, describes
the creative process throughout her career, but her words grow
more luminous when we recall that they are uttered in wartime
Berlin by a Jewish poet on the verge of deportation. Her
resolution to preserve the vigor of her imaginative life on her own

terms was her chief weapon against the world that was closing in on her. If it finally proved futile against such overwhelming odds, if dying with tragic dignity eluded her in the end, attributing fault is a vain and irreverent endeavor. The roundup deprived her of choice; extermination was not her human fate, but a violation of it. When the terms of her life "encountered" Auschwitz, how could they find appropriate terms for her death? The impasse is familiar to anyone who ventures forth in search of authentic versions of survival.

After the Holocaust, poetry about the event cannot be thought of as a weapon; the defeat was too universal. Not only the poet's voice was silenced by the event, but the way in which traditional vocabulary was used to imagine it. No wonder Adorno announced that after Auschwitz, poetry was no longer possible. Nelly Sachs, as we shall see, paid little heed to Adorno's fears, though she recognized the impulse behind them, since her verse draws on a landscape of images and memories that represent unexplored visual and verbal terrain. Gertrud Kolmar too, in her poems of the middle and late 1930s, investigated fresh visual and verbal terrain, though her vision responded to individual oppression rather than the memory of annihilation, and whatever form of suffering she anticipated cannot be compared to the history of atrocity that Nelly Sachs *knew*. Kolmar survived in spirit because she accepted as real the polarity between inner strength and outer pain, and the power of mind and language to express it meaningfully. As that polarity shriveled in the flames of Auschwitz, Nelly Sachs documented its fate and wondered—her poems are testaments to that wonder—whether it could ever be revived.

As woman and poet, German and Jew, Kolmar lived between the worlds of exile and hope. "Gloom and radiance surround me" she wrote in a poem called "*Mädchen*" ("Young Girl"), and these options animated the days of her life and the life of her art. As the perimeters of her daily existence shrank she took sanctuary, as her poems of the 1930s reveal, in the temple of her imagination. She filled it with images familiar and exotic, so that readers who enter its gates respond with mingled feelings of recognition and awe. In her poems she celebrated affirmation in the midst of potential tragedy, announcing her role almost prophetlike in one of the most moving stanzas of "*Wir Juden*" ("We Jews"):

> *And when your mouth is gagged, your bleeding shriek repressed,*
> *When your trembling arms are cruelly bound together,*

> *Let mine be the summons, that tumbles into the pit of eternity,*
> *Mine be the hand stretched out to touch God's high heaven.*[8]

She saw herself as an intermediary between the perishability of human effort and the permanence liberated by the poet's voice and language. Recognizing the impotence of one person against the realpolitik of the twentieth century, she acknowledged the "gloom" of an oppressive reality and sought some "radiance" beyond. There is an aching and desperate determination in these lines, also from "We Jews":

> *O could I, like a flaming torch in the dark wasteland of the world,*
> *Raise my voice: Justice! Justice! Justice!*

But the complexity of her vision included the very force that confined her spirit and prevented the fulfillment of justice in the world, for subsequent lines in this poem read:

> *Soul. The fluttering plea of a swallow in a barred cage.*
> *And I feel the fist that hauls my weeping head to the hill of ashes.*[9]

Foreboding lurks in her images, but does not dominate the poem; here, as in her letters, she concludes with an injunction to "her people" to embrace their sorrow, and with the promise that one day they will tread upon "the necks of the strong." She dwelt in a universe committed to the belief that, whatever one's personal fate, eventually justice would balance cruelty and restore order to a disturbed moral cosmos; chaos was simply not a permanent component of her reality.

Clearly such a poet needed to identify herself with a quality of experience more meaningful than mere daily routine. Although she has sometimes been likened to Emily Dickinson, there is a Whitmanesque tone to the cosmic dimension of her longings, corresponding to an untapped vitality deep within her soul. "*Die Unerschlossene*" ("The Unexplored Woman") begins with a declaration of this correspondence:

> *I too am a continent.*
> *I have unascended peaks, bushland unpenetrated,*
> *Inlets, stream-deltas, saltlicking coastal tongues,*
> *Caves, where giant crawling creatures gleam dark green,*
> *Landlocked seas, where orangeyellow jellyfish parade.*

She collects all the beckoning sexual power that the poet's voice can muster in this succession of primordial images, a kind of latent volcanic energy that amazes and terrifies the curious explorer. Throughout her poems we get a sense of this reaching out, a feeling that buried in herself (as in all human experience) is a potentiality for more complete expression and fulfillment, one that, because of the poverty of our imagination, we fail to achieve. The longing nevertheless governs vision and desire, seeking a balance between discipline and release while the goal— communion between the energy of self and the world outside— hovers in the distance. The closing lines of this poem explicitly link Kolmar's galvanic inner world with both tranquil and fiery resources in nature; for whereas its mysteries survive, she is limited by her mortality:

> *Above me often are skies with black stars, bright thunderstorms,*
> *Within me are lobed and jagged craters, quivering with a vigorous*
> *glow;*
> *But an ice-pure fountain too, and bluebells that drink there;*
> *I am a continent, that one day sinks silently into the sea.*[10]

In a sense "above me" and "within me" were the poles of her reality, as Nazism replaced nature and her art became a constant effort to validate her inner world, the life of her imagination, in an outer one at first indifferent and then increasingly hostile to her existence.

The tension in her life is thus carried over into her art, as eventually her silenced art will return its tensions to her life: on the one hand strangeness, alienation, the "apartness" or separation that the poet so often feels in a society committed to transient things, or to power without spirit; on the other, the ripe exuberance that transforms the simplest article or experience—a rose, a precious stone, the gesture of a dancing girl, or a mother's tenderness for her sleeping child—into a spontaneous delight with all creation. As the sources of that delight were eroded by her historical environment during her final years, she must have lost the impulse, and perhaps the ability, to link the items of reality with dynamic admiration—a sundering that she sadly transformed into *amor fati*, the love of fate. Earlier, the drama of her poems and the substance of her vision had been the freedom to forge this link. "I am a stranger," begins one of them; "I am in darkness and alone," begins another; and still another: "In my room I am totally lost. / The objects say that they do not know me." But the momentum in these poems enables the alienated woman to escape her *"Fremdheit"* and establish communion with another human being; the woman in darkness to regain the light; and the lost woman to discover acceptance. Fragments of experience evolve into unified forms, patterns of order, transcendence of disarray. When she surrendered the writing of verse to the incursions of history, Kolmar tried to translate her poetic inspiration into an equivalent moral vigor, shaping her attitude as her words had once shaped her vision. It was a fatal illusion, shared by millions, growing out of a futile hope: that somehow such vigor could preserve one's spirit from the contempt of one's persecutors. Few measured adequately the extent of that contempt.

But before she abandoned poetry Gertrud Kolmar, in one last burst of creative energy, produced the cycle of seventeen poems called *Welten* (*Worlds*), written in the latter half of 1937 and published posthumously a decade later. For this cycle she adopted an uncharacteristic free-verse line virtually absent from her earlier work, as if the mounting threats to self in the Hitler era required an assertion beyond the rhyme and controlled rhythms of those earlier poems. The poems in *Welten* are ripe with longing, profuse with upward-reaching imagery like towers and mountain peaks, as if the mere yearning to escape the shackles of history freed her imagination to soar into a dazzling heaven of light and color, motion and sound. But nature is now divided, as if the surging peaks no longer represented extensions of the caves within. Human figures inhabit her landscape, but they are dwarfed by the mysterious, magisterial force of nature, a cause for struggle in the poet rather than communion. In a poem like "The Urals" the poet wrestles to dominate her images, but they assume a life of their own: the artist's inner reality threatens to escape her imaginative mastery and to disclose a horror equal to the vision of Conrad's Mr. Kurtz.

Acknowledging the crags that rise through the darkness in "The Urals," the poet nevertheless at first exerts her authority: "the breath of my mouth weaves smokelike over the snow of the Yaman-Tau, my eternal summit." Roots of towering pines reach deep beneath ore-rich rock, and the image suffices for the treasures latent in the human spirit. But by the end of the poem

her vision turns sinister, though the exact nature of the evil,
corrupting the landscape and frightening its very creator, remains
elusive:

> But I have still other images, hostile, gloomy:
> Shadow gorges where a shapeless figure squats,
>   a half-creature that slipped away from me before I gave it
>   heartbeat.
> Mute, stifled, it shrieks to me, but I shudder; I do not look down.
> It waits for deliverance . . .
> One day, perhaps, one day
> In cold, starless gloom,
> When the night wind squeaks softly like a monstrous grey rat,
> When tree stumps, mouldy tooth stubs, chew in the mouth of the
>   earth,
> When snowflakes spread ghostlike shrouds over lifeless upland
>   moors—
> Then I will go there
> And, hands on my quaking breast, will bend over the abyss . . .[11]

One day indeed, far from her eternal summits, she confronted
that ominous abyss, which sucked her into its maw despite her
tentative imagined approach to its depths. The "half-creature"
hidden there, however we name it, achieved "deliverance"
without the artist's aid; neither words nor vision, as the poem
intuitively perceives, could give birth to its horror. This is the
closest Gertrud Kolmar ever came to the decay in nature and self
that culminated in the Holocaust. Its implications so transfigured—
disfigured—the sacred landscape of her imagination that she
postponed peering artistically into its reality until some future
time ("*einmal*") that never arrived.

Still, one must be cautious when searching for autobiographical
echoes in the pages of *Welten*. Kolmar was far from an escapist;
her strategy was to dignify the actions in these later poems by
infusing them with a quality of ritual, detaching them from daily
experience and floating them in a timeless pool of myth. It would
be tempting to read "*Das Opfer*" ("The Victim" or "The
Sacrifice"), in which a woman bravely offers herself to the
executioner, as a premonition of her own fate; but the poem is not
"about" that at all. If anything, like so many of her poems, it is
about the imagination; it celebrates the poet's power to imagine a

world more solemn and beautiful—and even more threatening despite its austere beauty—than anything the human being could possibly experience in real life. The poem may illuminate one individual's tragic destiny, but it cannot duplicate the ordeal of annihilation.

As the potential victim wanders through a courtyard to the sacrificial temple, "without will, bound in a dream," she is halfway between the disordered world of body and mind, vulnerable to violence, madness, and disease, and the tranquil realm of spirit—a parable of the human journey through life:

> *A young man stands tall and straight, impassive, with a broad*
> *   bronze sword,*
> *And a madman grovels in soft rapt laughter by the rosy granite*
> *   threshold.*
> *As she presses past, ailing hooded creatures snatch at the*
> *   amaranth-colored hem of her gown;*
> *But she moves on, a cloud, toward unreachable evening skies.*

Nothing terrifies her, not the writhing sacred serpents or even the stranger who will be her executioner. She enacts a timeworn ritual with timeless grace, and the progress of the poem becomes for Kolmar the archetypal pattern of all our lives, dreadful in the end but serene in its dreamlike certainty, controlled by the victim's dignity. Here human will and human fate collide to achieve human destiny—"So has it been decided for her, and she knows it":

> *She does not hesitate. No tremor shakes her limbs; she looks ahead,*
> *Aware of neither happiness nor grief.*[12]

In her letters to her sister subsequent to the writing of this poem, Kolmar spoke often of confronting her fate, whatever it might be, with a comparable equanimity; but unlike her art, her life could not guarantee a classical balance between what had been decided for her, and what she "knew." What *we* know of death in Auschwitz reduces the dramatic collision between human will and human fate to a moral shambles. But as long as Kolmar restricted her vision to the space between these terms—and her own spiritual survival before deportation depended on it—she could not follow Conrad's Kurtz to that darker place where the fascination of the abomination summoned the spirit into a chaos from which it could not return intact. One wonders how important a role the need to return intact plays in accounts of the deathcamp experience that adopt as a framework this questionable opposition between will and fate in Auschwitz.

The poem *"Das Opfer"* is both more and less conclusive than life; it does not end with the death of the victim but takes us outside her consciousness to a paradox beyond logic that only the language of art can sustain:

> *Yet in her heart is God.*
> *On her grave and lovely face is fixed his seal.*
> *But that she does not know.*[13]

Filled with a "burning darkness" within, she absorbs the burning darkness outside that will soon consume her; and she can accept this precisely because she has already established, through image and mood, a correspondence between her will and her fate (both of which, of course, are manipulated by the poet). As long as we cling to this correspondence, or insist on its relevance to the deathcamp experience, the "burning darkness" of Auschwitz can be interpreted as Kolmar interprets the execution of her "sacrifice"; despite the mysterious absence of God from human consciousness, the individual is still graced, through her bearing under oppression, by an indelible spiritual sign.

Under these circumstances, self-control or ruling one's own inner world becomes the only armor for the victim; one need not wonder why survivors and post-Auschwitz commentators rely so often on variations of this principle. For Kolmar, such fortitude in the face of death was a supreme virtue; survivors required little imagination to borrow it as a reason for their survival too. But it depends for its force on the desire to sustain a coherent image of the human; we have seen with what difficulty it flourishes in the incoherent atmosphere of annihilation. The dilemma is not that man must die, or even the eternally woeful truth that so many died innocent in the Holocaust. The dilemma is that it happened so in a world presumably presided over by the power of spirit. To surrender that power, even temporarily, to the nihilistic design of Auschwitz is to besiege the imagination with vexing questions undreamt of by the builder of Pandora's fabled box. Lacking exact details, Gertrud Kolmar could celebrate the dignity of human

creatures overwhelmed by a fate they might accept but could
never comprehend.

This uneasy alliance between the human creature and
something transcending the human is a theme that intersects
many of the poems in *Welten*, as it does so many survival
narratives. One feels that for all the fierce affirmations of her
individuality, Kolmar longed for consummation with some force
beyond the self, in requital of history's determination to
extinguish it. The end of *"Das Einhorn"* ("The Unicorn") finds a
woman encountering that strange mythical beast as if she hoped
for the fulfillment one gains from a lover:

> *Her greeting:*
> *Humility*
> *And the quiet shine of deep, expectant eyes*
> *And a breathing, a gentle swelling murmur from her mouth.*
> *A fountain in the night.*[14]

Woman as the source of satiation in the darkness; woman as
cloud, moving toward "unreachable evening skies"; woman (in a
poem called "Towers") wandering through the "hot, enchanted,
lifeless chambers" of an empty tower—the combination of vigor
(often sexual) and frustration in the imagery only confirms
Kolmar's ceaseless effort to extend the dimensions of her being
beyond the limitations of the physical self. Is this not one secret
agenda of almost all survival narratives too: a powerful, instinctive
desire to defy smoke and ashes as the ultimate images of man's
fate?

They were not, as I have been trying to suggest, expressions of
traditional fate at all, but rudely shifted the idea of "destiny" into
new and chaotic directions. When we consider that the millions of
Holocaust victims perished not because of divine wrath, natural
disaster, personal transgression, or the kind of moral corruption
that permits us to identify particular villains, but as the result of a
"program" of genocide based on a "theory" of racial purity, then
we are plunged into a realm of ethical confusion that cannot
regain its clarity merely by the verbal reassertion of prior sureties.
Whether we declare such "sureties" to be immanent in some vital
biological force, inherent in the moral will, or transcendent
through spiritual longing, whether we assert that survival was a
result of faith, hope, or cooperation, we are still left with the

paralyzing ethical enigma that the manner of the victims' lives
was in no way linked—not by tragedy, not by martyrdom—to the
manner of their deaths. They were not "fated" to die so; and the
survivors were not "fated" to suffer and live so. We need to
measure the various versions of survival by their fidelity to the
ethical (and physical) complexities of the deathcamp experience,
not by their success in repairing the ruptured connection between
human will and human fate until it is restored to its
pre-Auschwitz condition. If our age of atrocity has taught us
anything, it has taught us that the certainty of that connection will
never be as firm.

Thus when Gertrud Kolmar turned in "Asia," the last poem of
Worlds, away from a nervous Europe to the patient wisdom of the
Orient for a new image of certitude, she turned to a source of
being beyond time, a motionless existence that survived by
illuminating the creative moment. In the end, her vision *was* her
truth, reverence for her imagined universe the one solace left her
in the uncertain security of Berlin in 1943. The monument of
distant Asia, with its "enigmatic upward glance in the blue night
toward luminous wandering worlds," withstood the assaults of
men and time and inspired the rich fertility of her latest verse.
The stately ritual of return to a mysterious Eastern mother, whom
she invokes in this poem, joins her spirit to its ancient origins, to a
"proud hooded figure towering mightily from its mythic throne,"
whose brooding presence somehow survives and transcends its
own sinister progeny, the "vulture-demons" that hover ominously
over the poem's conclusion:

> . . . *you have plunged to the deepest core of our star, to a bath of*
>   *foaming fire . . .*
> *Burn . . .*
> *Hide with shame what foolishly is revealed, your midmost secret*
>   *that received the flaming seed,*
> *And let those born of you, the vulture-demons, circle eternally*
>   *about the towers of death,*
> *Towers of silence . . .*[15]

When by a slight alteration of image Nelly Sachs transformed
"*Türmen*" into "*Schornsteine*" and the "towers" of death became
"chimneys" of extermination, she shifted our entire perception of
man's traditional fate to his specific doom in the Holocaust. In the

final lines of Kolmar's "Asia," image continues to dominate deed, for whatever the womb of Mother Asia spawns, she remains in control, a riddling but essentially generative force. Words make reality, then survive the threat of the reality they create. But in the poems of Nelly Sachs, who knew what Gertrud Kolmar could not, we sense a constant struggle of words *against* reality, which smothers and chokes them with the sand and smoke and distorted limbs they themselves evoke. The "blue night" of Gertrud Kolmar turns black in Nelly Sachs, while the "luminous wandering worlds" become darker constellations in a cosmos where— because of the Holocaust that consumed so many millions—stars flicker intermittently—and occasionally go out.

Sachs accepted as a premise of her art what Kolmar could not have realized until it was too late to write about it: the Holocaust was not about living, but dying, and a kind of dying unimagined by her poetic predecessors. Death by atrocity, not survival is its legacy to future generations, though some commentators still confuse the two. Survival is a happy but accidental consequence, not the central gripping issue of the Holocaust. For the pre-Holocaust poet, night was still only an interval—prolonged by the renewed sorrow of ancient oppression—between twilight and dawn, but never a total eclipse. For the post-Holocaust poet, immersed in the memories of a murdered past, atrocity permanently altered the symbolic possibilities of night. In addition, at least for Nelly Sachs, it inflicted a perilous wound on the latent powers of language and vision themselves. She continues Elie Wiesel's dialogues and monologues with the dead, though their persistent refrains have been muted by the conciser aspirations of the lyric poet's voice. Her lyrics, like his essays and novels, rise from a dead landscape where the reborn phoenix can no longer flourish, where the mind seeks a more modest image for the future of the maimed human spirit.

Superficially, one might conclude that Sachs shares with Kolmar a sense of expectation and promise, of a distant, beckoning, mysterious source of fulfillment. And certainly for Kolmar, this is a potentially redemptive force; the Asia of her imagination is in harmony with a universal, transcendent power offering comfort and inspiration to the searching soul. But Nelly Sachs hears from her "landscape of screams" a shrill chorus of despair alien to Gertrud Kolmar's ears, sundering the vision of unity that the "earlier" poet yearned for. Sachs's lyric self passes from void to void, from the tomb of earth to a silent cosmos, whereas Kolmar is still able to mystify (and mythify) *her* cosmos with a fertile energy engendering images of growth. The images of blood and death that bind Nelly Sachs to a particular historical event generate a poetic energy that continually dissipates itself in the memory of atrocity, luring the reader back into that world even as words try to transform its localized pain into a larger human lament. The crematorium chimneys in "O the Chimneys," the initial poem of Sachs's first postwar volume (*In the Dwellings of Death*, 1947), are not signposts to the divine but accusatory fingers, each one an uninviting threshold "like the knife between life and death." This menacing image lingers through the later poems, a constant reminder that there will be no easy reconciliation between the smoke of Israel's body and the mysterious cosmos into whose distant regions that smoke slowly drifts.

In brief remarks acknowledging the award of the Nelly Sachs literary prize from the city of Dortmund in 1971, the distinguished Austrian writer Ilse Aichinger offered a versified tribute to the poet in whose name she had been honored. She spoke of Nelly Sachs as one standing on the brink, "where uncertainty begins to murmur"; as one who addressed "the sentries on the margins of the world," fearlessly bringing her voice to the "lion's den" and the "dens of men" (*Menschengruben*) too; as one always present when heaven fell "out of joint." They are places where the listener does not willingly venture, while the poet's voice whispers its illumination of misery into sparsely populated spaces. But for those with the courage to journey with Nelly Sachs to the margins of the world, her words quietly reconstruct a vision of things suffered and done that require a stern collaboration from those who accompany her on her verbal voyage. Perhaps this is what Ilse Aichinger meant when she said of the poet: "She encourages the scrupulous reader again and again to translate his muteness [*Stummheit*] into silence, into that involved silence [*engagierte Schweigen*] without which speech and dialogue are not possible." [16] Out of the nonbeing of the Holocaust grew a nonsaying, an inability to speak of certain things. A major challenge of Holocaust art, especially visible in Nelly Sachs's poetry, is to project from the very spaces between words (and images) a resounding silence that "engages" the reader and compels him to acknowledge and confront what is *not* said, not only by the poet, but even more by the tongue of the victim who can no longer speak of his doom.

Nelly Sachs is a spokeswoman for the consumed world of the victim: she mourns the loss, less in judgment than commemoration. The principle of *"engagierte Schweigen"* or involved silence allows the reader to enter as witness into a universe whose idiom at first is virtually alien to his ears. Quoting Ilse Aichinger on her own use of language after the Holocaust, Karl Krolow might have been reflecting the practice of Nelly Sachs too: I won't help you to unlearn the German language, Aichinger had said, but I will help you "to learn it anew, as a foreigner learns a new language—cautiously, prudently, as one kindles a light in a dark house and continues on one's way." [17] Sachs guides us through a cosmos whose darkness abides in memory even as the fragile beacon of her verse sheds dim light on its "margins" and "dens" and wavering displaced heavens, where once accessible spiritual truths now conceal the secret of their temporary disappearance behind a barricade of silence. As a post-Holocaust poet, she is a gardener in the greenhouse of words who knows that her precious language has been decimated by a terrible disease—whose lingering effects still afflict the slim seedlings remaining in the tiny new gardens of her shrunken world. In one of the last poems of *In the Dwellings of Death*, "Chorus of Solacers," she condenses into a few lines and images one of the main themes of this study: the inadequacy of our verbal and spiritual resources to express and transcend the wound of atrocity. There is progress in the poem, from total bleakness to a glimmer of hope, but we are never sure that the crossing from there to here, then to now, can be satisfactorily made. We are left with a vision of *difference* rather than organic growth, as memory and insight combine to remind us of the burden of a melancholy heritage.

The opening strophe defines that burden:

> *Gardeners are we, who have lost our flowers*
> *No healing herb can be planted anew*
> *From yesterday to tomorrow.*
> *Sage has drooped in the cradles—*
> *Rosemary has lost its aroma confronted by the new dead—*
> *The very wormwood was bitter only for yesterday.*

> *The blossoms of solace have budded too small*
> *Do not suffice for the anguish of a child's tear.*

Since the atrocity of the Holocaust cannot be undone, cannot be pardoned or redeemed, cannot be forgotten, the challenge is to find a source of consolation to mitigate the horror of the loss, of the child's tear and the empty cradles. Many, as we have seen, turn to the heroic spirit of the survivor as such a consolation, but Nelly Sachs, though she invokes that fragile spirit in several poems, refuses to let it sentimentalize her vision here. The blossoms of solace, the herbs (or words or values) that once balanced pain with comfort, do not flourish in this landscape of death, as if the very soil resists attempts to find a soothing balm. (Can it be accidental that the drooping sage, German *Salbei*, is but a letter away from *Salbe*, "salve," while *Wermut*, "wormwood," is but a letter away from *Wehmut*, "melancholy"? We will see later Sachs's sense of the sacred mission of the individual letters of the alphabet in reconstructing a language appropriate to the searing experience of the Holocaust.) The sharp rupture between yesterday and tomorrow was nowhere more dramatically delineated than in Gertrud Kolmar's response to the oppression that was closing in on her, using similar imagery but with an acceptance of "fate" that only an unsuspicious imagination could embrace: "To be sure," she had said of this *amor fati* in a line already quoted, "the germ has always been within me, perhaps even as a green stalk; but only now have blossoms developed and burst forth from their buds." [18] These blossoms of solace, Nelly Sachs knew, were withered on the stalk by tears that Kolmar never dreamed of.

The remainder of Sachs's poem traces the dilemma of those who would speak affirmatively after Auschwitz but cannot escape the pain of its legacy:

> *New seed will perhaps be nurtured*
> *In the heart of a nocturnal singer.*
> *Who among us may solace?*
> *In the depths of the gorge*
> *Between yesterday and tomorrow*
> *Stands the cherub*
> *Pulverizing with his wings the lightning bolts of grief*
> *While his hands hold apart the rocks*

> *Of yesterday and tomorrow*
> *Like the rims of a wound*
> *That must remain open*
> *That may not yet heal.*
>
> *The lightning bolts of grief do not allow*
> *The field of forgetting to fall asleep.*
>
> *Who among us may solace?*
>
> *Gardeners are we, who have lost our flowers*
> *And stand upon a star, that shines*
> *And we weep.*[19]

Cherubs no longer transfigure the spiritual landscape but fight a rearguard action, as it were, against unpacified time and unplaced grief; and whereas once the triumph of this divine agent would never have been in doubt, now the gardener-poet can only disclose the nature of the unhealing wound through her tentative refrain: "Who among us may solace?" The very images engage in a verbal struggle for domination—blossoms and tear, lightning and grief, aroma and dead, wound and sleep—and though the issue remains in suspension, the failure of synesthetic fusion between the visual and the aural promises little hope for harmony in the near future. The light of the star is diminished by the weeping of men.

But no single poem speaks for Nelly Sachs; she stands herself on the edge of her created universe and shifts her vantage point not in search of final truth but of multiple vision. She will not permit hope to supplant despair or despair to undermine hope. The logic of spiritual progress (or lapse) which the religious view has governed for centuries has been negated by the Holocaust. "Yesterday and tomorrow" no longer represent sequence, but simultaneity. In the final poem of *In the Dwellings of Death*, "Voice of the Holy Land," we encounter another refrain, again a tentative, unanswered question: "Where should the little holiness go / That still lives in my sand?" [20] The opening lines of this poem, lament rather than celebration (as so often in Sachs), explain the refrain:

> *O my children,*
> *Death has journeyed through your hearts*

> *As through a vineyard—*
> *Painted Israel red on all the earth's walls.*

The bright blood color, the conjunction of death with an image of nurture, cultivates the simultaneity of which I have been speaking, drawing us into two worlds—the living people of Israel, all Jews, and the memory of death that haunts their imaginations. Sachs does not deny the future, but seeks the outlines of its diminished holiness, diminished despite the comforting voices of the dead speaking through their "tubes of seclusion":

> *Lay on the land the weapons of vengeance*
> *To let them grow gentle—*
> *For even iron and grain are siblings*
> *In the earth's womb—*

The gesture of the child murdered in sleep that ends this poem, as it affixes a "white, breathing star / Once called Israel" to a tree's crowning branch and then invites it to spring back up to where "tears signify eternity," suggests that men must now include weeping as part of their permanent fate. It is a feature of the "little holiness" that has replaced the unlimited spiritual aspiration of the pre-Holocaust years; as this holiness still lives in the sand, the death of victims still lives in the heart. The poem's last line, more clearly in the original German than in translation, complements if it does not answer the question of the refrain (*"Wo soll denn die kleine Heiligkeit hin?"* "Where should the little holiness go?"), while at the same time stating the essential problem of definition and redefinition that has been generated by the Holocaust experience: *"Dorthin, wo Tränen Ewigkeit bedeuten"* (literally: "there, where tears eternity mean").[21] Individual words, as they jostle each other unadorned by superfluous epithets, suddenly reshape the reality that once inspired them. For the reader, the exhilaration of discovery contends with a forlorn revelation for priority in his imagination, thus duplicating the strategy of the poem itself. Israel's star may shine, but it shines through the tears of an eternally painful remembrance.

Nelly Sachs shifts our attention from survivor to victim by concentrating on *what* we have survived, rather than on the lucky accident *that* some thousands did in fact survive. One of the last poems she wrote before her death is called "Night, Divide

Yourself" ("*Teile dich Nacht*"—the name also given to her
posthumous volume of poems by its editor). Her first collection of
verse, as we have seen, was called *In the Dwellings of Death*. It
should come as no surprise that the two words she uses most
often in her poems are "*Tod*" and "*Nacht*," [22] death and night. In
the twentieth century we have lived in the habitations of death as
few previous generations have been compelled to, and no matter
how we "divide" night in our search for greater light, we only
seem to encounter the memory of more corpses—or reflections of
our own murdered past, as the boy at the end of Wiesel's *Night*
discovers. Sachs inherited a world whose darkness did not
dissipate with the daily rising of the sun. "Death" and "night" are
not merely metaphors for her, they literally describe the reality of
the experience she shared with the history of her time—and ours.
They define the terrain that the imagination must cross in its
search for a vision to restore to men a sense of justice and dignity
and a justification for the continuity of human life. Night and
death are powerful masters, springing not from romantic
atmosphere but lived pain; they challenge the poet to find
counterimages to resist their dominion. For Sachs, we survive the
memory of annihilation only by "seeing" into and through the
darkness that surrounds it; the poet's images are indispensable
beacons toward such insight.

The literary imagination has addressed itself to such questions
from the beginning, but the scope of the problem has not reached
genocidal proportions before. Near the outset of the *Odyssey*, Zeus
complains: "Oh, for shame, how the mortals put the blame upon
us gods, for they say evils come from us, but it is they, rather, who
by their own recklessness win sorrow beyond what is given."
Milton is even more explicit, for the opening words of *Paradise
Lost* sing of "man's first disobedience," placing the responsibility
for human suffering firmly in the hands of the human chooser.
The author of the Book of Job offers a vision potentially more
tragic, for here it is difficult to reconcile divine displeasure with
human agency. Unlike Adam and Odysseus, Job has not
consciously transgressed divine ordinance; if, as the magisterial
Voice from the Whirlwind chastises, he was not present when the
morning stars sang together, the fault can hardly be Job's. Beyond
the assertion of his moral innocence lies the melancholy fact that
we inhabit a universe where individual men often "win sorrow
beyond what is given"—of such stuff is tragedy born.

As a postwar writer immersed in the doom of her people, Nelly Sachs inherited a dual legacy: an ancient tradition of suffering far in excess of comprehensible cause but still compatible with spiritual aspiration and a tragic view of existence (the Voice in the Book of Job may disclose dim motives, but its presence is assured, and Job can be resolute before it); and a modern tradition of atrocity so far beyond the possibility of comprehensible cause or individual confrontation that the "tragic view of existence" collapses beneath its weight, carrying with it the vitality of the language once used to explore it. One can imagine Sachs the poet picking through the rubble to rescue separate words that may have survived the disaster, while sadly confessing that their place in the moral architecture of language will never be the same. Not inappropriately, she has been called one of the great language healers of our time.[23] George Steiner and Alexander Solzhenitsyn, among others, have commented on how an age of atrocity has wounded the word and thus victimized both art and the artist. For Nelly Sachs the dilemma was not merely restoring health to the word, as if language could be cured of corruption by a stroke of the imaginative pen, but recognizing that some words were "incurable." *Wahrheit* and *Würde*, for example, truth and dignity, scarcely appear in her poems, while other words, like death and night, achieve a resonance through repetition that draws us into a universe beyond tragedy, into the tangled landscape of yearning and despair that is Nelly Sachs's particular poetic domain.

Just as music is politically suspect to Thomas Mann's Settembrini in *The Magic Mountain*, all nominatives are untrustworthy for Nelly Sachs, including the commonest nouns in our vocabulary. Indeed, she argues that we must return to the separate letters of the alphabet if we are to reestablish a link between words and spiritual reality. "The alphabet is the land where the spirit settles and the holy name blooms," she insists in a note to one of her brief dramatic pieces (echoing the mysteries of the Zohar). "It is the lost world after every deluge. It must be gathered in by the somnambulists with signs and gestures." [24] A "nocturnal singer" like Nelly Sachs plays a major role in promoting connection with the spiritual powers, thereby saving the drowned word.

Sometimes it seems as if Nelly Sachs has narrowed her artistic goal, in a strictly verbal sense, to restoring the purity of the noun. Her poems are signs and gestures in tribute to this part of speech,

not to verbs and least of all to adjectives, as if her poetic mission
were little more than a renaming of the items of creation within
the perspective of the Holocaust, a resanctification of reality by a
reassertion of the noun. Forty-eight of the fifty most frequently
used words in her poems are nouns.[25] One would like to say that
she uses them precisely, so that the reader might perceive their
meaning unmistakably. Certainly she *chooses* her words precisely,
but their echo, the reverberations they generate when we drop
them like shining pebbles in the pool of our imagination—these
are less clear. We know what "night" and "death" have meant,
but she refuses to use them in familiar contexts; we must guess at
their allusions, while remaining only half convinced of our
solutions to their shadowy enigmas. It is not just that the
post-Holocaust bond between man and spiritual reality is
enigmatic, but that language, having shaken loose from its
original moorings, continues to float in a sea of uncertain currents.
Her nouns, unencumbered by descriptive epithets, are like
new-baked bricks thudding on the worn pavement of the mind.
Death, love, time, night, star, earth, blood—those favorite words
of Emily Dickinson too—seek to reconstruct a reality out of the
void, solid blocks of experience that will rebuild the edifice of our
lives while reminding us what we have paid for the spare
architecture of her vision.

Bereft of spirit for the time being, the universe is still inhabited
by words, though their proper use—or their misuse— is
determined only by men. In a poem addressed to "peoples of the
earth," Sachs warns those who climb into the confusion of
language—their legacy from the Holocaust—"as into beehives /
to sting and be stung / in the sweetness." Misplaced optimism is
no more serviceable than misplaced scorn, against which she also
cautions the "peoples of the earth":

> *do not destroy the cosmos of words,*
> *do not dissect with the blades of hate*
> *the sound, born in concert with the breath.*

Experience has caused purity of intention to dissolve into
ambiguity; a restored trust in the accuracy of words must precede
a faith in the human values they express or the actions they may
inspire: "O that no one mean death," she pleads, "when he says
life— / and no one mean blood, when he speaks cradle . . ."

Without identifying their source, the poet begs the peoples of the earth to leave the words there, to participate unhindered by the corruptions of history in a new process of creation:

> *for they alone can prod the horizons*
> *into the true heaven*
> *and with their side averted*
> *like a mask behind which night yawns*
> *help give birth to the stars——*[26]

An abstruse conjunction of images sustains a complex reorganization of our sense of time, space, and value. The reborn stars no longer simply illuminate the vacant cosmic spaces they shine forth from, but share their light with a gaping darkness in a form of dynamic coexistence that limits the spiritual vigor of each. Sachs does not accompany the verbal assurance of "true heaven" with the glorious celebration of a Milton or Dante, but offers us only a tentative expectation, as "stars" are divided from "night" by an anomalous "mask": in its presence, they glow with a different visual resonance, with a latent promise rather than an accomplished spiritual fact. Few writers on the Holocaust have expressed such faith in the power of words to rebuild what has been ruined by men, which is another way of affirming the essence of Nelly Sachs's vision: that saying must precede seeing—the star, after all, illuminates, it does not transform—and that seeing is itself a form of survival, an acknowledgement of the past rather than a triumph for the future.

As a *poet* of the *Holocaust*, Sachs participates simultaneously in a creative and destructive act, and as this idea seeps into our consciousness, we experience the paradoxical reality of our age of atrocity, when no affirmation can escape the powerful negations of such catastrophic times. She attempts nothing less than the propulsion of the reader's sensibilities into new dimensions of perception. The difference between her ambition and the aspirations of earlier poets is that she bases her demands not on a special inner vision but on history's outward facts. By entering the universe of her art, we embrace the history of the post-Holocaust era. Dichtung *becomes* Wahrheit, poetry truth, when we understand that our human future will never escape the delinquencies of our recently dehumanized past. Men now share their fate with their doom, and with the doom of others. To celebrate the triumph of survival as a positive spiritual act would divert the imagination from memories of annihilation. The proper exercise of this memory, for Nelly Sachs, is itself a version of survival, though it relegates rebirth to a state of permanent yearning that can never achieve fulfillment. And she attributes this loss not to the limitations of spiritual longing but to the events of history, which have radically altered both content and object of that longing.

Any hope of repairing this interrupted continuity requires an unprecedented revision of the vision of reality that made it possible in the first place. The dilemma, the abyss between God's will and man's fate, is introduced in the poem "O the Chimneys" in the very epigraph. The passage from Job is both paradox and affirmation: "And though after my skin worms destroy this body, yet in my flesh shall I see God" (Job 19 : 26). It reminds us that man's desire for continuity is eternally contradicted by his physical vulnerability, and that when his suffering exceeds the bounds of moral reason—as it did for Job, and even more during the Holocaust—the issue is not merely a difficult test of one man's faith, but the hope of a people, and the survival of a feeling for spiritual reality. How, asks Sachs, shall that feeling endure? Not, she replies (in the vestibule, as it were, to her creative endeavor), by returning to the terms offered by the Book of Job. Job still thinks of a personal God, demands a confrontation, whereas Nelly Sachs inserts her epigraph only to warn us against false expectations: a Voice from the Whirlwind would be choked—to men's ears, at least—by the smoke from crematorium chimneys.

The New English Bible translation of this passage from Job shifts the emphasis to judicial metaphor, making it an even stronger testament of faith, but the last such unequivocal statement we will find in Sachs's verse: "But in my heart I know my vindicator lives, and that he will rise last to speak in court. And I shall discern my witness standing at my side, and see my defending counsel, even God himself. Whom I shall see with my own eyes, I myself and no other" (Job 19 : 25–27). Sachs's poems comprise one long requiem to such certitude; its irrelevance to her imaginative world stands as a challenge to her search for a re-created universe more consonant with the experience of extermination. The poem "O the Chimneys" and its successors eschew such affirmations for questions; to the query "Who conceived you / and built, stone upon stone / The path for

fugitives of smoke?" we are left with anguish in place of an
answer, the perplexing fact of Jewry's annihilation but no
vindicator to justify or transcend that awful human doom.

If there is any doubt about the fundamental source of Nelly
Sachs's poetic inspiration, we have her own words as testimony:
"the dreadful experiences that brought me to the very edge of
death and eclipse have been my instructors. If I had not been able
to write, I would not have survived. Death was my teacher. How
could I have occupied myself with something else; my metaphors
are my wounds. Only through that is my work to be
understood." [27] Nothing could be more explicit: words as
instruments of survival and at the same time, reflections of the
near-fatal wounds themselves. The metaphors define the wounds,
they do not cure them. When Nelly Sachs moved from the
dwellings of death to her second volume of verse, she called it
Sternverdunkelung (Star/eclipse), annealing through metaphor the
two poles of her reality, a path back toward light that was paved
with the hot baked clay of extinction. If her imagination slowly
strained toward the healing mysteries of the cosmos, her feet
never forgot the disaster that had seared her soles—and her soul.

Uncertainty looms between grief and consolation in most of her
early poems. In a climate of justice, one knows one's loss, even if
the reasons are obscure. But in a poem like "If I only knew," a
gulf exists between mourner and victim, an ineradicable scar on
the memory, forbidding reconciliation between suffering and
justice:

> *If I only knew*
> *Where your last look rested.*
> *Was it a stone, that had already drunk*
> *Many last looks, until yours fell*
> *Blindly on its blindness?*
>
> . . . .
>
> *Or did this earth,*
> *Which allows no one to leave unloved,*
> *Send a birdsign through the air,*
> *Reminding your soul that it twitched*
> *In its body's scorched torment?* [28]

We are not in search of new images, but of new ways to assimilate
the old ones: earth and air, body and soul are not alien to our ears,

but appear strange to our imagination because of the uses to
which the human form has been put in their behalf.

We may speak of a shift in the content of epiphanies, from the
manifestation of spiritual reality behind human suffering to the
hint of a physical ordeal that in its anguish and cruelty excludes
usual consolations. Sachs condenses this issue in a poem called
"Abschied," which we might translate as "Departure," "Parting,"
or "Farewell," though one thrust of the poem is the very
inadequacy of the word itself to describe a kind of "adieu" for
which human beings have no orientation. Our own "involved
silence" plays a crucial role in this poem, since the reader must
supply the unspoken reality behind the lines, imagining that
moment of selection when friends or members of a family must
bid "farewell" as some are sent to work and others to their death.
How can the term *Abschied* ever evoke an episode like this? What
other resources does our vocabulary provide?

> *Parting—*
> *a word bleeding from two wounds.*
> *Yesterday still a word of the sea*
> *with the sinking ship*
> *as sword in the middle—*
> *Yesterday still a word*
> *stabbed by the dying of shooting stars—*
> *midnightkissed throat*
> *of nightingales—*
>
> *Today—two hanging tatters*
> *and human hair in a clutching hand*
> *that grasped—*
>
> *And we who bleed afterwards—*
> *fatally bleeding of you—*
> *we hold your source in our hands.*
> *We legions of those taking leave*
> *who build on your darkness—*
> *till death says: be quiet—*
> *yet here is: continue bleeding!* [29]

The poem, the last of a cycle within *Star/eclipse* called "Survivors,"
forces us to consider how closely allied to the survivor experience
is the need to redefine the words used to describe it. In this poem

Sachs distinguishes between the pre- and post-Holocaust worlds through clusters of images, and if the "farewell" of yesterday has a leisure of association—sea, shooting stars, nightingales—that makes the trial of parting more tolerable, whereas the "goodbye" of today is a spare, haunting, fragmented epiphany of rags and clawing limbs, this is only to confess that today's bleeding memories and bleeding words cannot stanch their hemorrhage of pain with yesterday's verbal tourniquets.

Just as the ship sinks into a sea that will roll on as it rolled five thousand years ago, so the shooting star erupts in the firmanent and vanishes into cosmic spaces concealing other vital secrets, like the nightingale's song that fades in the night and is both loss and harbinger of recurrence. These "deaths" men survive because they belong to larger rhythms in time and space; but the deaths of "today," the Holocaust dying, are wrenched violently from the contexts of tragedy or grace, leaving only the disconsolate image of "a clutching hand / that grasped"—with nothing to grasp at. That hand is now embedded in the veins and arteries of our memory, which continues to bleed from a different kind of wound that language has not yet been able to heal.

This was the quandary Nelly Sachs faced as a poet, as normal human relationships disintegrated and men lacked a frame for reshaping the ensuing chaos. It lies behind the lament of "Chorus of the Orphans":

> *World why have you taken our gentle mothers*
> *And our fathers, who say: my child, you resemble me!*
> *We orphans resemble no one in the world anymore!*
> *O world*
> *We accuse you!* [30]

Once again we are faced with unanswered and perhaps unanswerable questions, and no voice to speak with majesty *or* vindication as witness for man. Sachs is more concerned with recognizing the alienation that such unpecedented violations of natural feelings have imposed on the human spirit. At least this is a necessary first step. In "Chorus of the Stars" she makes clear that man must be his own witness, that only man can incorporate the catastrophe of the Holocaust into a cosmic vision that includes and begins to reach beyond disaster:

> *Earth, earth, have you grown blind*
> *Before the Pleiades' sister eyes*
> *Or Libra's examining look?*
> *Killer hands gave Israel a mirror*
> *In which while dying it beheld its death—*
>
> *Earth, O earth*
> *Star of all stars*
> *One day a constellation will be called "mirror."*
> *Then O blind one you will see again!* [31]

But if, to restore the lost connection between earth and stars, men and constellations, a mirror reflecting not man's destiny but his murdered past must ascend into the heavens as a permanent body in the "new" divine cosmology, then a reordering of how we perceive our fate is crucial. If "they" recognized their death while dying, *we* must renew acquaintance with their death while living, gazing into the skies of the mind to see their murdered past each time we seek a token of our eternal future. We pay a grievous price for the right to "see again." The unborn in "Chorus of the Unborn," "fragrant with morning," offer their potentiality as fragile promise—"We coming lights for your melancholy"—but mourning is now indistinguishable from hope, as each partakes of the other. If Nelly Sachs were to join two nouns to urge on us a fresh way of perceiving, she might call it *Trauerhoffnung*— "mourninghope."

In a world where "tears mean eternity," the key terms in Nelly Sachs's poetic vocabulary lose their original vigor and traditional symbolic possibilities. For example, atrocity has permanently altered the mind's associations with night as an interval between twilight and dawn, as the following lament confirms:

> *Night, night,*
> *once you were the bride of mysteries,*
> *decorated with shadow-lilies—*
> *In your dark glass glittered*
> *the illusions of those who yearn*
> *and love had brought forth its morning rose*
> *to bloom for you—*
> *Once you were the oracular mouth*

of dreampainting, mirror of the world to come.

. . . .

Night, night,
now you have become the graveyard
for a star's dreadful shipwreck—
time dives speechless into you
with its omen:
The tumbling stone
and the flag of smoke! [32]

Time sinks speechless into night as a kind of requiem to the doom of humanity at the hands of history. It will reemerge, baptized, as it were, in the dark waters of the Holocaust—as in the poem "That the persecuted may not become persecutors"—but accompanied by images that do not coalesce, that promise no illusions, that threaten disorder and disrupt the harmony that once allowed longing and despair to achieve some kind of balance in the cosmology of the imagination. The murdered past furnishes a different measure for time, while the clock hours of man and the eternity of God are stained by a violence that will not conform to older visions of temporal and cosmic order:

Steps
counting time with cries, groans,
flow of blood until it clots,
heaping deathsweat hours high—
Executioners' steps
over victims' steps,
second-hand in earth's circuit
dreadfully drawn from which blackmoon?

In the music of the spheres
where is your shrill sound? [33]

The *Schwarzmond* or "blackmoon" of Nelly Sachs is only one of many neologisms designed to thrust the imagination into a verbal universe both more authentic and more strange. It reminds us of the "*Schwarze Milch*" or "black milk" that sets the tone for Paul Celan's "Death Fugue," perhaps the most celebrated Holocaust poem ever written. In both instances, the poets take emotional opposites and fuse into a single image what once represented polarity, so that the mind experiences simultaneously spiritual options previously distinct. In Sachs's poem, our challenge is to find in the music of the spheres a note to harmonize with the steps of *such* victims and *such* executioners, who march now to a sinister drumbeat. God's will, in this matter, if it exists, is to be discovered, not revealed, as if the reader were present at the birth of a new creation from the chaos of time or history, superseding the original creation from vacant space. One commentator speaks of Nelly Sachs's need to pierce the "*Ungeist*" or "nonspirit" of the world, and goes on to describe this world in terms of Jakob Böhme and the Zohar that would have been familiar to the poet: "God is unreachable. He is the holy Nothing. . . . God has no qualities, no desires. He is eternal silence, eternal night. In this abyss of infinity life begins in that a will or longing arises, like light when it is born out of darkness." [34] But silence and night are eternal, and the light and life to be born from their womb possess only a tentative strength. Affirmations in spiritual space are limited by negations in historical time, as the Holocaust constricts what longing or yearning (*Sehnsucht*), another of Sachs's favorite words, seeks to liberate.

For Nelly Sachs the survivor does not inherit (or reinherit) a system of values that enables him to reassert a center of spiritual being. In her poems, again and again, memory with its stifling images interrupts the process of rebirth from the inert realm of infinity, as uncertainty of purpose in the form of interrogation looms between silence and longing and forestalls the natural sequence of growth. Sometimes the questions are explicit, as in "You spectators": "How much remembrance grows in the blood / Of the setting sun?" [35] Elsewhere, as in "Chorus of the Unborn," even nascent innocence cannot escape the implacable bond linking future to past:

> The shores of blood widen for our reception
> Like dew we sink deep into love.
> But the shadows of time still lie like questions
> Upon our mystery.[36]

Once more, the "involved silence" of the reader must help to endow that mystery with meaning, since the shadows of time darken his consciousness as well as the landscape of the poem. The unborn children of the poem address themselves to "you

yearning ones" (*Ihr Sehnsüchtigen*), but one need not read far in
Sachs's verse to learn that for her, yearning spreads in two
directions—not only forward toward new births to come, but also
backward toward the "old deaths" of those helpless infants
hurled, often living, into the flames. In such a context,
"mourninghope" assumes a vivid if melancholy reality.

Sometimes, as in "Numbers," which refers literally to the
numbers branded on the arms of deathcamp victims, time invades
space and matter afflicts spirit instead of being redeemed by it, as
the tokens of death become part of the heavenly orbits
themselves:

> *meteors of numbers arose*
> *summoned into those spaces*
> *where lightyears stretch out like arrows*
> *and the planets*
> *will be born*
> *from the magic substances of pain—* [37]

In "World, do not ask those rescued from death," Sachs rejects a
"picturebook heaven" that was not "honed for eyes / which
drank terror at its source." [38] Only when nature itself has been
transformed by cosmic pain can it offer solace to the survivors,
who in this poem welcome the setting sun because it shines with
an "agonylight" (*Marterlicht*) that reflects their own prior torment.
Men no longer aspire to the perfect bliss of heaven; the heavens
adapt to the unredeemable wounds of men. One feels that the
pathetic fallacy, attributing human qualities to nature, has finally
achieved validity, since men could not endure amid a nature
untouched (imaginatively) by the spoliation of atrocity.

Our place, in this redefined cosmos, is at best insecure,
enigmatic, surrounded by questions: man is caught in the
dilemma of responding to a universe itself altered by the very
experience that has transformed *him*. Old conjunctions between
man and his external world simply no longer exist, as the
following poem proposes:

> *O the homeless colors of the evening sky!*
> *O the blossoms of dying in the clouds*
> *like the fading away of the newly born!*

> *O the swallows' riddlequestions*
> *about the mystery—*
> *the gulls' inhuman cry*
> *from creation time—*
> *Whence, we who are left over from the star/eclipse?*
> *When, we with the light over our heads*
> *whose shadow death paints on us?*
>
> *Time murmurs with our yearning for home*
> *like a seashell*
> *and the fire in earth's depth*
> *already knows of our decay—* [39]

Not only the survivors, but all men, and the world they inhabit, occupy an undefined intermediate realm between "there" and "here," "then" and "now," until time and space themselves acquire new boundaries, to replace the ones permanently shattered by the experience of the Holocaust. To see beyond those boundaries, to see (as Sachs suggests in another poem) "beyond midnight" so that "whence" and "whither" (*"woher"* and *"wohin"*) once more contain between them the limits of human destiny, requires the very idea of destiny to absorb a particular doom: "We are in a sickroom / But the night belongs to the angels." [40] The problem is whether such images and the realities they represent can ever coalesce again, whether we can trust angels with the night, or men with the angels. Gertrud Kolmar believed that her inner world was invulnerable; hence she could establish private liaisons with the life of the spirit. Nelly Sachs's survivors—and here she is spokeswoman for all of them—tremulous with the memories of pain, hestitate to declare *any* truths safe, as if hidden shoals threatened their entrance into all harbors.

They seem to trust only questions:

> *Whither O whither*
> *you universe of yearning*
> *with dreams of lost earthrealms*
> *and the body's ruptured bloodpaths*
> *while the folded soul awaits*
> *its new delivery*
> *beneath the ice of the deathmask.* [41]

The soul has gone into hibernation, but the cave that keeps it warm is lined with the unforgettable portraits of victims. When the ice of the deathmask melts, what expression will be on the face that gradually emerges? Certainly that face will not be merely radiant with the joy of creation. The experience it has shared with those who did not survive the winter of destruction has infiltrated the chrysalis of its temporary nurture; as it rejoins the "universe of yearning," it will "fly" with a maimed flutter, reflecting the general mutation of spirit that has been bequeathed to the world by the "lost earthrealms" and "ruptured bloodpaths" and other violations of human continuity in the Holocaust era.

This unstable cosmos, pregnant with mystery and enigma, awes, perplexes, and dismays the reader accustomed to more familiar terrain. If we return for a moment to Viktor Frankl's evocation of this cosmos—remembering that he was in Auschwitz while Sachs was in Sweden—we may find it difficult to imagine that the two are writing of the same historical moment. Sachs speaks in one of her poems of a place where "emigrated love" has laid down its victory while "growth into the reality / of visions begins." [42] We might say that Frankl's vision of deathcamp reality assumes the stability of the cosmos that such reality temporari'y disrupts, whereas the reality of Sachs's vision sees the Holocaust not as a nightmare from which we awaken into the security of morning, but as one which both we and the dawn absorb as part of the atmosphere of contemporary existence. Consider Frankl's account of the journey from Auschwitz to a Bavarian labor camp, when the spectacle of "the mountains of Salzburg with their summits glowing in the sunset" caused him and his companions momentarily to forget their frightful circumstances. Such moments, says Frankl, offered constant solace to the prisoners, one of whom, he reports, was so moved by nature's grandeur to comment to his fellow laborer: "How beautiful the world *could* be!" [43] After Nelly Sachs's evocations of a nature stained and disfigured by human torment, Frankl's celebration of nature's sublime beauty sounds like a maudlin rhetoric embodying the most superficial features of an outmoded romanticism.

Unlike Sachs, Frankl cannot conceive of a reality that reshapes the very words used to describe it. For him, a light in a distant farmhouse "which stood on the horizon as if painted there [earlier he had compared the Bavarian landscape to a Dürer painting], in the midst of the miserable gray of a dawning morning in

Bavaria," [44] inspires nothing more original from him as analogy than the stale formula of *lux in tenebris*. By forcing us to view the Holocaust experience through associations from an intact reality (curiously, as I mentioned in an earlier chapter, from an intact *Christian* reality)—light shining forth from darkness—Frankl fetters the imagination, as if fearing to let the reader be distracted by unorthodox echoes from an indistinct verbal periphery. This is precisely the realm Nelly Sachs chose to investigate, discarding the conventional metaphorical values of "light" and "darkness" and building a poetic world on the premise that such words, though spelled the same, did not and never could again convey the simple opposition implied by Frankl's quoted formula. Their post-Holocaust meaning remained ambiguous, as signs *and* as words. Of one thing, however, she remained sure: the need to rewrite reality with the alphabet of atrocity, forcing her readers to recreate and reinterpret their relationship to physical facts and spiritual truths. She begins one poem:

> *Who knows where the stars stand*
> *in the creator's order of grandeur*
> *and where peace begins*
> *and whether in the tragedy of earth*
> *the bloody slit gill of the fish*
> *is destined*
> *with its rubyred to complete*
> *the constellation* Agony,
> *to write the first letter*
> *of the wordless language.*[45]

There are no hierarchies of values; there are no words to support them. The stars continue to exist, though their position in the cosmic realms may have shifted, as may have a creator's intentions. Between vision and truth hangs a veil of uncertainty, as the heavens themselves seek space for a new constellation (*Marter* = torment or agony), suggesting the multitude of victims who contribute to its glow. Speech has grown mute before it, while the sinister image of "the bloody slit gill of the fish" (with its hint of an earlier "agony," since the fish has long been associated with Christ) hangs suspended in the cosmos as an impediment to the rebirth of its previous splendor.

Later in the poem we learn the reason for that barrier:

> *Raspberries divulge themselves in the blackest wood*
> *through their aroma,*
> *but to no searching will the dead divulge*
> *the soulburden they have laid aside.*[46]

If the role of the constellation *Agony* in the new "heaven" is to be understood, it will not be through revelation; human risk, human courage, human persistence, human ingenuity must penetrate a secret whose bearers refuse to reveal its meaning. The terms of this poem suggest an uncompleted or aborted tragedy whose cosmic conclusion (unlike the other "agony" alluded to) must remain eternally in doubt. Despite the celebration of survival and the tributes to those virtues that enabled some supposedly to "choose life," the Holocaust is an unfinished drama because there is no place in the story for the "soulburden" of the dead. It hangs suspended in space, in time, in the mind and imagination, as a constant reminder that such an atrocity has introduced a literally unredeemable human agony into our vision of the future, and marred its appeal.

Marred, but not obliterated, and this is the problem that Sachs wrestled with in her increasingly condensed lyrics, as she sought a new place for human yearning in a universe permanently turned awry. Although the poet is driven by a passion to see anew, she knows that ordinary men and women, their eyes soiled by ashes, may not possess the power of strabismic insight that she demands of them. Although she longs for recovery herself, and knows the urgency of redirecting her readers' view, she is never certain how much is possible, as the following lines attest:

> *If the prophets*
> *should rush in with the stormwings of eternity*
> *if they should break open your earduct with the words:*
> *Who among you wants to make war against a mystery*
> *who wants to invent the stardeath?*
>
> *If the prophets should stand up*
> *in the night of mankind*
> *like lovers, seeking the heart of the beloved,*
> *night of mankind*
> *would you have a heart to bestow?* [47]

Neologisms like "blackmoon" and "stardeath" (*Sterntod*) represent attempts to use a process of linguistic annealing to squeeze fresh vigor into weary words and wearier men. The challenge to invent a stardeath is a challenge to revise the traditional relationship between heaven and earth, for even if the prophets, inspired by their access to eternity, have the strength to embrace a destiny that includes and transcends the Holocaust, is the human heart strong enough to endure such an encounter? The entire poem is written in the subjunctive mood, a conditional interrogative, a double reservation from a poet who ends so many of her poems with questions. Divinity has surrendered its absolute power to restore justice and offer love anew; that power is itself conditional on the heart's ability to respond. Once more the dark night of humanity looms between past and future, "whence" and "whither," extinction and renewal, a negation so pervasive that it threatens to wither the arteries of feeling through which once flowed the ardent blood of faith and love.

Nelly Sachs's later poems are testimonials to her hope that the withered arteries of Israel's body, and ultimately of humanity's body, are still flexible. Out of the viscous liquid of tainted blood, a vital future may yet flow, though its genesis must not be suppressed. The Dajan, a sober voice in Sachs's play *Eli*, cautions his more optimistic fellow survivors:

> *The new Pentateuch, I tell you, the new Pentateuch,*
> *is written with the mildew of fear*
> *on the walls of the deathcellars!* [48]

If the spiritual heirs of those cellars are to return to the beginning to re-create the universe and reconstitute its holiness, they must acknowledge the difference between the post-Holocaust era and the original moment of creation. That instant when pure being emerged from neutral nothingness is henceforth inaccessible to the imagination. Adam's was the innocence of not-yet-having-lived. Nelly Sachs's survivors inherit a legacy of annihilation, a sharing of the feeling of already-having-died: they are vessels of memory and longing who seek an equilibrium between an unaccountable past and an indefinable future. "All time," says Beryll in Sachs's brief dramatic piece appropriately

called *Beryll Sees in the Night*, "is conqueror- and conquered-time,"
while another character announces: "Always the pure from the
impure." [49] One is reminded here of Elie Wiesel's reformulation
of the old tragic dilemma: "The problem is not: to be or not to be.
But rather: to be and not to be." [50] We return to the question of
simultaneity, of inhabiting two worlds, not turning *from* darkness
to light in the spiritual journey so familiar to us through scriptures
and legend, but learning to dwell in both because now, says
Sachs, both dwell ineradicably in us.

Whatever principle of existence emerges from this duality, the
Urlicht or primal light will shine *through*, not in opposition to the
darkness, a light that cannot dispel the shadows it pierces. Beryll
is Hamlet-like in his hesitation, as he gazes at a stone floating in
the twilight of space and fails to perceive how little it takes—a
single letter—to transform this *Stein* (stone) into a *Stern* (star):

> *Is that the earth—is that a skull?*
> *I waver—I waver—*
> *In the dreamlike space of the world we live*
> *Do we sleep or do we wake?*
> *or in nothingness—*
> *I listen to a deathshead—*

For also swimming in space, alongside this sinister image, are the
letters of the alphabet, and another figure in this brief enigmatic
drama combines them into words, which light up in a message:
"Nothing—is the passion for Something." [51] This echo of Böhme
makes even more meaningful Nelly Sachs's dictum mentioned
earlier that the "alphabet is the land where the spirit settles and
the holy name blooms."

Although Beryll wavers between earth and skull, the poet is
more secure. "Song is suffering," says the voice of Night in this
mystery play. Poems penetrate death, the particular dying which
Nelly Sachs cannot forget, and renew life by forming letters into
lyrics, letters that peer "from the window of loneliness" in a
continuing "passion for Something" that is hidden not in light or
eternal being but in "the dark substance of the night." [52] Divine
(and human) energy is surrounded by a blackness that threatens
to engulf even as it encourages insight, while the conquering and
conquered word is man's chief weapon against nothingness. In
alliance with annihilation, the "dreamlike space of the word"

accommodates "stardeaths" that transform our vision of the universe, and our understanding of how recent atrocity has reshaped the human condition and the content of hope. If Nelly Sachs's poems grow more enigmatic during the last two decades of her life, certainly one reason is her determination to draw us into a lyric realm where the very nuances of words have shifted along with the spiritual possibilities of the world they describe. They seek nothing less than to alter the way in which our imagination imagines a once familiar but now disfigured reality.

That reality, as Sachs insists in "And we, who draw away," is a "heavy inheritance," and the task of the poet, whom she describes in imagery reminiscent of Ishmael's tribute to the ambiguous Whiteness of the Whale in *Moby Dick*, equally burdensome:

> *I here,*
> *where earth already grows featureless*
> *the Pole,*
> *death's white dead-nettle*
> *falls in the silence of white leaves.*

And Sachs even shares Captain Ahab's strategy for facing this polar vision—"If man would strike, strike through the mask!"—though her reverent tone would sound alien to Melville's monomaniacal hero:

> *Here, where ocean time*
> *muffles itself with iceberg masks*
> *beneath the last star's*
> *frozen scar*
>
> *here on this spot*
> *I bequeath the bleeding coral*
> *of your tidings.*[53]

Both the "your" and the "tidings" are ambiguous, since the verbal gesture may be turned inward toward the poem, toward the enigmas of earth, time, and the mysterious scar; or outward toward the reader, inviting him to interpret the message of the bleeding coral and find in its wound some means of sustaining the "heavy inheritance" it signifies.

Less hermetic is the image concluding "Landscape of Screams":

> *Ashen scream from seer's eye tortured blind—*
>
> *O you bleeding eye*
> *in the mutilated sungloom*
> *hung up for God-drying*
> *in the universe.*[54]

But Sachs never pursues the process of "God-drying," since the beneficence of divinity's once impregnable force must contend with a wound that memory repeatedly opens. Elsewhere she speaks of the bloodstain on the white feather of morning, reminding man that there is "no pure white on earth." [55] Old language cannot cure the wound:

> *But here*
> *always only letters*
> *that scratch the eye*
> *but long since become*
> *useless wisdom teeth*
> *remains of a dead age.*[56]

In bold metaphorical strokes she warns against gathering strawberries in the forests of speech, adopts instead a trumpet blown changeably in the dark: only the wind reflects the uncertainty of the world's course into the future. The unusual conjunction of images in single poems may suggest a universe of random chaos; but the total body of her work confirms instead a universe reborn with unfamiliar shapes, shapes that constantly shift our attention from the visual to the visionary. That vision, however, is not apocalyptic, springing from revelation, promising new unity; it evokes instead a passion for Something still undefined, but always haunted by a special past: "At the skin's frontiers / grope the dead / in horror of births / celebrating resurrection." [57] One enters a world where the language for reuniting body and spirit and gaining victory over death has perished. The final line of this poem—"Wordlessly summoned / godliness climbs aboard"—leaves us with a journey from silence into silence, as man reaches for divinity without speaking and divinity approaches man without being called. The groping dead again darken the horizon of hope.

Nelly Sachs ventures into verbal crevices where commentators like Frankl and Bettelheim will not even peer. Indeed, her confrontation with the deathcamp experience reverses Frankl's, since he depended on the spiritual associations of particular words and phrases to mitigate the anguish he survived, whereas she allows that anguish to transform some of those very words into echoes of atrocity. In "Behind the Lips" she speaks of "Letters dying like martyrs / in the mouth's urn / spiritual ascension / from piercing pain—," as if normal language were not an expression or fulfillment of inarticulate grief but one of its first victims. The concluding lines of this poem offer an alternative, a new source of vocabulary in alliance with less orthodox eschatological visions:

> But the breath of the inner speech
> through the wailingwall of the air
> breathes confessions freed of secrets
> sinks into the asylum
> of the world wound
> still in decline
> the awaited God— [58]

Alvin Rosenfeld describes the breath of this inner speech as a "poetics of expiration," shared by Sachs with Paul Celan and requiring the poet to be attuned to silence and to speak with a voice "empowered by a wind of waning currents." [59] The elliptical ending of the above poem cannot obscure the prevailing direction in which these winds drive the poet's imagination, or the barriers that hinder a completed voyage: wailing walls prohibit confessions from becoming traditional rites of purification, while the world wound like a whirlpool of pain draws those in pursuit of a new "inner speech" into its narrowing vortex. If Gertrud Kolmar during her last creative moments sought imaginative refuge in the towering peaks of the Urals, the dominant spatial impulse of Nelly Sachs's imagination is descent—not, like Dante's, as prelude to a more glorious ascension, but as an acceptance of the reservoir of human anguish where all immersions of the modern spirit must begin—and often end. Blackmoons and stardeaths in her verse do not betoken a reborn heaven but only remind us of the place in history where these luminaries themselves have plunged. And if the cosmic direction has been reversed, bringing heaven to earth, temporal momentum has likewise been inverted: how can one rebuild a future when the poet's glance is drawn steadily toward the past? Perhaps this is why the "awaited God" dangles so uncertainly (not only syntactically) at the poem's end: the poet has not yet discovered a fresh orientation for Him in time and space.

When Dante's pilgrim arrives in Paradise, he has left both the Inferno and Purgatory behind: the landscape of heaven reflects its own singular glories. It would be comforting to say that Nelly Sachs has made of Israel's anguish a similar legend, a descent into night, a period of suffering, and a return—a reascent—into light and firmer spiritual purity. But for Sachs the transfiguration of the ascent has been corrupted by the disfiguration of the ordeal below, so that for the reader there is no simple turning from despair to hope, but only another encounter with simultaneity: her version of survival requires the spirit to plunge *as* it mounts, tugged in two directions at once. It is worth noting that of the thirty most often recurring words in Sachs's poems, only two are verbs: *"ziehen"* and *"reissen,"* both of which, among other definitions, mean "to pull" or "to drag," suggesting a continuing motion between "whither" and "whence" and associating the experience of survival with a universe of constant reversals. Sachs tries to train the mind to view reality in terms of such reversals, abandoning the myth (with its many variations) that says we fall to rise and replacing it with the more strenuous burden of a rising that *includes* the prior falling, since the Holocaust is an event that the spirit is unable to leave behind. It forces us to experience time differently too, since the dead are present because of the *manner* of their absence, sometimes simply addressed as "you" in her poems, often infiltrating her lines merely through association with an image of flame or smoke. Dante could not have allowed his damned to intrude on heaven; they would have been inconsistent with the Love that moves the sun and the other stars. In Sachs's cosmos, the redemptive power of love is limited by the taste of ashes that accompanies its expression.

Some of these tendencies are illustrated by the following poem:

> *So climbs the mountain*
> *into my window*
> *Love is inhuman,*
> *transplants my heart*
> *into the lustre of your dust.*
> *My blood becomes a granite-sadness.*
> *Love is inhuman.*

Night and death build their land
inwards and outwards—
not for the sun.
Star is a sealed evening word—
torn in two [durchrissen, *from* durchreissen]
by the inhuman rising
of love.[60]

Both the landscape of nature and the landscape of love move here in unfamiliar ways. Gertrud Kolmar could coordinate her longing for spiritual freedom with an upsurge of the imagination into the towering peaks of her poems: the accompanying liberation swept her into a realm of strength and consolation, if not assured redemption. But in Sach's poem, nature invades the human, while the once human longing for love, drawn toward reunion with the victim, must see itself, must be perceived by us, in conjunction with the astonishing epithet "inhuman" ("*unmenschlich*"). Night and death obscure sun and star, whose usual potency to transfigure a gloomy universe with their heat and light vanishes in the presence of a granite sadness—its full implication once more draws on the "involved silence" of the reader—that deprives the blood of its usual vitality. By a kind of verbal osmosis, the inhumanity of the victim's doom afflicts—one is tempted to say infects—the memory of the survivor, whose love for what has been lost must be defined in terms of the nature of that loss. The need to love those annihilated can never be acknowledged as a normal form of affection. Both the impulse and the word now share their meaning with a world where night and death prevail.

Hence one cannot merely retreat to the durability of a pre-Holocaust value to sustain the spirit in the midst of chaos; when "emigrated love," as Sachs calls it in the following luminous poem, tries to resume its vision of reality, it discovers that through another reversal the original borders have dissolved into a new "reality of visions" that must somehow reconcile love with the murder of Jewish children:

I do not know the room
where emigrated love
lays down its victory
and growth into the reality
of visions begins

> or where is kept the smile of the child
> who as in play was thrown into the playing flames
> but I know, that this is the nourishment
> from which the earth with palpitating heart kindles her
>   starmusic— [61]

To the end of her life, Sachs refused to lapse into nihilism or despair; but she insisted that we be absolutely honest about the terms on which we accept our continued existence. Far more than Ivan Karamazov, she felt with all the force of her spiritual being how the annihilation of innocent children had corrupted a principle of universal love; and if she continues to yearn for a resurgence of human community, she knows that it must depend on visions that do not dazzle with beauty, as at the end of Dante's *Paradiso*, but that blind with horror. This poem is one of the last in a cycle called "Death still celebrates life," reminding the survivor of his dual cause for celebration: *that* he has endured, and *what* he has endured. The legacy is the reader's as well.

Sterntod and *Sternmusik*, stardeath and starmusic, thus generate their potency from an identical source, a literal holocaust, dying by fire. The sustenance that endows them with energy is an uncommon, unprecedented music of death, far from the *Liebestod* or lovedeath that enchanted an earlier romantic generation. In another poem from this cycle, "Night of nights," Sachs explicitly establishes the limits of the post-Holocaust universe, whose element is flame and whose meaning or interpretation depends on our acceptance of night as the dominant realm of being. The poem begins "The night was a coffin of black fire" and ends: "In the resurrection ashes music played." [62] But it is a phoenix with a difference, for resurrection cannot reconstitute what has already perished when the victim is not a single martyr but an entire people. Resurrection *here* is a mystery without a solution, one of those "glowing enigmas" that became material for Sachs's last completed long cycle of poems of the same name. At the heart of that mystery lay death by extermination, not life or rebirth or a new revelation. Like Elie Wiesel, Sachs was haunted by the memory of the dead, not by the miracle of survival; but unlike him, she could not populate her universe with their voices. Their disappearance introduced a dissonance into the music of the spheres, and made of her verse another form of simultaneity for the reader: a lamentation for their death and a requiem to the inadequacy of her poetic idiom. "Invulnerable / is your fortress," she begins one poem, "built only of benediction / you dead," and continues:

> *Not with my mouth*
> *which allows*
> earth
> sun
> spring
> silence
> *to grow on the tongue*
> *do I know how to kindle*
> *the light*
> *of your vanished alphabet.*[63]

Traditional verbal assaults cannot clarify the paradoxical blessing that surrounds and insulates these dead, who retain their secret until a revised cosmos finds room for their unique agony. Here the poet is intermediary, since she can help to give birth to this cosmos, if not to the enigma of their pain. Once we recognize how their pain has reshaped our universe, perhaps their ordeal will find a home in the vocabulary of tomorrow. The poet's role is to grieve through (*durchschmerzen.* literally "to pain through") their ordeal and liberate their wounds into the world we inhabit. We then can share with them, if not yet comprehend, their dwellings of death.

The ultimate reversal in this kaleidoscope of riddles occurs when, instead of God breathing life into the spirit of man, the dead breathe life into a new form of divinity, rescuing supernal presence from the banishment imposed by the events of the Holocaust. The dead, in still another example of simultaneity, make of their annihilation a necessary new act of creation: since the old creation has failed them, they remain the sole possible authors of a fresh one. In posthumous skies, says Sachs in a poem called "Rescued," their "dying discourse / in woe-filled winds"

> *will breathe through ages*
> *and*
> *like a glassblower, fashion*
> *a vanished form of love*
>
> *for the mouth of a God.*[64]

Expiration is thus inspiration, as multiple nuances accumulate and the reader is forced to reexperience and share in the re-creation of the verbal *and* spiritual foundations of his reality. We move through "a net of breath," as Sachs says in another poem, but no one can read this unorthodox holy scripture except lovers who have fled through the "dungeons of the nights" and climbed over the mountains of the dead. Only then, she concludes, will they be able to "bathe in the birth" of a sun that like potters, they have shaped with their own hands. The victim, the survivor, the poet, and the reader fuse into a single personality, and survival, whether of the living or the dead, requires simultaneous immersion and ascent (though never escape). We do not *rediscover* the sun, but *refashion* it so that it shines with a shadowed splendor, reflecting from its torrid core the night and death that gave it birth anew.

In her declining years, as illness besieged her body, Nelly Sachs addressed her "beloved dead" repeatedly in her "Glowing Enigmas," in search of some message that might unlock the mystery of their general doom and her personal fate. Somehow they were allied, as if their mass dying during the Holocaust held the key to her destiny as a mortal creature. Their doom and her fate fuse, and if we were to follow her habit of coining neologisms to illuminate post-Holocaust reality, we might speak of *doomfate* to signify the combination of natural decay with unnatural threat that now represents our legacy for the future. Although yearning and homesickness (*Heimweh*) continue to surface in her poems, human instincts that will not drown, the old goals of such longing have proved illusory, and new ones are still in the stage of gestation. Hence they drift without concrete object, orphaned feelings in search of a safe haven. "We freeze," she concludes one of her "Enigmas," "and struggle with the next step / into what is to come—." [65] The future of the spirit becomes real for the poet (and reader) when it is expressed; but reality has silenced the language of transcendence, and the quest for a new one often seems to be a vain and dangerous journey.

Sachs sums up this hazardous challenge in one of her gloomiest poems from "Glowing Enigmas," using the metaphor of an aborted voyage to pay tribute to the drowned word:

> *Hell is naked with pain—*
> *searching*

> speechless
> searching
> Passage into raven night
> girded with all the floods
> and ice ages
> to paint air
> with what grows behind the skin
> Pilot beheaded with the knife of leaving
> Sound of seashell drowns
> Search...Sear...Sea...S...[66]

She cannot lapse into dying or silence with serenity, since she connects her end with the heritage of violence that destroyed her people. With scarcely veiled sarcasm, in the poem immediately following the one just quoted, she laments the blindness of those "divers with divine greetings" who drop from heaven to earth but find no orphaned realm there: the same psalms pray with familiar language, as if nothing had happened below. Such an unseeing universe, as she suggests in the subsequent poem, confirms the futility of old revelations, since the pain that grows behind the skin of the victim (and his heirs) must follow an alien course and seek its own light, another kind of "creation":

> The circulation of the blood
> weeps toward
> its spiritual sea
> there
> where the blue flame
> of agony
> pierces the night— [67]

The unseeing universe may be redeemed from invisibility by the pen of the poet, though in the process of creating the artist employs a palette of destruction: "I make a line / write down the alphabet / paint on the wall the suicidal decree / from which the newborn sprout at once . . ." [68] One needs a firm heart to welcome such newborn, who do not sail into their spiritual sea trailing clouds of glory, but as offspring of some awful rite of passage, a paradoxical reversal from suicide to birth, surrounded by images of blood and flame, agony and night. Survival in this world permits no gentle delivery but a violent gesture, a piercing of the darkness (*durchbricht* is Sachs's verb), a re-creation reenacting the annihilation that spawned it.

The two are inseparable, requiring the reader to hold in delicate equilibrium a double vision of growth and decay, each maimed and supported by the other. The Holocaust has bequeathed to Nelly Sachs a crippled universe, which limps toward health on the hesitant crutches of her sturdy verse. In dialogue with herself, her dead, her readers, and her art, she offers both epitaph to a world destroyed and epigraph for the altered cosmos she helped to imagine from its ruins:

> *I write you—*
> *You have come into the world once more*
> *with the haunting strength of letters*
> *that probed for your reality*
> *Light shines*
> *and your fingertips glow in the night*
> *Constellation at the birth*
> *from darkness like these lines—*[69]

Earlier she had written that one day there would be a constellation called Mirror, in which Israel would see reflected its fate during its darkest years. Now that constellation has taken shape in the mirror of her art, gleaming beneath a re-created halo of language not simply in celebration of a reborn hope but as memorial to a wasted dying, that lives on in the minds of those devoted enough to scan the universe of her poems. Her final vision embodies our most paradoxical and exasperating version of survival: encouraging the spirit leaping toward heaven while simultaneously drawing it steadily backward into the vast anonymous grave of Jewish doom.

NOTES

Preface

1. Pam Bromberg, "Lillian Hellman's Uncertainties," *New Boston Review*, V (August/September 1980), 6.

Chapter One   Language as Refuge

1. Alvin H. Rosenfeld, "On Holocaust and History," *Shoah: A Review of Holocaust Studies and Commemorations* 1 (*1*) (n.d.): 20.

2. In *Survival in Auschwitz*, Primo Levi writes: "If I could enclose all the evil of our time in one image, I would choose this image which is familiar to me: an emaciated man, with head dropped and shoulders curved, on whose face and in whose eyes not a trace of a thought is to be seen" (p. 82). See note 9.

3. Benzion Dinur and Shaul Esh, eds., vol. 1 (Jerusalem: Yad Washem Remembrance Authority, 1957), pp. 18–19.

4. Charlotte Delbo, *None of Us Will Return*, trans. John Githens (Boston: Beacon Press, 1978), p. 128.

5. Ibid., p. 72.

6. Hermann Langbein, *Menschen in Auschwitz* (Wien: Europaverlag, 1972), p. 18. Translation mine.

7. Quoted in Langbein, *Menschen in Auschwitz*, p. 37.

8. Gitta Sereny, *Into That Darkness* (New York: McGraw-Hill, 1974), p. 171.

9. Primo Levi, *Survival in Auschwitz*, trans. Stuart Woolf (New York: Collier, 1961), p. 107.

10. Christopher Ricks, "Geoffrey Hill and the Tongue's Atrocities," *Times Literary Supplement*, June 30, 1978, p. 747.

11. Dorothy Rabinowitz, *New Lives: Survivors of the Holocaust Living in America* (New York: Avon, 1977), pp. 131–165.

12. George Steiner, *In Bluebeard's Castle: Some Notes towards the Redefinition of Culture* (New Haven: Yale University Press, 1971), p, 53. For a contrary view see Martin Walser, "Unser Auschwitz," in *Heimatkunde: Aufsätze und Reden* (Frankfurt am Main: Edition Suhrkamp, 1968), p. 11:

> The absolute illegality of this situation is simply unimaginable. And since we are unable to think ourselves into the condition of the 'inmates,' because the extent of their suffering exceeds any hitherto available conception of suffering—for this reason we also are unable to form a human image of the actual culprits—we call Auschwitz a Hell, and the culprits, devils. This explains why, when the subject is Auschwitz, we always use such an 'otherwordly' vocabulary [*aus unserer Welt hinausweisenden Wörter*].
>
> But Auschwitz was not Hell, it was a German concentration camp. And the 'inmates' were not the damned or partially damned in a Christian universe, but innocent Jews, communists, and so forth. And the torturers were no imagined devils, but men like you and me. Germans, or those who wanted to be considered Germans. *Translation mine.*

13. In *The Age of Atrocity: Death in Modern Literature* (Boston: Beacon Press, 1978), I discuss in greater detail the relationship between "normal" dying and "abnormal" atrocity. Here my concern is with "living" and "survival."

14. Henry Krystal, ed., *Massive Psychic Trauma* (New York, International Universities Press, 1968).

15. Robert Jay Lifton and Eric Olson, *Living and Dying* (New York: Bantam, 1975), p. 29.

16. Ibid., p. 121.

17. Ibid., pp. 122, 123.

18. Viktor E. Frankl, *Man's Search for Meaning: An Introduction to Logotherapy*, trans. Ilse Lasch (New York: Pocket Books, 1963), p. xi.

19. The title of the first American edition was *From Death Camp to Existentialism*. The original German edition (1947) was called *Ein Psycholog erlebt das Konzentrationslager* ("A psychologist experiences the concentration camp").

20. Frankl, *Man's Search for Meaning*, p. 183.

21. *Letzte Briefe zum Tode Verurteilter: 1939–1945*, hrsg. von Pietro Malvezzi und Giovanni Pirelli (München: Deutscher Taschenbuch Verlag, 1962), p. 252. Translation mine.

22. Langbein, *Menschen in Auschwitz*, p. 234.

23. Ibid., p. 277.

24. Irving Howe, *Politics and the Novel* (New York: Meridian, 1957), pp. 210–211.

25. See David Cohen, "The Frankl Meaning," *Human Behavior*, July 1977, p. 61.

26. Ibid.

27. Martin Buber and J. L. Magnes, "Two Letters to Gandhi," *The Bond*, April 1938, p. 39. The following note, quoted from Leon Poliakov, *Harvest of Hate: The Nazi Program for the Destruction of the Jews of Europe*, rev. ed. (New York: Holocaust Library, 1979), p. 220, seems relevant here:

> The Jewish historian Wulff, who was himself a survivor of Auschwitz, relates how during a discussion he had in the camp with his fellow prisoner, B. Kautsky, the question had been raised: What would have become of Gandhi in the camp? The speakers agreed that, after having been the object of some of the coarse jokes and pranks in which the SS and the Kapos shared, he would have passed into the category of the 'Moslems' in a few days, and would have succumbed at the first selection.

28. Bruno Bettelheim, *The Informed Heart: Autonomy in a Mass Age* (New York: Avon, 1960), p. 23.

29. Bruno Bettelheim, "Individual and Mass Behavior in Extreme Situations," *Journal of Abnormal and Social Psychology* 38 (1943): 417–452. This essay and *The Informed Heart* (which incorporates much of the essay's substance, with small but significant changes) have exerted undue influence on the thinking of numerous commentators on the psychology of Holocaust victims and survivors. For a severe but detailed criticism of these works see Jacob Robinson's pamphlet, *Psychoanalysis in a Vacuum: Bruno Bettelheim and the Holocaust* (New York: Yad Vashem–YIVO Documentary Projects, 1970). Recently Bettelheim has gathered many of his writings on the subject into a single volume, *Surviving and Other Essays* (New York: Knopf, 1979). In "The Holocaust—One Generation After" (1977) he seems to have reversed his position in *The Informed Heart*: "Confronted with the deathcamps, our old categories do not hold" (p. 97); nevertheless most commentators still regard his earlier work as authoritative.

30. Bettelheim, "Individual and Mass Behavior," pp. 434–435.

31. Bettelheim, *The Informed Heart*, p. 138. Apparently forgetting this change, Bettelheim later in the chapter says: "Earlier in this chapter, I recounted how hundreds of prisoners died one winter night, or soon thereafter, as a result of exposure on the parade grounds while the SS hunted two escaped prisoners" (pp. 178–179). This manipulation of figures is characteristic of Bettelheim's carelessness with details, as is his failure to correct the mistaken use of "Gestapo" for "SS" in some passages quoted directly from the earlier article. Inexplicably, when "Individual and Mass Behavior in Extreme Situations" was reprinted in *Surviving and Other Essays* ("with some small editorial changes"), the original exaggerated figure on death and frostbite was restored.

32. Delbo, *None of Us Will Return*, pp. 71–72.

33. Olga Lengyel, *Five Chimneys: The Story of Auschwitz*, trans. Clifford Coch and Paul P. Weiss (New York: Ziff-Davis, 1947), p. 211.

34. Ibid., pp. 100, 101. Cf. Bettelheim, *The Informed Heart*, p. 195.

35. Versions of this story abound: the desperate, unfortunate victim has entered into the mythology of the deathcamps. Bettelheim takes his details from the version of Eugen Kogon, who spent the war years in Buchenwald. Another version speaks of an Italian opera singer and actress: see Sylvia Rothchild, ed.,

Voices from the Holocaust (New York: New American Library, 1981), p. 162. For a far less heroic account than Bettelheim's, see "The Death of Schillinger" in Tadeusz Borowski, *This Way for the Gas, Ladies and Gentlemen*, trans. Barbara Vedder (New York: Penguin, 1976). Bettelheim seems more interested in using the details of Kogon's version for his own theoretical ends than in authenticating the evidence.

36. Lengyel, *Five Chimneys*, p. 154.

37. Bettelheim, *The Informed Heart*, p. 231.

38. Robinson, *Psychoanalysis in a Vacuum*, pp. 10, 18.

39. See "Reflections," *The New Yorker*, August 2, 1976, pp. 31–52.

40. *The Screenplays of Lina Wertmüller*, trans. Stephen Wagner (New York: Quadrangle, 1977), p. 332.

41. "Reflections," *The New Yorker*, p. 50.

42. Ibid.

43. Jacob Katz, "Was the Holocaust Predictable?" *Commentary*, May 1975, p. 44.

44. Terrence Des Pres, *The Survivor: An Anatomy of Life in the Death Camps* (New York: Oxford University Press, 1976), pp. v, vi.

45. Jorge Semprun, *The Long Voyage*, trans. Richard Seaver (New York: Grove Press, 1964), p. 60. Cf. Des Pres, *The Survivor*, p. 141.

46. Jozef Garlinski, *Fighting Auschwitz: The Resistance Movement in the Concentration Camp* (Greenwich, Conn.: Fawcett, 1975), p. 183.

47. Langbein, *Menschen in Auschwitz*, p. 37.

48. Lengyel, *Five Chimneys*, p. 212.

Chapter Two   **Auschwitz: The Death of Choice**

1. Primo Levi, *Survival in Auschwitz*, trans. Stuart Woolf (New York: Collier, 1961), pp. 112–113.

2. *In the Hell of Auschwitz: The Wartime Memoirs of J. S. Newman* (New York: Exposition Press, 1963), pp. 42–43.

3. Ella Lingens-Reiner, *Prisoners of Fear* (London: Viktor Gollancz, 1948), p. 29.

4. Levi, *Survival in Auschwitz*, p. 36.

5. Even Des Pres quotes only part of this passage, ignoring Levi's subsequent disclaimer. See *The Survivor: An Anatomy of Life in the Death Camps* (New York: Oxford University Press, 1976), pp. 64–65.

6. Lingens-Reiner, *Prisoners of Fear*, p. 90.

7. For many years it was believed that there was only a single survivor of Belzec. According to Jaffa Eliach, director of the Center for Holocaust Studies in

Brooklyn, New York, a second very elderly survivor of Belzec recently turned up in New York City. Of the other deathcamps, four are said to have survived Chelmno, about fifty Sobibor, and about forty Treblinka. See *NS Vernichtungslager im Spiegel deutscher Strafprozesse: Belzec, Sobibor, Treblinka, Chelmno*, hrsg. von Adalbert Rückerl (München: Deutscher Taschenbuch Verlag, 1977), p. 13, note 8.

8. Joost A. M. Meerloo, "Delayed Mourning in Victims of Extermination Camps," in *Massive Psychic Trauma*, ed. Henry Krystal (New York: International Universities Press, 1968), p. 73.

9. Editha Sterba, "The Effects of Persecution on Adolescents," in *Massive Psychic Trauma*, p. 51.

10. Ibid., p. 55.

11. Even distinguished authorities like Richard Rubenstein and Raul Hilberg have lent partial support to this oversimplified view, discounting the idea that after a certain point the situation itself forestalled effective resistance.

12. Quoted in Charlotte Delbo, *Le Convoi du 24 janvier* (Paris: Editions de Minuit, 1965), p. 90. Translation mine.

13. From "The Manuscript of Salmen Gradowski," in Jadwiga Bezwińska, ed., *Amidst a Nightmare of Crime: Manuscripts of Members of Sonderkommando*, trans. Krystyna Michalik (State Museum of Oświęcim, 1973), p. 96.

14. Bernard Naumann, *Auschwitz: A Report on the Proceedings Against Robert Karl Ludwig Mulka and Others before the Court at Frankfurt*, trans. Jean Steinberg (London: Pall Mall Press, 1966), pp. 294–295.

15. From "The Manuscript of Salmen Lewental," in Bezwińska, *Amidst a Nightmare of Crime*, p. 145.

16. George Steiner, *In Bluebeard's Castle: Some Notes towards the Redefinition of Culture* (New Haven: Yale University Press, 1971), p. 44.

17. Viktor E. Frankl, *Man's Search for Meaning: An Introduction to Logotherapy*, trans. Ilse Lasch (New York: Pocket Books, 1963), pp. 132–133.

18. Hermann Langbein, *Menschen in Auschwitz* (Wien: Europaverlag, 1972), p. 132.

19. Ibid., p. 134.

20. Ibid., p. 112.

21. Ibid., pp. 138–139. Langbein neglects to mention that 300,000 Hungarian Jews were gassed in the spring and summer of 1944.

22. Bezwińska, *Amidst a Nightmare of Crime*, p. 138.

23. Langbein, *Menschen in Auschwitz*, p. 166.

24. Ibid., p. 225.

25. This seems to be the consensus of most authorities, though opinions differ on the issue. In addition to accounts in Langbein and in Jozef Garlinski's *Fighting Auschwitz*, those interested should consult Olga Lengyel, *Five Chimneys*, Reuben

Ainzstein, *Jewish Resistance in Nazi-Occupied Eastern Europe,* and Ota Kraus and Erich Kulka, *The Death Factory: Documents on Auschwitz.*

26. According to Kraus and Kulka, they cut the still-electrified barbed wire with insulated shears.

27. Levi, *Survival in Auschwitz,* p. 111.

28. Langbein, *Menschen in Auschwitz,* pp. 167, 220.

29. Tadeusz Borowski, *This Way for the Gas, Ladies and Gentlemen,* trans. Barbara Vedder (New York: Penguin, 1976), p. 175.

30. Andrzej Wirth, "A Discovery of Tragedy: The Incomplete Account of Tadeusz Borowski," trans. Adam Czerniawki, *Polish Review* 12 (Summer 1967): 45.

31. Quoted by Jan Kott in "Introduction," *This Way for the Gas,* p. 22.

32. Perhaps we see here a clue to the practice of blaming the Jews for collaborating in their own destruction. The search for "agents" must end somewhere.

33. Kott, "Introduction," p. 26.

34. Wirth, "A Discovery of Tragedy," p. 51.

35. Langbein, *Menschen in Auschwitz,* pp. 405–406.

36. Wirth, "A Discovery of Tragedy," p. 52.

37. Frankl, *Man's Search for Meaning,* p. 213.

38. Ibid., p. 110.

39. Bruno Bettelheim, *The Informed Heart: Autonomy in a Mass Age* (New York: Avon, 1960), p. 291.

40. Ibid., pp. 291–292. In some of the later essays appearing in *Surviving and Other Essays* (New York: Knopf, 1979) Bettelheim adopts a somewhat more flexible view.

41. Bezwińska, *Amidst a Nightmare of Crime,* p. 147.

42. Bettelheim, *The Informed Heart,* p. 277.

43. Des Pres, *The Survivor,* pp. 65, 202, 94.

44. Ibid., pp. 87–88.

Chapter Three   **Elie Wiesel: Divided Voice in a Divided Universe**

1. Most extended analyses up to now have concentrated on Wiesel's religious ideas. This imbalance will be corrected when Ellen Fine's critical study of Wiesel as a writer of fiction appears.

2. See especially Josephine Z. Knopp, *The Trial of Judaism in Contemporary Jewish Writing* (Urbana: University of Illinois Press, 1974) and Irving Halperin, *Messengers from the Dead: Literature of the Holocaust* (Philadelphia: Westminster Press, 1970).

3. Since I have discussed *Night* in detail in *The Holocaust and the Literary Imagination* (New Haven: Yale University Press, 1975), I avoid duplication here.

4. Elie Wiesel, *Legends of Our Time* (New York: Avon, 1970), p. 212.

5. Elie Wiesel, *A Jew Today*, trans. Marion Wiesel (New York: Random House, 1978), p. 15.

6. Albert Camus, *The Rebel: An Essay on Man in Revolt*, trans. Anthony Bower (New York: Vintage, 1958), p. 4.

7. Alvin H. Rosenfeld, "The Problematics of Holocaust Literature," in *Confronting the Holocaust: The Impact of Elie Wiesel*, ed. Alvin H. Rosenfeld and Irving Greenberg (Bloomington: Indiana University Press, 1978), p. 2.

8. Elie Wiesel, *Dawn*, trans. Anne Borchardt (New York: Hill & Wang, 1961), pp. 65, 41.

9. Ibid., p. 65.

10. Elie Wiesel, *The Accident*, trans. Anne Borchardt (New York: Avon, 1970), p. 113.

11. Elie Wiesel, *The Town beyond the Wall*, trans. Stephen Becker (New York: Atheneum, 1964), pp. 74, 78.

12. Elie Wiesel, *The Gates of the Forest*, trans. Francis Fresnaye (New York: Avon, 1967), p. 174.

13. Wiesel, *Legends of Our Time*, pp. 112–113.

14. Elie Wiesel, *One Generation After*, trans. Lily Edelman and Elie Wiesel (New York: Avon, 1972), p. 17.

15. Elie Wiesel, *A Beggar in Jerusalem*, trans. Lily Edelman (New York: Random House, 1970), p. 133.

16. Wiesel, *A Jew Today*, pp. 128–129.

17. Ibid., p. 152.

18. Wiesel, *Legends of Our Time*, pp. 223–224.

19. Ibid., pp. 229, 222.

20. In November 1943, meeting in Moscow, Roosevelt, Churchill, and Stalin issued a "Declaration of German Atrocities," warning the Germans that they would be tried and punished for their crimes. The "Declaration" had no deterrent effect. See Joseph Borkin, *The Crime and Punishment of I. G. Farben* (New York: Free Press, 1978), p. 111.

21. Wiesel, *Legends of Our Time*, pp. 231–232, 141–142, 126.

22. Ibid., p. 206.

23. Cf. Chapter 1, note 27.

24. Wiesel, *A Beggar in Jerusalem*, p. 208.

25. Ibid.

26. Wiesel, *One Generation After*, pp. 61–62.

27. Ibid., pp. 53, 56.

28. Wiesel, *Legends of Our Time*, p. 31.

29. Wiesel, *One Generation After*, p. 57.

30. Elie Wiesel, "Why I Write," in *Confronting the Holocaust*, p. 200.

31. Ibid., p. 201.

32. Ibid., pp. 201, 202.

33. Bruno Bettelheim, *The Informed Heart: Autonomy in a Mass Age* (New York: Avon, 1960), p. 109.

34. Viktor E. Frankl, *Man's Search for Meaning: An Introduction to Logotherapy*, trans. Ilse Lasch (New York: Pocket Books, 1963), p. 3.

35. Wiesel, *The Accident*, p. 81.

36. Wiesel, *Legends of Our Time*, pp. 77, 78.

37. Wiesel, *One Generation After*, p. 14.

38. Wiesel, *Dawn*, p. 122.

39. Wiesel, *One Generation After*, p. 209.

40. Ibid., p. 10.

41. Ibid., p. 12.

42. Wiesel, *The Accident*, p. 25.

43. Ibid., p. 53.

44. Rosenfeld, "The Problematics of Holocaust Literature," in *Confronting the Holocaust*, p. 30.

45. Wiesel, *The Accident*, p. 72.

46. Wiesel, *One Generation After*, p. 216.

47. Wiesel, *The Town beyond the Wall*, pp. 43, 47.

48. Wiesel, *The Gates of the Forest*, p. 13.

49. Wiesel, *A Beggar in Jerusalem*, p. 5.

50. Wiesel, *A Jew Today*, p. 188.

51. Elie Wiesel, *The Oath*, trans. Marion Wiesel (New York: Random House, 1973), p. 12.

52. Wiesel, *One Generation After*, p. 224.

53. Wiesel, *A Jew Today*, pp. 198, 200.

54. Ibid., p. 188.

55. Ibid., pp. 197, 200.

56. See Jozef Lánik (pseud. for Alfred Wetzler), *Was Dante Nicht Sah* (Berlin: Verlag der Nation, 1964).

57. Elie Wiesel, *Souls on Fire: Portraits and Legends of Hasidic Masters,* trans. Marion Wiesel (New York: Random House, 1972), p. 240.

58. Wiesel. *A Jew Today,* p. 200.

Chapter Four   **Gertrud Kolmar and Nelly Sachs: Bright Visions and Songs of Lamentation**

1. Heinz Politzer, "The Blue Piano of Elsa Lasker-Schüler," *Commentary* 9 (1950): 337.

2. Ibid., p. 344. Translation mine.

3. Ibid., p. 343.

4. Gertrud Kolmar, *Briefe an die Schwester Hilde: 1938–1943* (München: Kösel Verlag, 1970), pp. 23–24. Translation mine.

5. *Dark Soliloquy: The Selected Poems of Gertrud Kolmar,* ed. and trans. Henry A. Smith (New York: Seabury Press, 1975), p. 51.

6. Viktor E. Frankl, *Man's Search for Meaning: An Introduction to Logotherapy,* trans. Ilse Lasch, (New York: Pocket Books, 1963), p. 107.

7. Terrence Des Pres, *The Survivor: An Anatomy of Life in the Death Camps* (New York: Oxford University Press, 1976), p. 202.

8. Gertrud Kolmar, *Das Lyrische Werk* (München: Kösel Verlag, 1960), p. 101. All translations of Kolmar's letters and poems are my own. Many of the poems I discuss also appear in facing German and English texts in *Dark Soliloquy.*

9. Ibid., p. 102.

10. Ibid., pp. 12–13.

11. Ibid., pp. 585, 586.

12. Ibid., pp. 582, 584.

13. Ibid., p. 584.

14. Ibid., p. 578.

15. Ibid., p. 592.

16. Ilse Aichinger, "Laudatio," in *Ansprache und Dokumente zur Verleihung des Kulturpreises der Stadt Dortmund* (Stadt- und Landesbibliothek Dortmund), Heft 3 (1971), p. 32. Translation mine.

17. Ibid., p. 30.

18. Kolmar, *Briefe,* p. 196.

19. *Fahrt ins Staublose: Die Gedichte der Nelly Sachs* (Frankfurt am Main: Suhrkamp, 1971), pp. 65–66. All translations of Nelly Sach's poems and prose are my own. Most of her poems may also be found in facing German and English texts in *O the Chimneys* (New York: Farrar, Straus & Giroux, 1967) and *The Seeker and Other Poems* (New York: Farrar, Straus & Giroux, 1970).

20. Ibid., p. 68.

21. Ibid.

22. See Paul Kersten, *Die Metaphorik in der Lyrik von Nelly Sachs: Mit einer Wort-Konkordanz und einer Nelly Sachs Bibliographie* (Hamburg: Lüdke, 1970).

23. See Werner Weber, "Laudatio annlässlich der Verleihung des Friedenspreises des Deutschen Buchhandels an Nelly Sachs im Oktober 1965," in *Nelly Sachs zu Ehren: Zum 75. Geburtstag am 10. Dezember 1966. Gedichte. Beiträge. Bibliographie* (Frankfurt am Main: Suhrkamp, 1966), p. 41. Translation mine.

24. See Nelly Sachs, "Anhang zu *Beryll sieht in der Nacht*," in *Zeichen im Sand: Die szenischen Dichtung der Nelly Sachs* (Frankfurt am Main: Suhrkamp, 1966), p. 354. Translation mine.

25. See Kersten, *Die Metaphorik in der Lyrik von Nelly Sachs*.

26. *Fahrt ins Staublose*, p. 152.

27. Quoted by Gisela Dischner, "Zu den Gedichten von Nelly Sachs," in *Das Buch der Nelly Sachs*, ed. Bengt Holmquist (Frankfurt am Main: Suhrkamp, 1968), p. 311. Translation mine.

28. *Fahrt ins Staublose*, p. 31.

29. Ibid., p. 124.

30. Ibid., p. 55.

31. Ibid., p. 61.

32. Ibid., p. 76.

33. Ibid., pp. 77–78.

34. Olof Lagerkrantz, "Die Wunde zwischen Nacht und Tag," in *Nelly Sachs zu Ehren*, p. 47. Translation mine.

35. *Fahrt ins Staublose*, p. 20.

36. Ibid., p. 67.

37. Ibid., p. 110.

38. Ibid., p. 114.

39. Ibid., p. 117.

40. Ibid., p. 138.

41. Ibid., p. 140.

42. Ibid., p. 382.

43. Frankl, *Man's Search for Meaning*, pp. 12, 63.

44. Ibid., p. 64.

45. *Fahrt ins Staublose*, p. 169.

46. Ibid.

47. Ibid., pp. 93–94.

48. *Zeichen im Sand*, p. 51.

49. Ibid., pp. 291, 302.

50. Elie Wiesel, *The Accident*, trans. Anne Borchardt (New York: Avon, 1970), p. 77. Being and nothingness are not opposites or alternatives here: they exert force simultaneously on human efforts to endure. Being is *part of* nothingness, as nothingness is an expression of being.

51. *Zeichen im Sand*, pp. 301, 302–303.

52. Ibid., pp. 303–304.

53. *Fahrt ins Staublose*, p. 183.

54. Ibid., pp. 222–223.

55. Ibid., p. 309.

56. Ibid., p. 288.

57. Ibid., p. 316.

58. Ibid., p. 319.

59. Alvin Rosenfeld, *A Double Dying: Reflections on Holocaust Literature* (Bloomington: Indiana University Press, 1980), pp. 82–95.

60. This poem is omitted from *Fahrt ins Staublose*. The German text appears in *O the Chimneys*, p. 240.

61. *Fahrt ins Staublose*, p. 382.

62. Ibid., p. 384.

63. Ibid., p. 272.

64. Ibid., p. 279.

65. *Suche nach Lebenden: Die Gedichte der Nelly Sachs* (Frankfurt am Main: Suhrkamp, 1971), p. 41.

66. Ibid., p. 57.

67. Ibid., p. 59.

68. Ibid., p. 63.

69. Ibid., p. 76.

INDEX